Embodied Visions
Bridget Riley, Op Art and
the Sixties

Frances Follin

EMBODIED VISIONS
BRIDGET RILEY, OP ART AND THE SIXTIES

Thames & Hudson

First published in the United Kingdom in 2004 by
Thames & Hudson
181A High Holborn, London WC1V 7QX
www.thamesandhudson.com

Designed by Richard Hollis, London
Typographic assistant: Jasmin Sieke

British Library Cataloguing-in-Publication Data
A catalogue record for this book is available from the British Library

ISBN 0-500-97643-0

Printed and bound in the United Kingdom
by BAS Printers

For Alan

Contents

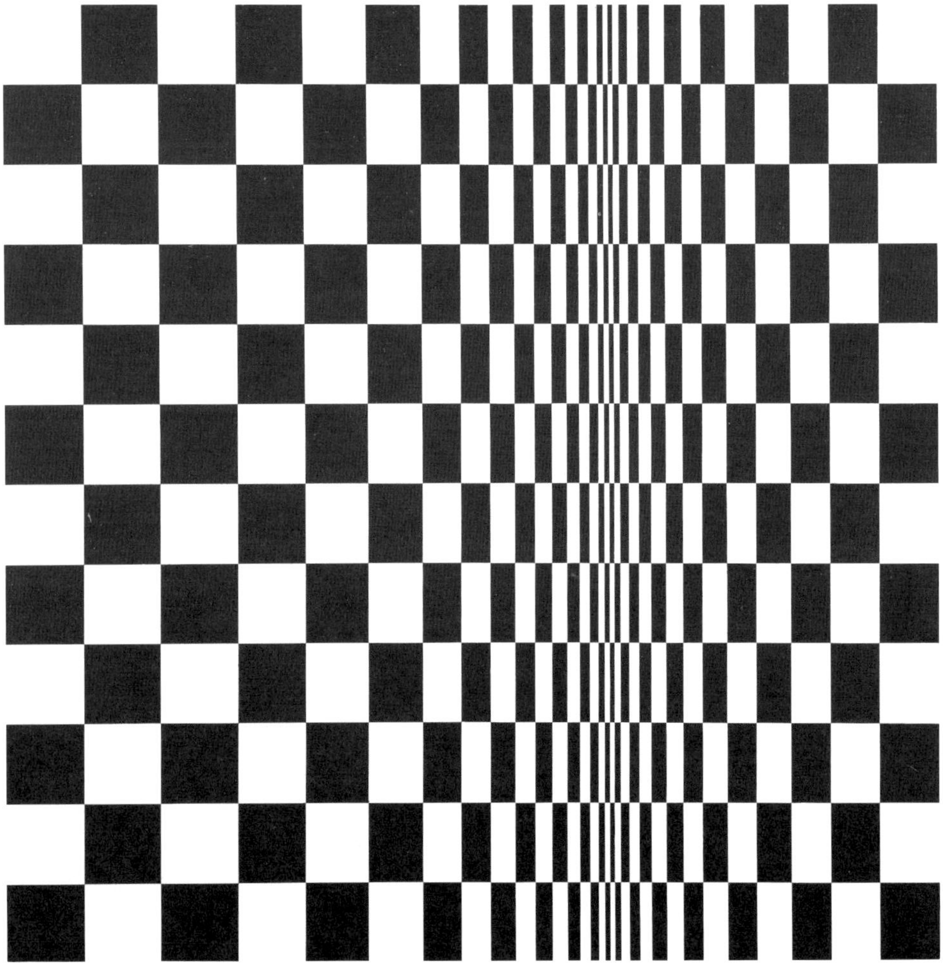

1. **Movement in Squares** 1961

Introduction

It is not until art expresses the immediate hopes and aspirations of humanity that it acquires its social relevance.

Herbert Read 1963[1]

This book is about the work created by British artist Bridget Riley between 1961 and 1965 – in other words, from works exhibited at her first one-person show at a private gallery in London, to her contribution to 'The Responsive Eye', an international show at New York's Museum of Modern Art (MoMA). These works are familiar to many people – they have been used on book jackets and elsewhere to signal 'the Sixties'; they remain icons of the period. Why should this be? What do we see when we look at these paintings, and, more to the point, what did people see when they looked at these paintings in the early 1960s? I believe that they always carried within them a multiplicity of meanings and associations that were so bound up with the concerns of the period that they produced a sensation of immediate recognition in their audience which was visually compelling then, and which has made them evocative of the period ever since. For a modern audience, however, the precise nature of these meanings and associations has become blurred. It is time to re-examine them.

Accounts of twentieth-century art tend to neglect Op art, as if it does not quite fit into the familiar narratives of modernist and postmodernist art as it 'developed' from Abstract Expressionism after the Second World War (1939–1945). It has become difficult to appreciate its central role in the early 1960s, when it was seen by some critics as the most important art of the period. We need to examine what these critics had to say about Riley's work and other Op art, and so reposition these works in relation to other art of the 1960s. In doing so, we will see that Riley's work relates in subtle and unexpected ways to much of the other art of the period, from Happenings to Minimalism, to earlier work such as Pollock's and to later developments in postmodernism, and to areas of culture that might seem to have little to do with art at all, such as the 'space race' or the development of the 'hippy' movement. This book cannot hope to cover fully this enormous area of history and culture, but it explores some of this territory in relation to Riley's art, and considers her art in relation to this complex context.

T.J. Clark has written 'I do not want to talk about history as 'background' to the work of art – as something that is essentially absent from the work of art and its production, but which occasionally puts in an appearance'.[2] Clark warns us to be wary of a concept of history as 'a support, a determination, a background, something never actually there when the painter stands in front of the canvas'.[3] One might add, 'something never actually there when the spectator stands in front of the finished painting', for the spectator – the contemporary critic, newspaper pundit or visitor to the art gallery – can hardly avoid the presence of the 'history' of their own time. It is this presence of history within the work that I wish to keep in view. In 1961 Bridget Riley painted her first black and white pictures, later to be known as 'Op' art; from 25 February to 25 April 1965 she participated in 'The Responsive Eye', the largest ever international exhibition of Op art, at MoMA in New York. This was a passage from obscurity to both artistic recognition and celebrity. It was a period in which much of Riley's work attracted controversy, and this spilled beyond the confines of the art press into the wider media. It is this relatively brief period that we will look at in this book.

The genesis of 'Op' as a term

Although work that is now classified as 'Op' art appeared at least as early as the 1950s (when the Hungarian artist Victor Vasarely experimented with geometric devices that induced optical illusions), it first appeared as a descriptive term in 1964 in an article in *Time* magazine.[4] This was explained by artist and critic Lil Picard: 'The new mathematical art equation reads POP – P = OP. That means simply: drop the letter P and op we go'.[5] Unlike their counterparts in the USA, European commentators did not seem to feel the need for a 'snappy' tag. *Time*'s act of naming this art form 'op' art (note lower case 'o'), in the run-up to the opening of MoMA's exhibition, suggests that the author felt that such a naming was necessary, at least from a journalistic perspective. Previous 'movements' in art had attracted names, usually with the suffix '-ism': Realism, Impressionism ... Abstract Expressionism, and one might have expected a name such as 'Optical Illusionism' to be bestowed on the 'new' art. The most recent art to attract international attention and controversy, however, was not an 'ism' but Pop art ('pop' in *Time*). Pop had none of the potential portentousness of an 'ism': it was a journalist-friendly, direct, casual, modern term, free of the art-historical, academic associations of an 'ism'. By 1964, it had also been in use for some time – at least since the activities of the Independent Group in

Britain in the mid-1950s. It was familiar both as a term and and as an art style, and was thus no longer 'news' for general interest magazines such as *Time*. The writer of the *Time* article may have assumed that a major exhibition at MoMA heralded the arrival of a potential, and newsworthy, successor to Pop. As such, it would need a name: how convenient, therefore, to 'drop the letter P and op we go'. *Time* needed to find an angle to market artistic matters to its readers. They needed to be persuaded that this art was, above all, fashionable. Future sales would then be generated by continuing to comment on the new art. No doubt other journalists found the term just as useful, and for the same reasons. Therefore, 'Op' may be regarded as a marketing term, but one coined not by the art market itself but by the publishing industry. Nonetheless, the term soon found acceptance in more 'serious' journals. Writers variously used 'Op Art', 'Op' art and 'op' art with the London *Times* preferring 'optical' art, perhaps considering 'Op' to be slang. More recent writers[6] have favoured 'Op' art, the capitalization preferred by Riley herself.[7]

A new look at Riley's work

In 1966, art critic Jasia Reichardt wrote: 'Op paintings do not lend themselves to intellectual exploration'.[8] I came across this comment early in my research but already I had found that it was not true. Op art was, nonetheless, largely unmapped territory and Reichardt's comment gives a clue as to why this might be. She argued that Op's subject matter is the technique by which it is created and its experience by the viewer is of 'an intense sensual and often sensational impact'.[9] Contemporary reviews and published comments about Riley's Op art emphasized the intensity of physical effects produced by these paintings, which have encouraged the view that responses to these works are unmediated by thought processes and, therefore, have no intellectual basis. Against this, I argue that an intellectual exploration of Riley's paintings of the period 1961–65 is needed in order to find clues to the meaning they had for viewers at that time. I have investigated six important issues: science; drugs and perception; national identity; Happenings and the theatrical; the commercialization of Op; and the implications of Riley's being a woman for the reception of her work. As I explored these very different areas, I detected three underlying and recurring themes which connect them. These themes are physical aggression and violence; the body (rather than the less physical notion of 'mind') as a site of perception and experience; and an apparently deep concern with the future of Western societies. These themes themselves are interlinked,

2. **Horizontal Vibration** 1961

violence most obviously being directed at or enacted by the body, but imagined futures also having strongly physical aspects, from the effects of space travel on the body to the changing relations of the sexes. As I shall show, concerns as diverse as space travel and the changing social roles of women have relevance to the reception of Riley's work.

I began my research by considering claims that Op was in some way scientific, because I was intrigued by a claim made by Norbert Lynton that Riley had used 'diagrams through which scientists were studying perceptual processes' in the creation of her Op art paintings.[10] As a biology graduate whose early education had been predominantly scientific, I was interested to find a form of art that apparently had a scientific genesis. I soon discovered, however, that Riley and others denied that any such basis existed. Some critics suggested that Op artists such as Riley were merely reproducing, or possibly extending, the work of scientists investigating visual perception. Such assertions appeared to deny the individual creativity of these artists, reducing their work to the mere application of a scientific method. While one would expect most artists to deny working in such a mechanistic fashion – as Riley certainly did – intriguingly, not all artists did so. Furthermore, I found that these paintings could have 'scientific' connotations independent of methodological concerns. Hence, in Chapter 1, I have attempted to open up the debate about the 'scientific' aspect of Riley's work and recast this in relation to contemporary concerns with science and technology, and with the future of Western technocracies. Intriguingly, I also found indications that Op art was regarded as aggressive, and induced feelings of nausea in spectators, in relation to these concerns with Op's 'scientific' aspect. I have attempted to analyse the possible connections between science, aggression and Riley's work.

No one looking at early press coverage of Riley's work could escape the references to psychotropic drugs that crop up repeatedly around the time of the MoMA exhibition 'The Responsive Eye' in 1965. When some of her 1960s' work was shown retrospectively in 1998, this aspect again drew press attention. As with the issue of science, this debate has been cast in terms of accusation and denial. In Chapter 2 I look again at the contemporary debates about perception, itself so radically affected by the use of psychotropic substances, and at the social meaning that such substances and their use had in this period. I also consider the language used to describe drug experiences, the experience of looking at Riley's work and aesthetic responses to art, to indicate where correspondences may exist and where they do not. I explore what it might mean for art to be aligned with 'drug culture', or opposed to it. Again, concerns with possible futures for Western societies emerge in relation to this debate. Notions of 'the body' also arise here as central to questions of perception: psychotropic drugs affect the mind through physiological effects on the body – specifically, on the central nervous system. French philosopher Maurice Merleau-Ponty was much concerned with the centrality of the body in the creation and perception of art. There are striking correspondences between his work and views on Riley's paintings expressed by her contemporaries.

The theme of national identity is important because of contemporary comments in the press that suggest there were new efforts to promote British art both in Britain and abroad, in which Riley's work features prominently. With Abstract Expressionism, the USA had challenged Paris' domination of the international art scene, and this success promoted the idea that an Anglo-Saxon culture could produce internationally significant art. Enthusiasm for the possibilities created for British artists was countered not only by recurring concerns that British art had qualities inappropriate for 'international' art but also that if artists rejected these qualities, they might lose their 'Britishness' and appear simply to plagiarize 'foreign' art. Riley's art is central to such debates. As I show in Chapter 3, her work was widely argued to have its roots in Russian Constructivism (an 'origin' that Riley herself has supported[11]), rather than in, say, landscape art (which has long been promoted as 'British'). Riley was associated with new ideas of the British artist as a young urban professional, 'ruthlessly' pursuing an international career. Riley's paintings found considerable press attention and critical support – and controversy – in New York when shown there in 1965, as discussed in Chapter 4, and this in turn was subject matter for much contemporary British press coverage. Riley's work attracted this attention in the wake of Pop art, which had garnered accusations of commercialism on both sides of the Atlantic, with the added concern, in Britain, that it celebrated specifically American commercial values associated with US cultural imperialism. Riley's work apparently resisted such engagement with either commerce or US culture, yet it was taken up by American (and later British) manufacturers of a range of consumer goods. Her work could thus be seen as either a flagship for British art abroad, or as a foreign (Russian) import that attracted the wrong sort of attention in the country whose premier position British artists had to challenge if they were to establish a major presence on the international art scene.

The relationship between Riley's work and another prominent form of artistic expression in the 1960s, the Happening, is explored in Chapter 5.

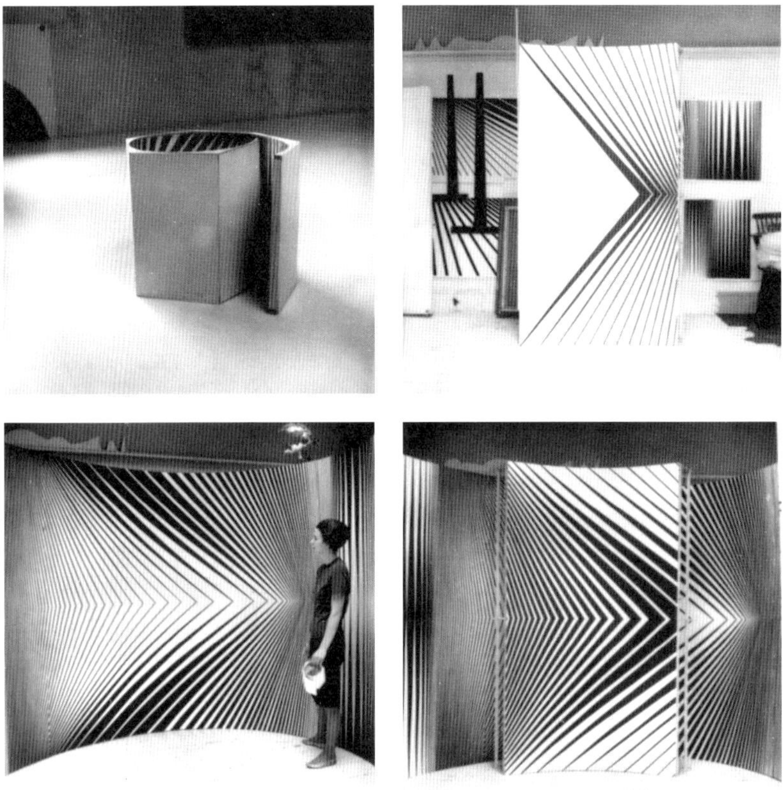

3.
Stages in the development of *Continuum* from the maquette to the final construction, 1963

I relate this to arguments concerning the 'theatrical' in art initiated by Michael Fried in his consideration of Minimalist art[12]. Although Fried specifically excluded Op from his argument, I have found significant parallels between his comments on Minimalism and contemporary comments on Riley's work. This leads to a consideration of the relation between theatre and Happenings, and between Happenings and other forms of art in this period, to show how Riley's work relates to a considerable body of work by her predecessors (such as Jackson Pollock) and contemporaries (such as Michelangelo Pistoletto and Yves Klein) in very diverse areas. The importance of the body – of the artist and spectator as corporeal entities, not merely perceiving intellects – emerges here again. This leads to further consideration of Merleau-Ponty's work on the perception of art as essentially a bodily phenomenon, as well as an engagement with the Russian philosopher Mikhail Bakhtin's ideas regarding the centrality of the body in experience, and particularly his concept of the Carnivalesque.

Op art suffered considerable commercialization around 1965, coincident with MoMA's 'The Responsive Eye' exhibition. Riley's paintings (and those of some other Op artists) were adapted by manufacturers of consumer goods, particularly for use on women's clothing. Op-inspired patterns appeared on wallpapers, fabrics and household goods, which Riley argued trivialized and debased her work, and she tried to stop this practice as I show in Chapter 6. I look at the ways in which consumer culture itself was seen as 'feminized' and debased, and the ways in which such perceptions may have interacted with the public image of Riley's work. I also consider what the reasons may have been for the development of 'Op' fashions and why women, in particular, may have purchased and used such goods. This leads on to a discussion, in Chapter 7, of how the reception of Riley's work may have been affected by her position as a woman artist. There are not many direct allusions to this in the press reports of the time and it may not have been thought appropriate to comment on it. The instances where this happens, and the ways in which writers and critics address the subject of Riley as a woman artist without, for instance, claiming that there was anything unusual in being one, or anything that made art an unsuitable job for a woman (while nonetheless implying that this area is problematic), are thus all the more interesting. I consider the views of Andreas Huyssen and Peter Wollen on the 'masculine' nature of modernist culture, and those of feminist writers Kate Millett and Mary Anne Doane on the position of women in the mid-twentieth century as the feminist movement developed, and examine how these ideas might be related to perceptions of Riley's work and ways in which she was represented, as an artist, in the press.

My aim in considering these aspects of the reception of Riley's work has not been to show that one side in any given debate was right, but rather to demonstrate the complexity of the issues involved and the impossibility, in many instances, of taking up a fixed 'for' or 'against' stance in relation to contemporary views on Riley's work. Hence my seven chapters are not meant to represent single separate viewpoints from which one can comfortably stand back and assess this work. It is my contention that there is no single viewpoint from which a clear, unwavering, unambiguous assessment may be achieved. A viewer standing before one of these pictures finds that s/he cannot bring it into focus but experiences, as an unattainable quest, the involuntary attempts of the eye to find stability. When considering the question 'What does/did this work represent?', one likewise finds that a precise answer is elusive.

Another interesting aspect of Riley's work of this period, from an art-historical perspective, is its relationship to modernism at a time when the latter had come under threat from developments that may now be characterized as 'postmodern'. Throughout this book, I relate Riley's work to the ideas promulgated by a number of art historians, usually writing on other artists and other art historical problems, to explore how Riley's work relates to various conceptions of modernism. Her work can be seen as challenging what were then ascendant views of the nature of modernist art, specifically by contesting notions of aesthetic appreciation as what Roger Fry called 'clear, disinterested contemplation'.[13] We might say that her work asks 'What is mind?' and suggests that it is part of the body, something that cannot be divorced from physical experience. I will show that some critics implied that Riley's work was expressive of the highest pleasure experienced by and through the body.

Riley's paintings of 1961 to 1965 invite a range of interpretations and meanings through which we may look again at this period of art – and social – history. In a Riley painting of this period, the eye is rarely allowed to settle; there is no point at which the viewer can stand and perceive a static entity. The image is always both 'here' and 'there', sliding between points of focus. I argue that this slide, this constant movement of focus, is also part of any meanings that may be associated with these works. It is not, for example, that they may be understood in relation to science or to an absence or negation of science, but rather in relation to both. When exploring the historical specificity of these paintings, one returns, repeatedly, to a concern with the body. From the ideas of Merleau-Ponty to those of Bakhtin, from a critic writing in *The Times* to a woman purchasing a dress of fabric based on one of Riley's paintings – relationships between these works and the human body seem inescapable. In the words of Merleau-Ponty:

> *It is by lending his body to the world that the artist changes the world into paintings. To understand these transubstantiations we must go back to the working, actual body – not the body as a chunk of space or a bundle of functions but that body which is an intertwining of vision and movement.*[14]

Bridget Riley's Op art paintings from the early 1960s manifest this 'intertwining of vision and movement' to an extraordinary degree, and this is a vital aspect of understanding the paintings' impact at that time. What one might call an embodying of vision links Riley's work with the very different work of Jackson Pollock before her, and that of the performance artists who were her contemporaries. It is fruitful to speculate on why her work appealed both to those who looked forward to the 'Space Age' with eagerness, and to those who recoiled from such a future with dread. It is time to look afresh at Bridget Riley's Op art and recognize its place in the cultural history of the twentieth century.

Chapter 1 Venus and Mars
The Marriage of Art and Science

> *It . . . surprises me that some people should see my work as a celebration of the marriage of art and science. I have never made any use of scientific theory or scientific data, though I am well aware that the contemporary psyche can manifest startling parallels on the frontier between the arts and the sciences.*[1]

Bridget Riley wrote this in 1965 after taking part in the Museum of Modern Art's 'The Responsive Eye' Op art exhibition in New York earlier that year. Riley praised the exhibition itself but she objected both to its sensationalized treatment in much of the US press and to persistent suggestions, by some critics, that her work was the product of mathematical calculation and scientific theorizing.

Other artists, such as the Hungarian painter Victor Vasarely (based in Paris) and his adherents in the Groupe de Récherche d'Art Visuel (GRAV – founded in 1960), had published manifestos and given interviews in which they claimed to be researching visual effects in a scientific manner, and that their art was based on such 'research'.[2] Some commentators drew attention to similarities between Op paintings and optical illusions, which had been used since the 1940s to investigate visual perception.[3] Riley considered that any similarities with scientific work were coincidental – 'startling parallels'. Similarly, the influential American critic Clement Greenberg, who dominated American art criticism in the 1950s and 1960s, had claimed:

> [art's] *convergence with science happens to be a mere accident ... What their convergence does show, however, is the profound degree to which Modernist art belongs to the same specific cultural tendency as modern science, and this is of the highest significance as a historical fact'.*[4]

What were the implications of a 'marriage of art and science' in relation to Bridget Riley's Op art production in the early 1960s? Why might such a connection have been both promoted and disparaged? On what evidence was any such connection based?

Both art and science may be seen as quests to discover 'truths' about the world and the place of human beings within it. While the 'objective' 'scientific method' relies on empirical observation to establish 'facts' about the universe, art is associated with the subjective individual 'genius' of specific artists. Science is supposedly concerned with practical matters that, in theory, could be discovered by anyone armed with the correct methodology. If Riley's work were produced following such pre-established rules or formulae, it would conflict with the romantic notion of the 'intuitive genius' befitting a true artist. Riley later commented on the complexity of the artist's situation in relation to these stereotypes:

> *No matter what I do it will always be subjective, and so to develop as much objectivity as I can, is simply counterbalancing this inevitable presence of myself in the work. De-personalisation is, I think, a bogus hue and cry.*[5]

Riley's words suggest that there was considerable tension around the notion that art and science could interact in some way; for some, the idea was attractive but it repelled others. The terms she chose for her denial of scientific methods provide clues to the appeal of Vasarely's claims. The phrase 'a celebration of the marriage of art and science' is strongly romantic, suggesting a joyful union. There is an implication (whether intended or not) that some people might have been happy to bring about such a union, but Riley emphatically denied that this was either her object or her achievement. There may have been 'parallels' between her work and some aspects of contemporary scientific thought but, for her, art and science remained separate, if contiguous, continents. Whilst artists such as Vasarely argued that Op was the product of a merging of art and science, others, including Riley, rejected the possibility, even the desirability, of any such union.

There were strong reasons for any artist or critic to take up *either* of these positions: reasons relating to Op art's position in relation to the wider field of contemporary art practices, to the position and relative importance of art itself in an age apparently dominated by technology, and to the significations of concepts of 'science' and 'technology' in the wider cultural context in which Op rose to prominence.

1. Science versus aesthetics

The MoMA exhibition's title, 'The Responsive Eye', suggested the physicality of the spectator's response to art, whereas the language of modernist critics – from Roger Fry, in the early twentieth century, to Clement Greenberg[6] – had previously emphasized the aesthetic aspect of this response.[7] By contrast, the title 'The Responsive Eye' drew attention to the contraction and expansion of the iris, and the muscular action to adjust the focus of the lens: the eye's physical response to what it sees. The contemporary US critic Thomas Hess argued that Op achieved its psychological effects through the exploitation of neurological phenomena that had, at least potentially, a definable physical nature, rather than through some indefinable sense of the transcendent 'aesthetic' that some modernists espoused. Much Op art was based on firmly late-modernist principles: the lack of distinction between figure and ground, the avoidance of large internal divisions in the work, the repetition of units and the use of a grid structure. These were characteristics shared with modernist works such as the grids of Mondrian or the 'all over' (Greenberg's term) paintings of Jackson Pollock or Mark Rothko. The emphasis on the *physical* reaction to Op, on the active role of the eye–brain neurological system, in the very title of this exhibition, however, apparently challenges modernist emphasis on a transcendent aesthetic. Whereas the title of an exhibition usually expresses some characteristic of the works on show, 'The Responsive Eye' emphasized the *spectator* of the work. It is as though visitors to the gallery were invited to experience themselves at least as much as anything that might be on show. This is particularly significant because, since its opening in 1929, MoMA's management had formulated a set of aesthetic criteria which not only defined a certain view of modernism but also positioned the gallery as a central institution of US modernism.[8] This version of modernism – emphasizing Fauvism, Cubism, Surrealism and the Bauhaus – was wider in scope than that later espoused by Greenberg. As we shall see, Op art relates to MoMA's modernism through its connections with Constructivism, an early twentieth-century Russian art movement which had influenced the Bauhaus aesthetic.

Reviews and statements made in the first half of the 1960s (which find echoes in much later discourse[9]) show that there was a very active debate in progress over the nature of Op, its importance as a movement in the wider context of contemporary art practice and its relation to contemporary culture (in many senses of that term). At stake was its acceptance as a valid kind of art by an art establishment dominated in the US by formalist critics such as Clement Greenberg and in Britain by the views of Roger Fry (still influential nearly thirty years after his death). Greenberg had strictly divided cultural production between 'avant-garde' and 'kitsch', notions that were given new relevance with the contested rise of Pop art. Fry and his disciple Clive Bell had promoted a notion of 'aesthetic emotion' and later the influential British critic Herbert Read promoted the notion of an 'aesthetic sense'.[10] Op challenged such ideas. The supposed connection with science was used both in support of Op's claims to consideration as a major art form and as an attack on such claims. If Op succeeded as art, did it do so by finding new expression (through some conception of science) for modernist ideals or by undermining them (again, through science)?

The Op art/science debate

These considerations raise a number of issues. What connections were posited between Op art and science and what were the accepted meanings of the terms 'science' and 'technology' in contemporary cultural discourses? How did these conceptions of the scientific and the technological relate to notions of modernity, and to hopes or fears about the direction of social development and 'the future'? These questions had implications for the interpretations of Riley's work as a 'new' kind of art, whether accepted as modernist or seen as oppositional to modernism. What were the strategies used by supporters and opponents to position her work, and other Op art, in relation to modernism? How were notions of science involved in these debates and how did such notions relate to the perceived conventions of modernism? Could a connection with science be seen as 'disqualifying' Riley's work as a modernist art practice and instead place it in opposition to modernism?

We must first consider what 'science' and 'technology' meant, as terms in common use in the 1960s, and their relationship to people's conception of the society in which they lived, and their hopes and fears for the future development of that society. Although explaining only part of the fascination that Riley's work had for her contemporaries, this is an important aspect of the reception of her work.

'Science', 'technology' and hopes for the future

The meanings of both terms were various and contradictory. Then, as now, they were often used interchangeably in general parlance and the division between the two was unclear. In Britain, for instance, when Lord Hailsham was made the first Minister for Science in 1959, the (unsupportive)

Federation of British Industry commented: 'The first essential in this country is for science to penetrate more widely and thoroughly into the more backward industries'.[11] As it usually takes scientific research a long time to have any beneficial effect on industrial output and competitiveness (central concerns of the Federation), what the Federation probably wanted was investment in up-to-date technology. Neither the government nor the Federation seems to have had clear ideas concerning the nature or potential of science (or its limitations) but there appears to have been a belief, perhaps akin to either superstition or religious faith, that science could solve Britain's economic problems. The science journalist Tom Wilkie sums up this attitude: 'In Britain around 1960, science and technology seemed the talisman that would, through modernization, solve the problems of relatively slow economic growth and relative decline'.[12] It is notable here that Wilkie describes 'science and technology' (two things) as 'a [single] talisman', reinforcing the notion that they were perceived as the same thing or, at best, two sides of the same coin. The word 'talisman' suggests a magical aspect; what if there were a certain attraction in the idea that if science could infuse art, in the form of Op, something magically powerful might result?

If 'science' and 'technology' were so closely associated in the public mind, why should science be singled out, as it often was, in relation to Op?[13] The answer may be rooted in the British public's attitudes to social class, which made a distinction between science and technology. The British physicist and novelist C.P. Snow argued (in 1959) that there was an:

> *instinct – perhaps sharpened in this country by the passion to find a new snobbism wherever possible, and to invent one if it doesn't exist ... to take it for granted that applied science was an occupation for second-rate minds.*[14]

Snow was suggesting that, rather than being conflated, the two terms had distinct connotations, science being intellectually, even socially, superior to technology ('applied science'). This notion was not confined to Britain. In 1965, in the USA, art critic Thomas Hess described Op as 'pseudo-scientific', 'gadgetry' and '[science's] obsolete apparatus'.[15] These terms make belittling reference to technology. Because Pop art was associated with the depiction of technology and its products (cars, gadgets, mass media), forging an association between Op and 'science' may have represented an assertion of the intellectual and class superiority of Op. Both Snow's and Hess' words suggest that any association with technology was likely to be detrimental to perceptions of Op.

The talismanic power of science, as an idea, and its association with middle-class values were both evident during the 1964 General Election, when 'science became a main platform and a rallying cry for both political parties'.[16] The Labour Party, under its new leader, Harold Wilson, saw a chance for power after more than twelve years of Conservative rule and the scandal that had engulfed that party in the wake of the Profumo affair.[17] Labour still needed to modernize its image and win over middle-class voters. The party campaigned in 1964 with claims that it would exploit science to revitalize industry. Wilson announced:

> *We are redefining and we are restating our socialism in terms of the scientific revolution ... the Britain that is going to be forged in the white heat of this revolution is no place for restrictive practices or outdated methods on either side of industry.'*[18]

Science was presented as the key to the fulfilment of a new and progressive social vision. Its promotion by the Labour Party also had the social class connotations implied by Snow: the party saw the espousal of science as a means of achieving greater appeal among the middle classes. Wilson also used the concept of science as a means of unifying a membership divided over the question of retaining Clause 4 (concerned with nationalization policy) of their constitution. 'Unity was Wilson's central theme. He argued that the party must "unite on policy, not divide on theology"'.[19] Science was used to provide a new 'theology' for a party seeking new supporters and a new image.

Harold Macmillan, Conservative Prime Minister from 1957 to 1964, also believed that science had, potentially, a wide popular appeal, as indicated by the creation of the much-criticized Ministry of Science in 1959. Once in power, Labour responded by replacing this with a Ministry of Technology, which was appropriately named, having no concern with pure science at all. Again, Wilson seems to have used the term 'science' as a rhetorical talisman in his pre-election speeches, an imprecise promise of a better tomorrow. Science represented a means of revitalizing not just industry but, in some way, the country itself. The public faith in science that both the major political parties sought to exploit electorally was based not on knowledge of either science or technology, but rather on a quasi-religious belief in a power beyond most people's understanding which acted in mysterious ways to transform the world. Just as Christianity had once provided ample subject matter for art, in the 1960s science potentially offered appropriate subject matter for an age requiring new faiths.[20]

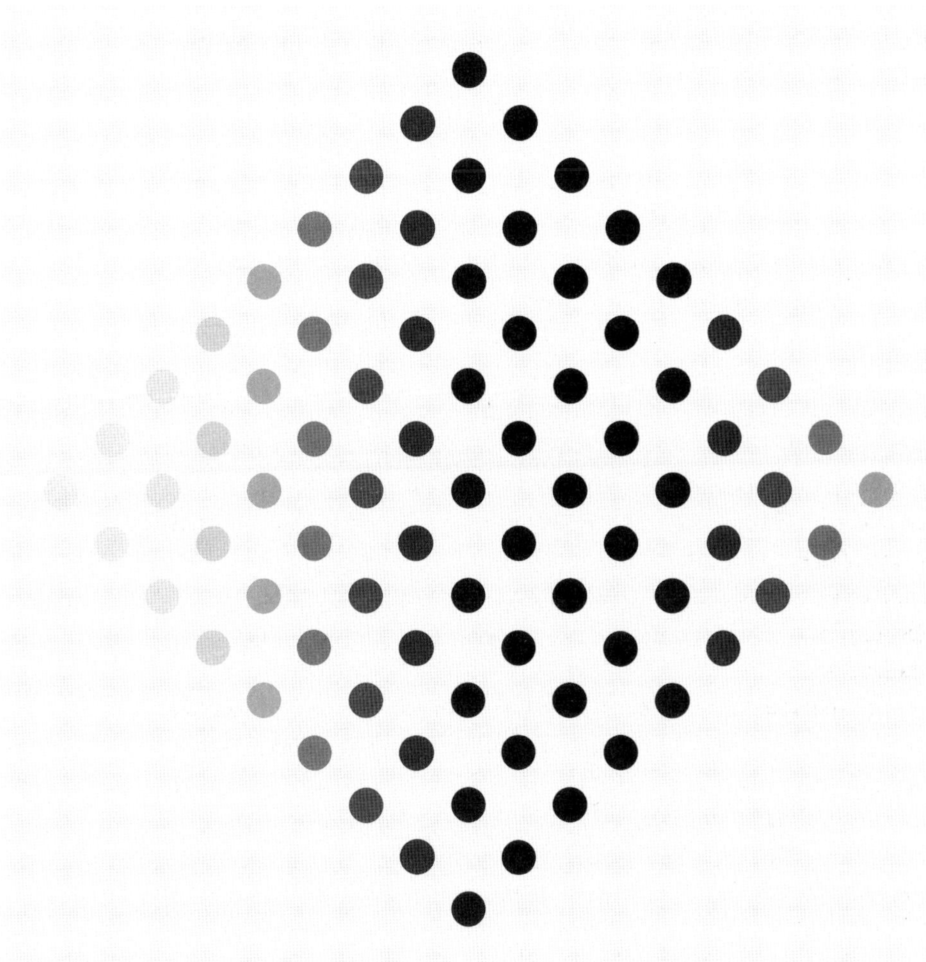

4. **Black to White Discs** 1962

Since the 1950s, Pop art had featured motifs culled from the new, technological aspects of contemporary life, but for some critics this was not enough to create a genuinely powerful art to express the new age. The subject matter of much Pop was the commodified aspects of technology, and because of this it risked becoming identified with mass culture rather than with the aesthetic values of 'high' culture. In Pop, technology appeared as the commodification of science, where science was reduced to a provider of (possibly frivolous) consumer goods. Depicting technology itself connoted the intellectually and socially 'second class', compounded by associations of commercialism. Nonetheless, in its technological manifestations, science was coming to dominate the environment in a physical sense, as industries expanded and their products proliferated. In the intellectual environment that bred the rhetoric of Snow and Wilson, we may detect an anxiety that art would lose its central cultural role. Hence a union between art and science might appear as more to the advantage of the former, endowing it with a new credibility as an expression of the age.

The notion that Op art could effect such a union – that it had pretensions to significant scientific content – seems to have developed over time. Initially, some critics reviewing Bridget Riley's work used vocabulary that was merely suggestive of scientific discourse. The *Observer*'s review of Riley's first show at Gallery One in 1962 described her paintings as 'experiments in perceptual experience' in which 'black and white patterns of geometrical shapes bring the flat picture surface alive and vibrant to an extraordinary degree' [Figs. 4 and 5].[21] Scientific and mathematical language (experiments – perceptual – geometrical) was used unproblematically in this early review without any overt suggestion that the work was based on scientific or mathematical principles. The reference to the 'flat picture surface', which was 'brought alive' without any suggestion of the illusion of depth, suggests that the reviewer saw the work as anchored within the conventions of modernism as promoted by Fry, Bell and Greenberg, however novel the artist's interpretation of those conventions might be.

In his review of 'The Responsive Eye' for the *New York Times*, American critic John Canaday found the relevance of Op to a technological society to lie not in the scientific credentials of the artists or their methods but in the works themselves [Fig. 6]. Writing broadly of the paintings, sculptures and painted constructions in the exhibition, Canaday commended them as: 'the only objects being created today, as art, that can compete with launching pads and industrial machinery as expressions of

5. **Tremor** 1962

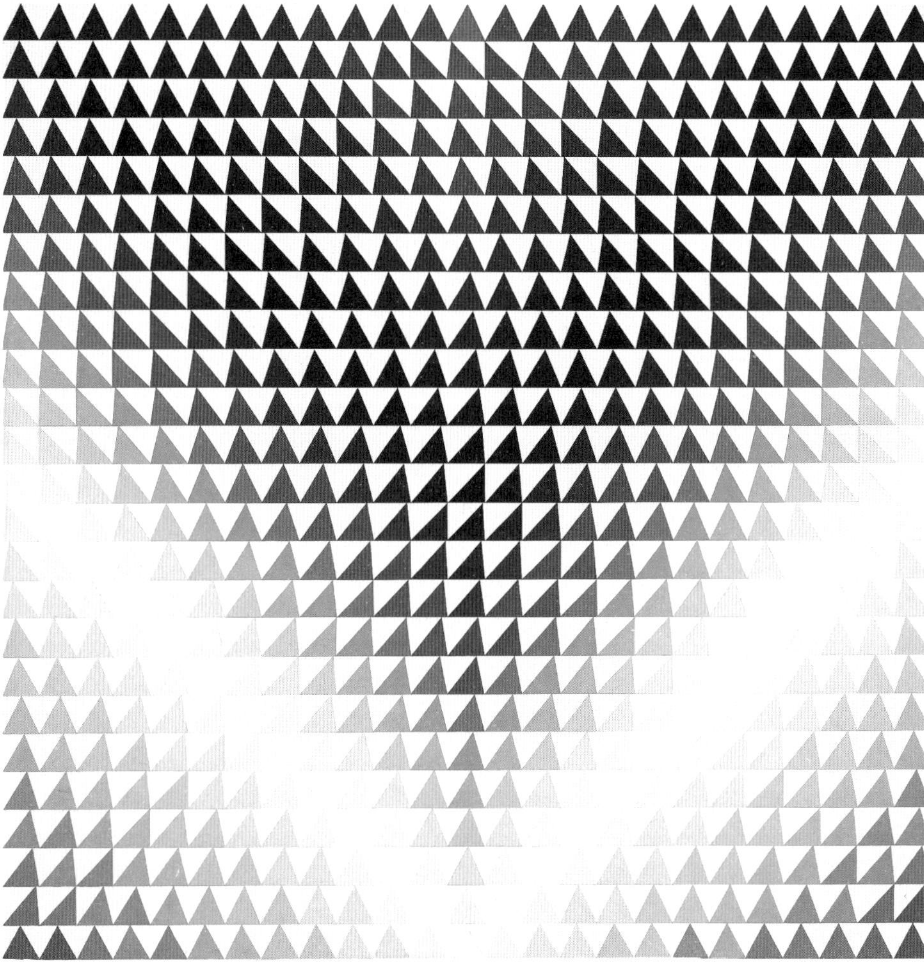

6. **Burn** 1964

the character unique to our civilization'.[22] This was echoed by an unnamed artist quoted by US art critic Harold Rosenberg: '"The most romantic place on earth" an [Op] artist declares in his exhibition announcement "is Cape Kennedy"'.[23] Here the romance of exploration was coupled with the 'scientific' notion of a 'space age' – and perhaps with extensions of US military power into space.

Canaday's comment makes it clear that art and science, far from being potentially unified, were in direct competition. The visible progeny of science – technology – had produced visual emblems that dominated Western civilization's conception of itself. The most significant images representing contemporary life were those conveyed by the television screen, where technological products featured more often than works of art. Thus one of the traditional functions of art – to supply society with self-images – was now performed by science and technology. The high level of media exposure given to 'The Responsive Eye' may have contributed to the sense that art had at last found a form in which it could compete with science. American art critic Barbara Rose argued that this notion of Op art as a response to the cultural ascendancy of science had contributed to the media interest in 'The Responsive Eye':

> *Another idea that a show of this nature puts across is the ... false one that art and science have something to do with one another. The reconciliation of art to science is (from the amount of to-do 'The Responsive Eye' has elicited) a particularly attractive rationale to a science-oriented technological society. Thus, if it was the task of the Renaissance to reconcile Plato with Christ, it is ours, one might argue, to reconcile Orpheus with Einstein, and Optical art is hailed as the offspring of that blissful union. This is the pseudo-humanism of* The Two Cultures *and equally nonsensical.*[24]

Rose's 'blissful union' anticipates Riley's expression, 'a celebration of the marriage of art and science'. Like Riley, Rose dismissed the notion but admitted its currency, which is also indicated by another review, written later in 1965 when 'The Responsive Eye' had moved to Pasadena:

> *behind the organization of this exhibition there seems to be an implicit belief that Op art offers a maximum of scientific (or rather, technological) attitude as applied to contemporary art and may represent a beginning of that third culture so avidly sought by those who bemoan the gap between the humanities and the sciences.*[25]

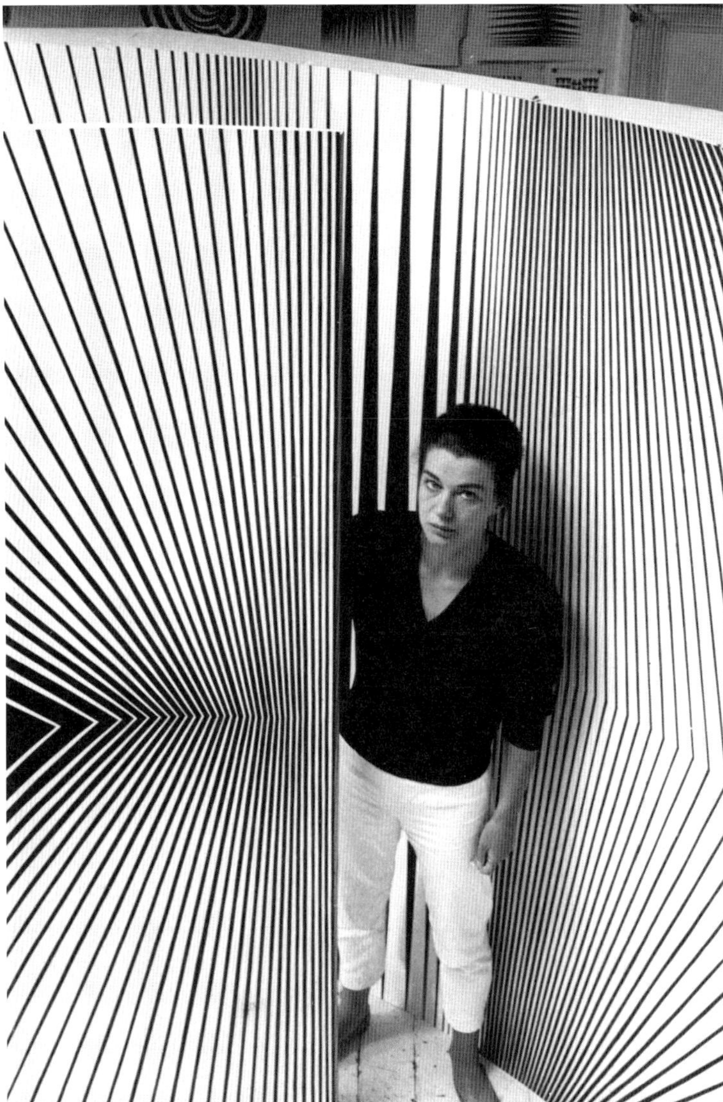

7. **Continuum** 1963

'Science', 'technology' and fears for the future

The widespread view that science and technology were beneficial was not uncontested. The journalist Bernard Levin expressed the unease felt by some sections of the public:

> *Stealthily the computer advanced, vanguard of the technological revolution, hailed as the cure for all mankind's ills and denounced as the baleful force which would first enslave and then destroy us all.*[26]

It seems strange that in the mid-twentieth-century Britain, the land where the Industrial Revolution had begun two hundred years previously, computers should have been seen as the 'vanguard' of a technological revolution, rather than a further progression in one instituted long ago. It is as if technology were perceived as something new in itself, with an untested power to change society for good or ill, to enslave where American-style labour-saving devices had promised to liberate. Levin's words present a more troubled conception of the future than Canaday's optimistic space-age vision.

To C.P. Snow, a lack of understanding of science and technology existed because the scientist and the non-scientist did not communicate and knew nothing of each other's work. Twentieth-century science had developed ideas such as relativity and quantum phenomena that were difficult for the layperson to grasp or to relate to everyday life. At the same time, since the First World War (1914–18) British governments had used scientific expertise and achievement to achieve military success: the development of more effective weapons and of the intelligence systems that gave rise to the first computers.[27] This may have created a perception of science as being primarily for military purposes. Films such as *The Dambusters*, which showed science as a key to military victory, may have reinforced this idea. Science could be blamed for the horrors of the atom bomb and, in peacetime, phenomena such as myxomatosis (introduced in Britain and Australia in the 1950s to reduce rabbit populations), the thalidomide tragedy (from 1961 recognized as the cause of deformities in babies born to mothers who took it during pregnancy) and nuclear power (an accident at the Windscale nuclear reactor in Cumbria had released radioactive fumes, in 1957).

In this context, some commentators feared that art might be rendered hard, aggressive and even violent, while science might be 'emasculated' by the subjectivity of art.[28] The most notable signs of the former concerns were the many assertions that Op was an 'aggressive' art form and such charges were often levelled at Riley's work. A 'trivia' page in the *Daily Mail* in September 1963 made much of a correspondent's claims that her cylindrical 'walk-in' painting *Continuum* (1963 – now lost) [Figs. 3 and 7] produced sensations of seasickness in the spectator.[29] In a more serious piece, artist and critic Andrew Forge was to accuse Riley of 'swaying the audience by tilting the seats'.[30]

I will return to the theme of violence/aggression later in this book, and show that there was widespread concern with this in various areas of culture in the 1960s, and hence its importance for the reception of Riley's work.

Apart from the more obviously troubling aspects of scientific developments, even more apparently benign aspects caused concern. From the 1950s, science – in the form of technology-based consumer goods such as television, numerous household gadgets and the motor car – had perceptibly changed most people's lives. This was not seen as an unalloyed good. In Britain, there were fears about the effects of greater materialism, as crime rates were higher in this period than in the much less prosperous pre-war society.[31] A generalized notion of science was linked not only with ill-defined visions of future improvements in industrial performance and national well-being, but also with the idea that valued aspects of British culture might be under threat from the little-understood powers of the scientist.[32] Science represented a certain vision of the future and was therefore associated with deeply felt hopes and fears because of its apparently god-like power to create and destroy. The debates about science in this period lent a cultural vitality and even glamour to the idea of 'the scientific', increasing the likelihood that it would become linked in some way to contemporary art. As Pop art had been associated with a world of commodified technology, so Op art (often treated in the media as the successor to Pop[33]), with its use of images apparently drawn from the science-linked phenomenon of optical illusions, lent itself to appropriation as the art of Wilson's 'scientific revolution'.

Venus and Mars – a new kind of culture?

So, in the 1960s, both in Britain and the USA, a seductive new kind of culture – a 'technoculture' based on the little-understood power of scientific knowledge and the technologies that followed in its wake – was seen as creating a new kind of society.[34] Labour-saving devices in industry and the home promised greater leisure and comfort. There were perceptions of greater prosperity for the bulk of the British population, partly created by the availability and affordability of domestic technological products, many of which had not existed, or had been generally unavailable, a generation previously. Pop art was a self-conscious product of this new society (or, in Britain, of the tantalizing dream of it before it began to materialize). As we have seen, in using motifs and themes drawn from commercial sources, it risked being seen as 'commercialized' itself. Could painting enjoy a position of cultural dominance in a world of television and the 'space race' unless – instead of depicting a commercialized technology – it forged an alliance with science on equal terms?

Now, in a marriage of Mars and Venus, warlike science (with its military/aggressive connotations) could be tamed by the beauty of art and rendered not only harmless but accessible. If an Op painting *were* a result of mathematical calculation or scientific theory, there was no question that the viewer needed to understand either maths or theory, because they had been transmuted into art. The term 'marriage' connotes an element of wooing, even seduction: had art seduced science or vice versa? Hence reviews of the period that claimed that Op had scientific content were vague about its precise nature. In a society where art and science were perceived as so separate as to form two cultures, such a marriage, if attempted at all, could hardly be promoted without provoking powerful reactions, whether for or against. Just when this marriage may have seemed to offer a way ahead for art, Op emerged,[35] apparently with the right credentials. Some of its practitioners claimed to be scientists (for example, US artist and exhibitor at 'The Responsive Eye', Gerald Oster), whilst others claimed to work in a scientific fashion (for example, GRAV). Furthermore, visual perception, the branch of science with which Op was most closely associated, may have seemed particularly well suited to effect such a match, and not merely because of the obvious connection between art and visual perception. The psychoanalyst C.G. Jung had commented in 1954 on what he claimed was a new awareness of perception as the governing factor in an individual's knowledge of and interpretation of the physical universe. Jung was aware of earlier work in physics[36] that could be seen as supporting the concept of the subjectivity of all experience.

> *Now that the formerly hypostatised 'universal' ideas have turned out to be mental principles, it is dawning upon us to what an extent our whole experience of so-called reality is psychic; as a matter of fact, everything felt, thought or perceived is a psychic image and the world itself exists only so far as we are able to produce an image of it.*[37]

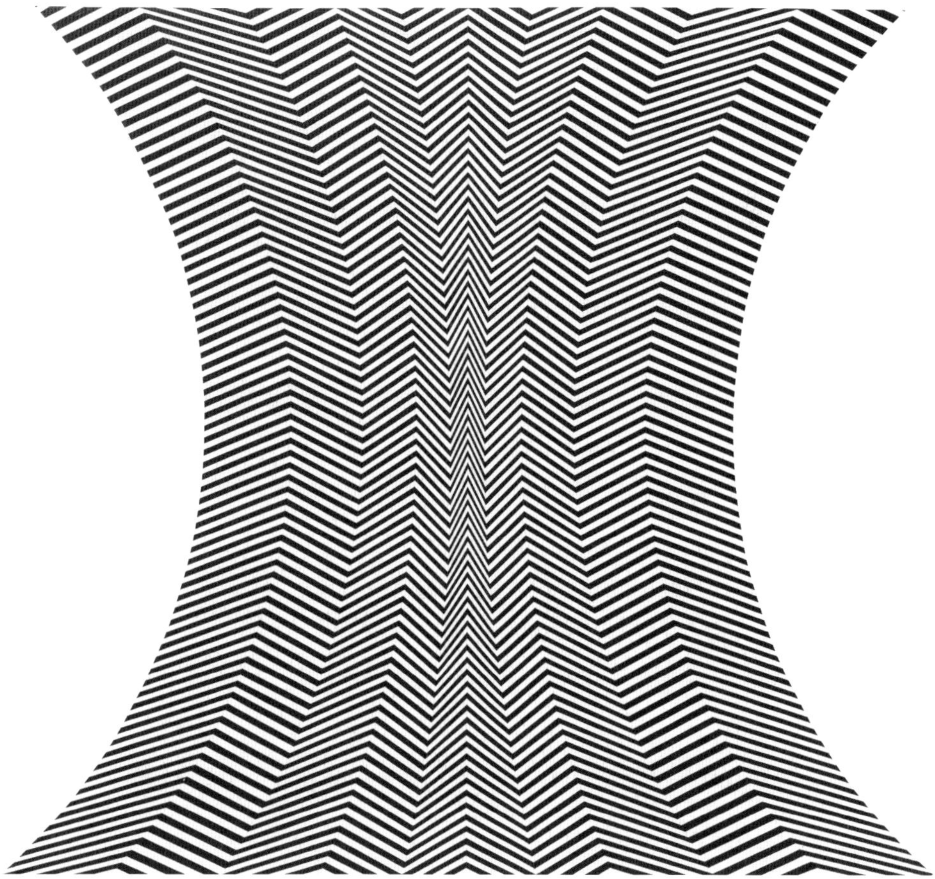

8. **Climax** 1963

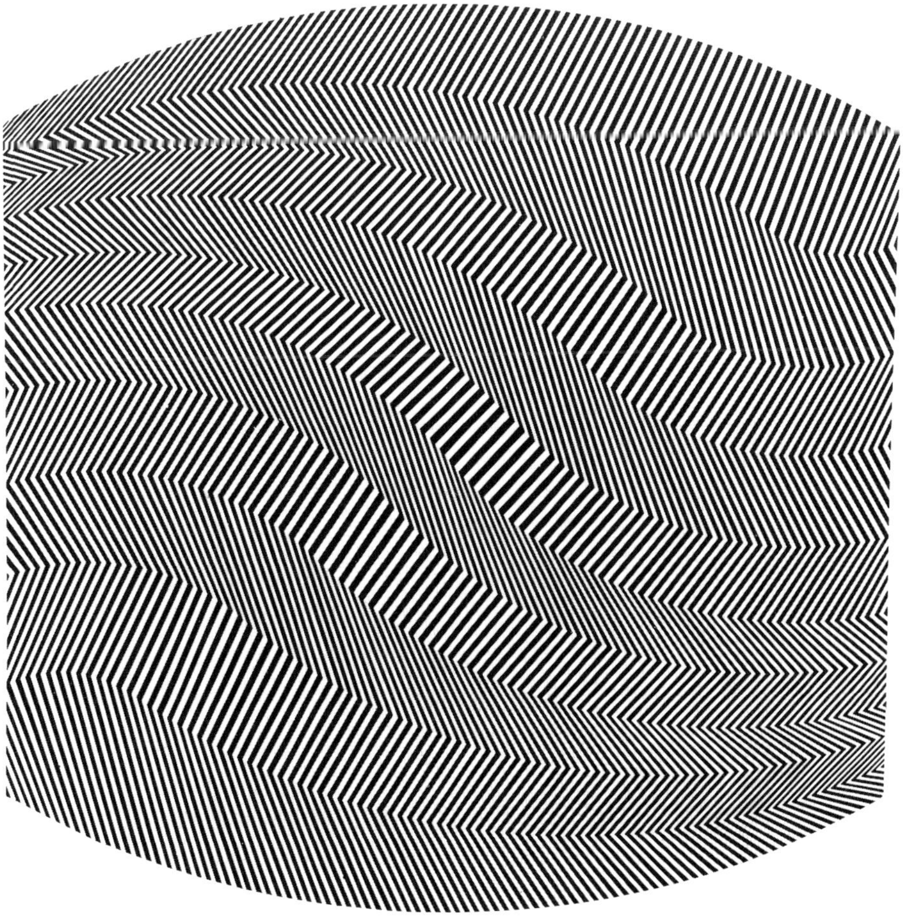

9. **Shuttle** 1964

Here, reality is no longer seen as an objective phenomenon but as a construct of the human mind, so that perception becomes central to conceptions of 'the real', and 'scientific objectivity' is seen to be simply subjectivity in disguise. If the only possible understanding of the universe is a subjective one (and art is seen as essentially subjective), then the possibility arises that barriers between art and science may be overcome. Furthermore, if subjectivity depends on perception, an art which foregrounded the very experience of perceiving would be an ideal candidate to unite art and science.

2. Modernism in dispute[38]

Modernism was a contested field with key figures, such as Fry and Read in Britain, and Greenberg and Michael Fried in the USA, influencing interpretations of what constituted modernist art. William Seitz, a senior curator at MoMA, was a contender here, wishing to position his institution as the arbiter of modernist taste. His championing of Op art, particularly exemplified by Riley's work, was a deliberate attempt to seize the initiative in this debate and renew MoMA's earlier role as a determining force in the trajectory of modernism.[39]

Op and the future of culture

The emerging popularity of Op art indicated to some people that contemporary aesthetics were moving away from the models widely associated with modernism, and that science and technology were implicated in this. This in turn was related to hopes and fears about the future of Western culture, as cultural production and aesthetics are inevitably interlinked. Riley's paintings can be seen as points of convergence for contemporary concerns about the future of science, of artistic modernism and of the wider culture in which they appeared.

In May 1964 Jonathan Miller reviewed three exhibitions held in London: a Rauschenberg one-man show held earlier that year, the just-closed 'New Generation' show at the Whitechapel Gallery (which included work by Riley, Figs. 8, 9, 10 and 11) and the still-running show of paintings from the Lisbon-based Gulbenkian Foundation at the Tate.[40] Miller saw all this as 'Mod'[41] art, especially the Whitechapel show: 'cool, "go" and very purple heart'.[42] After describing the repetitive patterns used by Anthony Donaldson, Miller went on to discuss how:

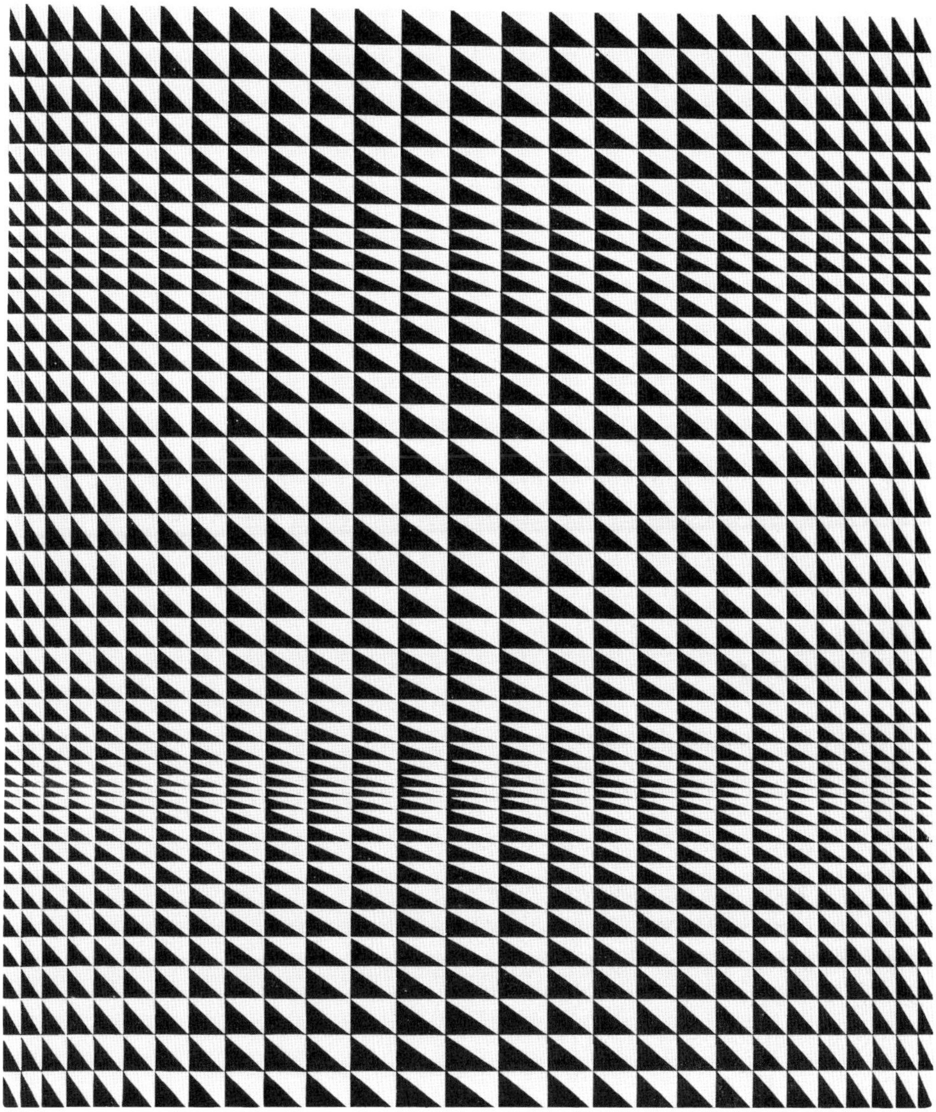

10. **Straight Curve** 1963

the optical painters, Bridget Riley and Vasarely force this exploitation of repetitive rhythms to an almost physiological extreme with patterns derived from the striped, dotted or chequered cards used in experimental optics. This is painting by dint of ruthless mathematical calculation, whereby in pitting carefully calibrated patterns of stimuli against the rhythmic action of the observer's brain and retina a fantastic vibrato is established. In the same mathematical idiom we get the strange moiré appearances produced by imposing grids or gauzes one upon the other ...

In the work of these artists one can see how the enduring impulse for ornament has fleshed itself out with the new rhythmic themes of science and technology.

As if to reinforce his claim for the role of science and technology in contemporary art, Miller also asserted that:

if the revolution in aesthetics was begun by the invention of movable type, it has been extended almost beyond recognition by the visual fecundity of TV, cinematography and experimental optics.

Miller saw the work of Riley and Vasarely as unequivocally 'scientific' in its origins; he did not doubt that their paintings derived directly from experimental optics and were products of mathematical, scientific and technological phenomena. Here, Op art was an expression of a certain concept of science and technology – one in which the use of mathematics was 'ruthless' (an oddly emotive term for a field often regarded as 'emotionless' and 'intellectual') and science was always 'experimental'. Miller implied that artists such as Riley and Vasarely were using the fully-fledged results of earlier scientific experiments, 'carefully calibrated' to achieve predetermined effects, which anyone could achieve simply by following the rules. This suggests that Op was even more dependent on science for its content than Pop art had been on technology, a view shared by Harold Rosenberg, who commented in the mid-1960s that '"Op" art is far more extreme than Pop in subjugating art to the social power, this time the power of science'.[43] He interpreted dependence on science as subjection to it; the position of the artist as a creator of unique works of the imagination was undermined; a marriage of equals was not possible, and this sort of argument underlies resistance to the suggestion by Riley and others.

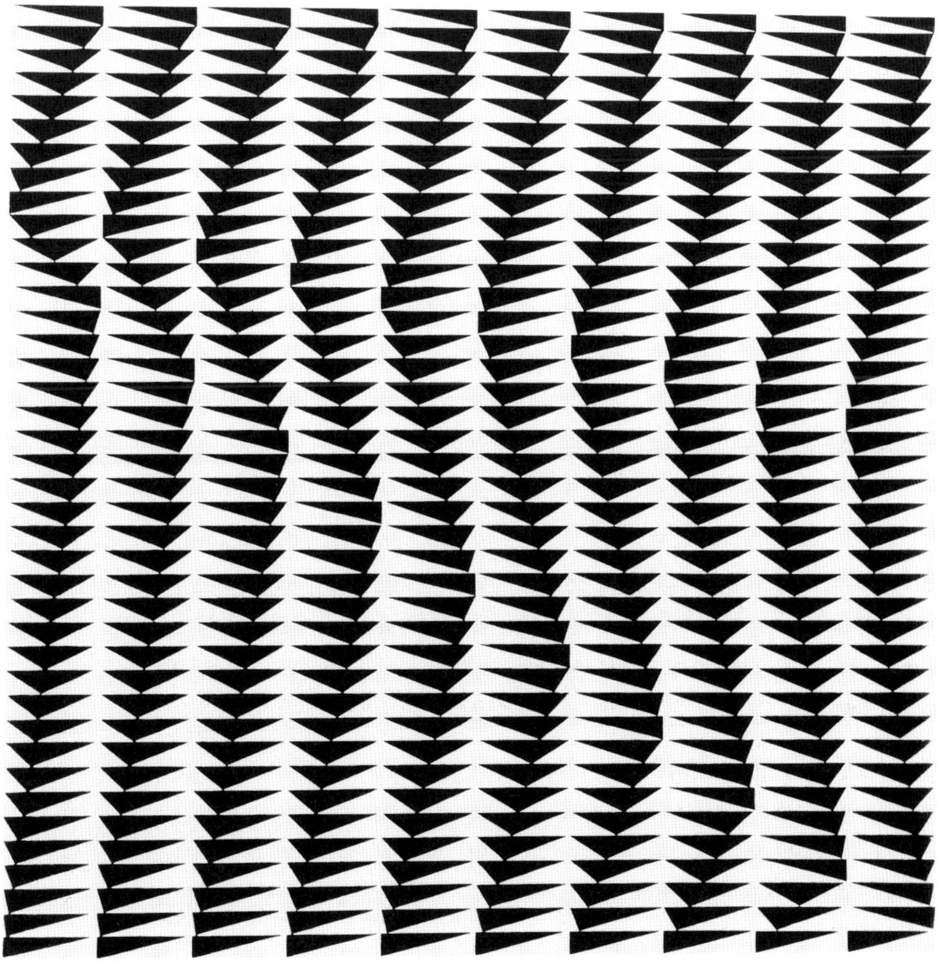

11. **Shift** 1963

Miller's 'revolution in aesthetics' was a revolution of the people, not of an elite: Caxton introduced to Britain a process whereby books and their contents eventually became available to a mass audience. During the twentieth century, the information technologies of television and cinema continued this process of making information and ideas available to a wide public. Miller's claim that experimental optics was having a comparable effect to that of cinema and television on contemporary aesthetics implied that Op was now a pervasive, widely-known and influential art form. The idea that contemporary aesthetics could be affected by experimental optics suggested that the discoveries of this branch of science had become general knowledge. The only point of access to such knowledge that Miller suggests is Op art itself: for him, the methods and results of optical experimentation had been used by Op artists in an aesthetic revolution which could trace its history back to Caxton. History was used here to support the artistic claims of a new form of painting. Miller placed Op in an historical relation to the concept of 'the aesthetic', but without invoking modernism.

Miller's reference to 'the enduring impulse for ornament' is ambiguous. His review is 'cool' (to use a 'Mod' slang term often applied to Op art at the time[44]): he was intrigued by the new art and presented it as full of potential. In the early 1960s, however, it would have been read in the context of older models of modernism, which remained influential.[45] To describe Op paintings as 'ornamental' could mean that they were not modernist – perhaps even anti-modernist. In 1964, whatever Miller's own views, this would probably have been interpreted as derogatory. A reference to an 'impulse for ornament' implied that Op paintings were derived from ancient human needs that predated modernist dogma. This is Op as a rejection of modernism and an assertion of older, more 'human' values, despite the 'ruthless mathematical calculation'. The 'enduring impulse' expressed in Op had 'fleshed itself out with the new rhythmic themes of science and technology'. This can be read as an assertion, in effect, that contemporary art – and contemporary aesthetics – could be modern without being modernist.

Miller expressed a guarded enthusiasm for British versions of Op but much less for the US versions. He devoted just a few lines to the Gulbenkian exhibition but noted that it:

> *abounds in pieces which could have come from the pages of* Scientific American. *There are conglomerates of lunar dust, elegant meson tracks, printed circuits, spectroscopic shadows of*

> *nucleoproteins or the wrecked left-overs of archaeological digs. One wanders Crusoe-like through the league-long reefs of the Tate hoping against hope to be thunderstruck by the print of a human foot.*[46]

The reference to *Scientific American* hinted at a pre-packaged, simplified version of science that the artists concerned had simply transferred to canvas. It also suggests that there is something specifically 'American' about this, echoing debates about the post-war 'Americanization' of Europe. Apart from lunar dust,[47] Miller's list of supposed influences on/subjects for the art shown in this exhibition consists almost entirely of the creations of scientists. Yet Miller looked for evidence of human involvement in the creation of these paintings and did not find it. Printed circuits, meson tracks, spectroscopic images and archaeology simply 'existed' without human contrivance and could not themselves constitute 'the print of a human foot'. Science was presented here as not merely alien to art, but alien to humanity. Miller expressed uneasiness over the directions in which both art and science were taking Western culture. There was an implication that Humanity itself might be driven from art by its apparent preoccupation with 'science'. Miller pondered:

> *One wonders how things will go from now on ... / ... the image of man has slipped like a Boojum into the night, leaving a sort of unmanned, indifferent art like something snapped by a self-operated space probe.*[48]

Was Humanity to be exiled from its own culture? Miller echoed earlier concerns that the advance of technology and the accompanying 'revolution in aesthetics' would have deleterious moral and psychological effects on human beings.

'...bitten by art, dreaming about science'

As we have seen, not all the connections made between Op and science took the form of claims that Op was directly based on scientific theories or concepts. Other links were perceived, often with technological developments rather than with pure theory. Reviewing Riley's Gallery One show in August 1962, Robert Melville described her painting *Escaping Centre* (1962) as: 'the fifteen phases of the well-planned escape of a dot from an encompassing circle' – a description suggesting the escape of a spacecraft or satellite from a planet's sphere of gravity.[49] The telecommunications satellite *Telstar* had been launched with much publicity only a month before this review appeared, while the US space probe *Mariner 2* was due to be launched shortly afterwards, suggesting a link between Melville's use of this language and the media coverage of, and public preoccupation with, these events.

Television was a primary form of technology which had entered the domestic sphere for the majority of people in the 1950s and 1960s. It had the potential to show the launches of spacecraft and other major technological developments that would otherwise have been invisible to the general public. Television seemed to break down the distinctions between the private, domestic space and external public space. Furthermore, from a British sitting-room, one could look straight in to an American sitting-room or kitchen in an imported sit-com and see 'the future' – those elements of domestic gadgetry that were not yet available in Britain or were still too expensive for most people. There were worries about the influence of television on society and these were not always about the content of specific television programmes. The critic and painter Andrew Forge commented in April 1964:

> *[w]hen one comes within range of Bridget Riley's violent black and white dazzle and one's whole field of vision begins to jump and flicker, it is exactly as though, like some cool TV mechanic, she had reached out and started to twiddle knobs in one's box.*[50]

Here, technology had taken over completely, as though the viewer of the painting were trapped inside the television set, at the mercy of the manipulative artist-mechanic – the latest manifestation of the mad scientist who wants to rule the world. 'Cool' was a term much used in the period to describe new, geometrically-based art forms that were regarded as breaking away from, or reacting against, Abstract Expressionism, as well as in the 'Mod' sense, used by Miller, to describe an attitude of detachment, a lack of emotional involvement regarded as 'chic'.[51] There is a link here between Riley's work and the contemporary 'new wave' (not just Op painting) and a suggestion of the artist's fashionable detachment from the viewer, whom she manipulates with casual power. Forge echoed common fears of the power of television. It was seen as a threat to cultural values that emphasized the importance of literature and the development of individual taste and discernment.[52]

Modernist dogma also emphasized individual discrimination while suggestions that Op 'manipulated' the viewer's visual perceptual system implied that it denied an individual and discriminating response. Other critics also saw television as a sinister and manipulative medium, and connected these qualities with Op art. Thomas Hess, in his extensive review of 'The Responsive Eye', also closely linked Op art to television. Hess asserted that, while Pop art took its content from the printed media:

> *Op uses T.V. – its image made up of hundreds of tiny dots which the eye reads by filling in the gaps; in times of distress the screen is covered by appealing moiré patterns. There is the same quivering glare to the light, the same ping effects, the radar blips. And there is the same immediacy. Like the T.V. viewer the Op audience passively participates, conditioned into giving up critical faculties or at least suspending disbelief. Peripatetic zombies ... the image acts on and for the placid viewer. It lures him to watch.*[53]

Television was presented here primarily in terms of technology rather than in terms of its cultural content. It was depicted as highly suspect, a technological artefact hypnotically taking over the mind of the viewer, rendering him or her 'passive' – with that word's suggestions of weakness and helplessness – and now infiltrating art. Furthermore, Op art works were argued to have an effect on the retino-neuro-physiological system that might be mild or strong, according to the work in question, and which was assumed to affect everyone in the same way. The disorientating or dizzy feelings reported by many spectators indicated to Hess that the viewer looking at an Op painting was not engaging the critical and intellectual faculties which had traditionally been considered necessary to the appreciation of 'good' art. He commented that:

> *Op effects only function as they mesh with the physiology of the eye-brain system. In other words, Op works with what is already there, in your nerves ... Op plays with increasingly complicated now-you-see-it, now-you-see-something-else illusions ... (Op) has the craftsman's awe of craft secrets and the technician's relish of a good job neatly done.*[54]

Although all visual phenomena are dependent for their perception on the eye-brain system, the point about optical illusions is that they exploit the way that this system has evolved to interpret certain visual stimuli in particular ways. Perspective drawing exploits the same phenomenon – smaller objects are perceived as being further away than larger objects, even though the spectator of a painting knows that such objects occupy the same flat plane. Hess was prepared to accept perspective as a valid artistic technique whereas he regarded Op artists as mere 'craftsmen' and 'technicians', implying that craft and technique are inferior to true art (and to science).[55] He argued that a new art should not be 'popular', 'especially when its style is new and it has not yet been assimilated in a body of accepted ideas'. For Hess, Op's public and media acceptance undermined its claim to be art – however, he did not claim that Op was science rather than art. This might have seemed a serious, even important, association for this kind of painting. His approach was to trivialize, not to validate. 'Op is not involved with science but with the pseudo-scientific crafts of display – shop window designs, textile patterns, eye-catching wrapping-papers'.[56] This reference to 'display' echoes Miller's 'enduring impulse to ornament' and is effectively a denial of Op's modernist credentials by linking it to the frivolity of the ornamental, the ephemeral and the commercial. Hess saw Op as a commodity, not an art form.

Hess dismissed Op as 'gadgetry, bitten by art, dreaming about science'.[57] Whereas, for Hess, Pop art took inspiration from the contents of the printed media, Op actually was a sort of 'gadgetry' – and the only piece of 'gadgetry' to which he compared it was the television set. Whereas Canaday saw Op as an art that could 'compete' with technology, Hess saw only another manifestation of technology – and not in a form anything like as impressive as Canaday's 'launching pads and industrial machinery' but rather in the guise of the humble domestic television set. This notion of domesticity itself was used to argue that Op was not modernist because the domestic sphere was alien to contemporary constructions of modernism.[58] Hess presented the 'scientific' aspect of Op, such as it may have been, not as ultra-modern but actually as rather passé, consisting of ideas with which even relatively uneducated members of the public were familiar.

> *The ideas about color, after-images, moirés, etc. which attract certain* Popular Mechanics *coteries to the mode, are rooted in late eighteenth century experiments which were exploited in the early nineteenth century by Central Europeans (especially in Austria) and reached France just before the mid-century in time for Chevreul and the experiences of impressionism.*[59]

Here, history was not brought in to defend Op but to attack it as a product of passé science. Hess claimed that Op appealed to the readers of *Popular Mechanics*, a tribe that one feels he would have labelled 'nerds' had he had this word at his disposal in 1965. If the existence of a widespread audience for Op in itself undermined Op's claims to be art, readers of *Popular Mechanics* were beyond the pale!

To sum up, there were a variety of connections made by critics between Op art and science and/or technology. The connections they perceived evoked fears about the effects of science and technology on wider aspects of culture. In particular, television was deeply distrusted and presented as manipulative (although the forms of this manipulation and its effects on individuals were somewhat non-specific). Others made links with space technology, apparently concerned that artists were creating a dehumanized art. Op art was intimately linked with ideas of 'the future' and fears that this future was to be dominated by technology, whether in the home (the television) or outside it (where space exploration represented the most extreme aspect of the 'outside' to which human beings had ever had access). There were fears that this future would also be a dehumanized one. At the same time, the idea of 'progress' was central to a view of modernism that had held sway at least since MoMA's first curator, Alfred Barr had published his art history 'genealogical tree' in 1936.[60] Progress was seen as inevitable in art just as, since the 'Enlightenment' in the eighteenth century, it had been seen as inevitable (and desirable) in science. Long-standing anxieties about progress were being reformulated in the 1960s to encompass more than just material culture. Art was apparently travelling along the same highway as technology and, to critics such as Miller, neither was being directed by Man but rather both were *directing* Man. The perceived links between Op and science/technology made Op a focus for these fears and encouraged its rejection by some modernists as embodying the 'wrong' sort of progress.

Op, modernism and the idea of a scientific art

Bridget Riley certainly saw herself as a modernist artist and was seen as such by many of her contemporaries; as we have seen, there were differing views of what might constitute modernist art, and modernism's relation with other aspects of modernity was problematic. Science had epitomized modernity for some time, hence the desire in some quarters to incorporate science into art. T.J. Clark sees this as a recurring phenomenon: 'Some avant-gardes ... believe that artists can be scientists, and new descriptions of the world be forged under laboratory conditions, putting aside the question of wider intelligibility for the time being'.[61] Clark's use of 'avant-gardes' indicates that the artists who believe that they 'can be scientists' are also modernists, and Georges Seurat certainly comes to mind here. By the 1960s, nonetheless, a gulf had opened between dominant conceptions of modernism and science.

Riley was herself influenced by Seurat's art, in which an important aim was to eliminate the expressiveness of the brushstroke as a signature of the artist's individual personality, so as to create an objective, anonymous mode of expression, which in turn connotes a scientific approach.

This anonymity of surface facture runs counter to, say, Fry or Greenberg's view of modernism: that the work of art should be a work of self-expression characterized by individuality of facture, the kind of art most recently epitomized by Abstract Expressionism.[62] This version of the modernist ideal was challenged throughout the 1960s by Pop art, Minimalism and other movements such as Conceptual art, so Op art was an early part of this contemporary debate.

Because notions of a scientific art could be associated with early forms of modernism such as Seurat's or the Russian Constructivists',[63] the supposed connection between Op and science was not necessarily seen as either new or progressive. When Edward Lucie-Smith organized the show 'One Year of British Art' at the Tooth Gallery, London in February 1963, Nigel Gosling described the Op exhibits as 'a throwback to the scientific experiments of the pointillists' and:

> *perhaps the ultimate in abstraction – pure retinal sensation divorced from form or content – and by definition a dead end, though it is impressively reached by Bridget Riley and Gwyther Irwin.*[64]

Here, Gosling seemed to be referring to Riley's expressed interest in Seurat but saw her work as paradoxically a 'throwback' *and* 'the ultimate in abstraction' – from this, one might infer that it was the ultimate in modernist painting. This was not Gosling's position, however, as the term 'dead end' makes clear. Despite the precise geometric construction of her paintings, they had no 'form' and any references to 'the scientific experiments of the pointillists' did not constitute a 'content'. Gosling believed that mathematics and science had nothing to do with art; his conviction that Riley's work had a scientific or mathematical basis disqualified it as art of any importance. The term 'dead end' indicated that art was expected to progress constantly – just as people had come to expect a continuous process of change in the social and economic spheres, so too did they expect it in art. Inspiration for new art forms had to be found and while Gosling evidently believed that science would not provide it, other commentators were more open to the possibility that it could.

A romantic approach to Op

In 1964, when Riley's *Blaze 1* [Fig. 12] won a prize in the John Moores Competition, the critic Robert Melville described her work as 'a romantic approach to the science of optics'.[65] In other words, what was previously thought of as objective and independent of the observer – the science of

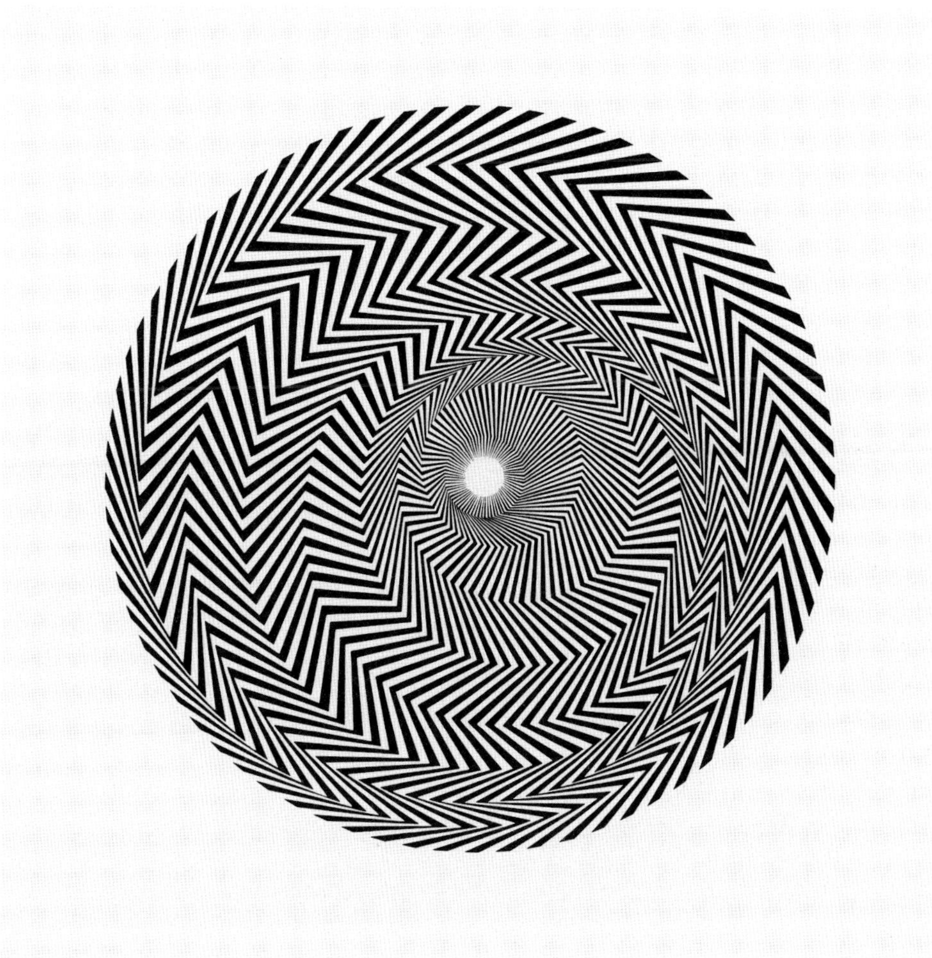

12. **Blaze 1** 1962

optics – was susceptible to different approaches, including the highly subjective 'romantic' approach.

In contrast to post-Enlightenment ideals of objectivity and rationalism, Romanticism emphasized subjectivity and harmony with (rather than domination of) nature. Although it had originated in the late eighteenth century, there were links between Romanticism and modernism. Greenberg's formulation of modernism was partly based on the philosophy of Kant (1724–1804), which he applied to the production and appreciation of art. A Kantian privileging of sensory perception is central to Romanticism, in which in turn we find that privileging of the notion of artistic genius and subjectivity seen in concepts of the modernist artist. Melville's review emphasized the way that *Blaze 1* subverted the processes of visual perception to create impressions that the viewer understood as purely subjective.

> *The stripes* appear *to shuttle back and forth, the hole in the centre* appears *to be a long way off and the stripes going one way* appear *to be a different colour*[66] *from the stripes going the other way.*[67] [Emphases added.]

There was no discussion of what this manipulation of appearances might signify for the viewer. What it signified for Melville was implicitly a process of appropriation – either of a form of science by an artist or of art by science – and this (equivocal) appropriation would appear to be an end in itself. His review also suggested that the dynamic effects of the paintings were achieved through a set of 'scientific' procedures that could be followed by anyone, with the same result.

It is difficult to dissociate any concept of a 'science of optics' from perception – optics must be studied via 'what is seen' and 'the seen' is known through visual perception. In optics, more than in many other branches of science, it is clear that observation is subjective. The large amount of work on optical illusion published during the 1950s meant that this was widely known by the 1960s. Hence, it may be difficult to conceive of a 'romantic' approach to the science of thermodynamics (for instance) but optics lends itself to such treatment.

In linking optics and art, however, the critics were not making an unprecedented connection between art and science. Seurat and the Neo-Impressionists had been influenced by the 'psychophysics' of Charles Henry, in an earlier attempt to create a 'scientific' basis for art, but there had been a much more recent attempt to 'marry' art and science. In the early 1950s, crystallographic images had been used to create the so-called 'Festival Style' of design associated with the Festival of Britain, 1951. Films on the growth of crystals were shown at the Independent Group's first exhibition, 'Growth and Form' at the Institute of Contemporary Art in London, also in 1951. The group's interest in science went much deeper than a contemporary fashion associated with the Festival.[68] It had been sparked by such books as D'Arcy Wentworth Thompson's *On Growth and Form* (1917) and Sigfried Giedion's *Mechanisation Takes Command* (1948), the former concerned with biological development and the latter with effects of industrial mechanization on art and culture. In the early 1950s, Constructivist artists[69] took particular interest in these books' rejection of Aristotelian, teleological explanations of natural phenomena. The Independent Group took up Thompson's argument that physical processes, rather than goal-directed development, accounted for natural forms. One member of the Group, Pop artist Richard Hamilton, claimed that the exhibition would influence designers by showing how beauty, derived from physical processes, had evolved by chance.[70] This viewpoint connected the Independent Group to the Dada movement and Duchamp, and they rejected the influential British critic Herbert Read's notion of 'timeless'[71] art. The Independent Group saw themselves as oppositional to Read's Aristotelian aesthetic.[72] Read's position was not as clear-cut as this, however, as his own writings show that he was interested in science as an aspect of culture but deplored what he saw as the materialistic aspects of technology.[73] Read had encouraged debates on the subject of art and science at the ICA in the early 1950s and one of these, the 'Aspects of Form' symposium, had been organized by a physicist and had also involved biologists and a crystallographer.[74] Read argued that both art and science depended on 'sensuous perception and imaginative experience' and it could be said that not only Read, but also the Independent Group and the Festival had a romantic approach to the science of crystallography. All shared a desire to privilege the 'natural' over its opposite, whether the latter were defined as 'technology' (in Read's case) or outmoded aesthetic values (in the Group's case). When Melville described Op as 'a romantic approach to the science of optics' he might instead have said 'here is the latest attempt at a romantic approach to a science'. Melville's review was itself another attempt to find a 'romantic' link between art and science.

Hence the Independent Group, Read, and the designers[75] who had created the Festival Style were all seeking expressions of modernity and sought to fertilize art with the modernizing power of science. Science and technology enjoyed a prominent rôle in the Festival, being celebrated in two major exhibitions, in the Dome of Discovery at the principal Festival site on the South Bank and in a series of new galleries at the Science Museum in South Kensington. It was notable that science was not contained exclusively within these appointed sites, however, but affected other areas of the exhibition as well, including those concerned with the fine arts

> *(T)he great screens that separated everyday London from the South Bank world, one strung with balls like an atomic structure line up.... could be regarded as a novel and functional sort of sculpture. The Skylon, turbines and propellers, the coal-faced tetrahedron sheltering Minerals of the Island* [sic], *the highly strung observation platforms beside the river: every major feature or exhibit seized the attention and left the fine art looking prim and out of sorts.*[76]

In the economic crisis that followed the Second World War, government and industry were desperate for exports; thus, whatever the state of the fine arts, they could not afford industrial designs that looked 'prim and out of sorts'. Science rather than art was seen as the potentially rejuvenating force. Moreover, science was presented as a source of national pride at the Festival. As early as 1949, the Council of Industrial Design (CoID, later the Design Council) was keen to use the fruits of scientific research to 'revitalize' industrial design. Paul Reilly (director of the Design Council in 1976), claims that, at that time, Britain led the world in crystallography.[77] Hartland Thomas, CoID's chief industrial officer in 1949, wrote an account of his work in this period.

> *I had it in mind that we are at a stage in the history of industrial design when both the public and the leading designers have a feeling for more richness in style and decoration, but are somewhat at a loss for inspiration. Traditional patterns that have come down to us from ancient Greece and elsewhere had lost much of their sparkle by now ... But these crystal structure diagrams had the discipline of exact repetitive symmetry; they were above all very pretty and were full of rich variety yet with a remarkable family likeness; they were essentially modern because the technique that constructed them was quite recent, and yet like all*

successful decorations of the past, they derived from nature – although it was nature at a submicroscopic scale not previously revealed.[78]

A number of points arise from this passage. If there were a new tendency for the public to seek out 'more richness in style and decoration' in design, in reaction to the drabness of wartime Britain, then surely the same social and psychological forces were at work in the production and perception of the fine arts. The desire to find inspiration in nature is something that design may also have had in common with the fine arts and, in the 1960s, may also have underlain the claims that Op was based on optical science (perception being as much a natural phenomenon as crystallographic structure). It is interesting that Thomas refers to crystallographic patterns as being 'constructed' by crystallography, the technique that had revealed them. It is as though these patterns did not exist until the crystallographers got to work; as though they were not uncovering a hidden, but previously existing, order of nature but actually constructing it as they worked. Science is shown here as literally making the world anew. For Thomas, 'timeless' patterns much older than the human race were 'essentially modern' for this reason.

This view of science as creative rather than merely observational contrasts strongly with views of science as a purely objective process of discovery and suggests that science could, in some way, form a valid inspiration for the modernist artist – a scientific aesthetic. Connotations of scientific creativity were compromised, however, by the association that Thomas sought to forge between the new science of crystallography and industrial design. Designs based on crystallographic patterns would be used on all manner of goods for domestic consumption – crockery and other ceramic ware, and textiles such as carpets, curtains and upholstery. Contemporary modernist ideas rigidly separated fine art from the applied arts and crafts; anything associated with the latter was likely to be deemed beyond the pale of the fine arts. To modernist critics and artists in Britain by the 1960s, therefore, memories of the scientific connotations of the Festival Style could have created strongly negative associations. Furthermore, the Style had been short-lived and had not given rise to obvious progeny; despite Thomas' hopes it had been a dead end itself, perhaps also sowing doubts that science could provide a new source of inspiration for the visual arts, whether fine or applied. Outside Britain, of course, connections between the Festival Style, with its scientific connotations, and the fine arts were much less likely to be either perceived or made.[79]

Connections between fine art and notions of the scientific were certainly made, nonetheless. Writing in the mid-sixties about the 1963 exhibition 'Americans' at MoMA, Harold Rosenberg considered the work of Richard Anuszkiewicz, whose work, by 1965, was to be categorized as Op by some critics.

> *The pictures first met on the gallery floor were exercises in eyeshifting dispositions of crosses, rectangles and circles in variations of color values and size. The statement by the artist, Richard Anuszkiewicz, in the museum catalogue helped put the spectator in the proper* tiled-laboratory *mood: 'My work is of an* experimental *nature and has centered on the* investigation *into the effects of complementary colors of full intensity when juxtaposed and the* optical *changes that occur as a result' and so on.*[80] [Emphases added.]

Here, Rosenberg picked up the scientific connotations of Anuszkiewicz's description of his work and intensified them by his preceding reference to the 'tiled-laboratory'. The notion of the laboratory may have connoted the Constructivist experiments in the Soviet Union, and caused unease for political reasons.

In 1964, *Time* magazine also picked up scientific references and expressed uneasiness about them. William Seitz, the curator of 'The Responsive Eye' Op show due to be held at MoMA in 1965, in which Riley's work was to feature prominently, was quoted: 'These works exist less as objects than as generators of perceptual responses'.[81] The same might be said of any work of art but the language used – the phrase 'generators of perceptual responses' – suggests the scientific or technological. The *Time* article nonetheless assured readers that:

> *Op has a legitimate ancestry. Cézanne, Seurat and Monet seized upon newly proposed theories of optics when they painted. In this century, such constructivists as Mondrian and Malevich were the forebears of op art's dry, highly controlled use of color which sometimes ... amounts to rejecting color.*[82]

Here the use of optical theory as a basis for art was legitimated by the precedents of nineteenth- and early twentieth-century modern masters, including Seurat. The implication was that without such precedents, there might be doubts about the validity of contemporary practices. Outside Britain as well as within it, the validity of art was called into question by close association with science.

The *Time* article went on to discuss the work of Josef Albers and Vasarely – the latter, it claimed 'dons the craftsy lab coat instead of the smock and refers to his work as visual research' (p. 42). *Time* presented a very quaint picture of the 'traditional' artist, wearing a smock, and contrasted this with the 'scientific' Op artist wearing a lab coat, like the six members of GRAV in Paris: 'six researchers who resemble the Atomic Energy Commission more than café-sitting artists'.[83] With this stereotypical view of both artists and scientists, *Time* was evidently concerned to draw a dividing line between art and science. Artistic identity was apparently threatened by too intimate a connection with science – the inference is that it really *mattered* for an artist to be readily identifiable as such. Readers were told that 'Germany boasts a group called Zero, begun in 1959 by three artists who hold PhD degrees'.[84] There was no indication of which subjects these degrees were in – implicitly, they were in 'scientific' subjects. There was also an implication that working in groups is peculiarly scientific, in opposition to Romantic claims for the unique individuality of the artist-genius. One artist was quoted as saying: 'We consider ourselves technicians, in the medieval sense, rather than artists'. While the term 'technicians' suggests the science lab, taken in the context of the whole sentence it is more suggestive of craftsmen. Ultimately, the author wanted to claim all these practitioners for *art*, not for either science or craft:

> *Much op art is removed from the artist's subjective discovery. It is the result of a mechanical muse and the artist becomes a computer programmer churning out visual experiences. ... But is it therefore science and not art?*
>
> *Perhaps. By analyzing wavelengths of visible light, scientists might well make the paintings on these pages. But they have not bothered, and if they had tried, the man hours would have far outnumbered the time spent by artists using intuition'.*[85]

So scientists did not create Op paintings because they could not be 'bothered' (a statement suggesting that there would be some purpose in a scientist making such a painting, but no actual purpose or motive for a scientist to do this was suggested[86]). Moreover, if they did, their methods would necessarily be slower than artists using 'intuition' (a phenomenon suddenly presented after all the previous 'evidence' of the emergence of the new 'scientific' artist – by implication scientists did not use intuition). The artist wished to 'play' and achieve 'insight' – the reader must infer that scientists did neither. A great deal of space in this article was devoted to presenting the Op artist as a scientist of some kind – a 'visual researcher' in a lab coat – but ultimately he (decidedly 'he') was reclaimed for art by the simple assertion of his intuition, playfulness and insight and the implication that these qualities were not shared by scientists. *Time* was essentially reassuring readers that, whatever they might read to the contrary elsewhere, the Op artist was not really different to his smock-wearing predecessors, he was merely wearing new 'clothes' (in the sense of new jargon and pronouncements).

In Europe there was the same concern with the 'scientific' aspects of Op. In *Kunstwerk* Lil Picard reviewed 'The Responsive Eye' exhibition and its catalogue for a European readership. She discussed William Seitz's preoccupation (in the catalogue) with the scientific aspects of the optical phenomena exploited in Op art.

> *He also mentions the German scientists of the 19th century, Ewald Hering and Hermann von Helmholtz, who were involved in a controversy, whether the phenomenon of simultaneous contrast of colours was physiological (Hering) or psychological (Helmholtz). 'To this day' Harry Asher wrote in 1961, 'it is not known for certain whether the process underlying the effect takes place in the eye or in the brain'.*
>
> *Mr Seitz has studied the field of visual research from A to Z and has made it his task to explain why retinal phenomena occur, bother the eye nerves, in short do many unexplained things which are a mystery to painters and lay men. By no means is this optical perception something new. Chevreul, Seurat, Signac, Herbin were occupied with optical research and today's artists again are involved with the problems and with the study of visual perception and are busy reading the articles in* Scientific American, *a monthly magazine, to find out about the secrets of light, color and visual effects, as Moiré pattern, reflexions, refractions of color.*[87]

Picard saw artists as unable to discover and investigate such phenomena empirically; they must have read about these 'secrets' in a popular science magazine. She claimed that *Scientific American* was in fact 'indispensable in artists' studios' at that time, a claim that echoes Jonathan Miller's comments quoted earlier in this chapter. What we see here is a fascination with science, at least on the part of Seitz and Picard. It is not clear from this how many artists sought information, inspiration or explanation from the pages of *Scientific American* or elsewhere; what is significant is that they should be thought to need 'scientific' information in order to produce works of art susceptible to scientific analysis. Picard indicated that it was fashionable for an artist to have copies of *Scientific American* lying about his/her studio but her readers were assured that such interest was 'by no means ... new'. Like the *Time* article, Picard produced solid names from nineteenth-century art history to validate current interest in scientific matters. It is as if the 'scientific' aspects of Op art might otherwise have looked suspiciously fashionable – Op was strongly identified with concepts of fashion[88] – which enhanced its market value while threatening to undermine it as art. An association with science, whilst enhancing Op's claims as an appropriate art for a scientific and technological era, could also be interpreted as evidence of its possible transience and irrelevance to the modernist avant-garde project. It was a more direct, obvious use of historical support for the validity of a new art form than Miller's 'revolution in aesthetics' but was similar in its use of historical precedent to validate contemporary practice. Picard's approach forms an interesting contrast with Hess' use of the same historical information to attack Op's claims to be taken seriously as art.

The idea that connections with science were dangerous for Op persisted. For American critic Carlo McCormick, writing in the mid-1980s:

> [Op] *confronts the standards by which we Westerners like to define art; it runs close to the shaky footing where the slightest slip tumbles one out of creativity and into the abyss of rules and design.*[89]

McCormick also claimed that 'Op has remained volatile and subversive as the mechanical mirage of a synthesis of art and science'.[90] This suggestion of 'subversiveness', I would argue, formed part of the perception of Op from the beginnings of its popularity in the 1960s and helps to explain its rise to prominence. McCormick's use of 'mechanical' again suggests technology, as though the technocracy itself had generated the 'mirage' of the union of art with science. McCormick and others associated this union with an 'abyss of rules' which was antagonistic to the creativity of art.

Dangerous liaisons II: the danger to science

As we have seen, diverse connections were made between Op art and science. While some art critics saw this as a dangerous liaison for art, there were also concerns that it was not good for science either. Several articles that referred to Op art appeared in *Scientific American* in the early 1960s. It was argued that these articles, such as one in May 1963 on moiré by scientist/painter Gerald Oster and a colleague, influenced artists.[91] Whether they did or not, they influenced critics' perceptions of Op. Oster's article was illustrated on the front cover of the journal by an illustration of a moiré effect. The authors were enthusiastic about the decorative beauty of these patterns (well known in the form of oriental watered silks) but were more concerned with the uses to which such patterns could be put in a scientific context. They claimed that:

> *A moiré pattern can be regarded as the mathematical solution to the interference of two periodic functions; hence the moiré technique can be used as an analogue computer. When line figures representing periodic functions are moved about in a continuous manner the resulting moiré patterns provide a continuous series of curves corresponding to the solution of mathematical problems ... The use of moiré patterns in this way would be applicable to complex problems involving electromagnetic radiation, acoustical waves or water waves.*[92]

If this article were really as widely read as is suggested both by the allusions to 'moiré' and to *Scientific American* in writings of the period, the question arises of how Oster's ideas were interpreted by non-scientists. Some may have thought that any moiré pattern would hold hidden, secret information, like an oracle, so that Op paintings based on such effects would have hidden complex, 'scientific' meanings. *Time* magazine claimed that 'Some [Op paintings], like moiré patterns, suddenly reveal new sensations that man never knew were within his visible province. But is it therefore science and not art?'[93] Explicit claims for any 'scientific' content in Op paintings are hard to find but critics referred to the presence of moiré patterns in Op works, and assumed that artists were familiar with *Scientific American*. It was as though the presence of any element with scientific connotations might give access to things 'that man never knew' and raise the question of whether the work concerned was itself art or science. *Time* implied that such content was probably not enough to change the status of such work from art to science, and the question 'But is it therefore science and not art?' seems to invite a negative answer.

Some articles in *Scientific American* nonetheless reflected a concern among the scientific community that art was invading 'their' territory. Writing in July 1965, in the wake of the MoMA show, the mathematician Martin Gardner appeared to be making an attempt to counter this. He claimed that not only was Op art 'the new name for a form of hard-edge abstractionism that has been around for half a century' but also that

Scientific American had been using images on its front cover since 1958 which were 'almost pure Op. They leave little doubt about Op's close kinship with modern science'. Gardner noted the

> *cold, rigid, precise, unemotional and impersonal qualities* [of Op]. *Its astonishing popularity revives ancient questions about art and mathematics. To what extent is art ruled by mathematical laws? To what extent can pure mathematical structure arouse esthetic emotions?*[94]

Gardner quoted other authors, including Aristotle, to argue that mathematics is the source of the greatest true beauty that human beings can apprehend. The tenor of this lengthy article, illustrated with various Op-like images derived from mathematical sources, is that Op art was a recent fad, which owed any beauty or value it might have to the scientific discipline of mathematics. The unexpressed fear here is that a 'marriage of art and science' would see science as the lesser partner, dominated by its publicly popular 'spouse'. Did Gardner fear that Op represented a public distraction from more intellectual, scientific disciplines – that it threatened to reduce mathematics, in the public's perception, to an artist's assistant?

There appears to have been good reason, therefore, for Bridget Riley to claim, in 1965, that some people saw her work as a marriage of art and science. In fact, Op in general was widely perceived as either the consummation or the issue of such a match. This view was the result of a general perception of science and technology as dominating everyday life and creating a new society. At the same time, a lack of public understanding of science and technology meant that hopes and fears were invested in them, almost as earlier epochs had invested theirs in the deity. Ideas derived from quantum physics had found their way into wider cultural discourse and gave rise to suggestions, such as Jung's, that science was as subjective as other areas of human experience – and art was already regarded as a product of the artist's subjective viewpoint. Some artists encouraged the supposed connection with science but others denied it, while scientists did not necessarily welcome the idea of a 'scientific' art. We can see in this debate a struggle for the 'soul' of the technocratic society: was art or science to provide the new 'religion' for modern Man? Rather than risk defeat in this struggle, would Mars and Venus agree to a 'marriage'?

The latest form of modernism?

Throughout the reviews quoted here, references to *Scientific American* are commonplace. It was presented as the most important source of information on science for the interested non-scientist. Seitz quoted from a *Scientific American* article in his text for the catalogue for 'The Responsive Eye' to support his own belief in the triumph of subjectivity.

> *But now, as Paul Kolers writes in a recent issue of* Scientific American, *most contemporary investigators regard illusions as 'genuine perceptions which do not stand up when their implications are tested' and as 'putting in question any belief in "objective" perception'.*[95]

Seitz saw science as a useful confirmation of history. If the possibility of objective perception is denied and replaced by an acceptance that only subjectivity is possible, then the importance of art, as perhaps an extreme form of subjectivity, must be enhanced. Hence Seitz, whilst admitting that perception was still only incompletely understood, could claim that 'Laforgue's definition of an impressionist can be borrowed whole for the perceptual artist of 1965: "a modernist painter with an uncommon sensibility of the eye"'. Seitz's project was to establish Op[96] as the latest form of modernist art, a natural progression from earlier forms of modernism.[97] His argument suggested that some degree of contact with science was helpful to the cause; as this chapter has shown, this was not a universally accepted idea.

As the dominant paradigm for the creation and interpretation of art in the early 1960s, notions of modernism were central to most of the arguments constructed around the validity of Op art *as* art. Riley's work had to be positioned in relation to modernism by its supporters and detractors alike. Any possibility that Op was a 'scientific' art had also to be considered *in relation* to modernism, and hence repeated references to Seurat, placing Op in a purported historical context within the modernist paradigm. Such claims involved a degree of 'sleight of hand' however, and were therefore not convincing to all observers. For some, the 'objectivity' of early modernist artistic practices had been superseded by the subjectivity of Abstract Expressionism. Notions of the subjectivity of *science* were very new – the *Time* article with its stereotyped 'intuitive' artist and plodding scientist was a much more generally accepted view of the relation – or rather difference – between art and science. In Britain, there were additional problems for the acceptability of a 'scientific' art in that, as we have seen, the earlier Festival Style may have imbued the concept with connotations of industrial design and domesticity, at odds with the ideals of modernism. As the *Time* article demonstrated, it was easy to trivialize the claims of some artists for a 'scientific' content in their work and treat this as the latest attention-seeking 'gimmick' of those involved.

If Op were not modernist, then it was either not art or it represented a challenge to modernism. A critic could adopt the position that Op was not modernist and not really art; that it was not modernist but was still art and therefore represented a challenge to modernism; or that it was in fact a valid form of modernism. It is plain that whatever position a critic took with regard to Op, he or she had to engage with the debate over Op's 'scientific' credentials.

Op art attracted considerable public and critical attention in Europe, Britain and the United States in the early to mid 1960s. Hess claimed that there were 'some forty or fifty-thousand Op-Art [*sic*] group shows 1963–65'.[98] In many cases perceived connections with science took the form of claims that Op was derived from scientific studies of perception and 'scientific' methodologies were even attributed to the artists, but less direct connections were suggested by others (for example, Canaday's vision of Op as 'competition' for the highly visible new technologies of the 'space age'). The concepts of science and technology were prominent in cultural discourses of the period. Pop art had already encouraged the notion that the new 'technological' age could supply subject matter for art. A perception that society was becoming a technocracy and that art was losing its position of cultural dominance may have supplied an incentive to promote connections between art and science. Furthermore, in increasingly secular societies there may have been a need for a new 'faith' to replace conventional religion. Would this be supplied by the scientist's promise of ever-improving material well-being or by the aesthetic experience provided by art? As I have argued above, Op presented an opportunity, grasped by some artists, scientists and critics, rejected by others, to 'marry' the two and avoid the possible 'defeat' of art in a perceived struggle for the 'soul' of the technocratic society. At the same time, such a 'marriage of art and science' threatened Op's claims to be a truly modernist (as opposed to a modern) art form; it could be seen as trivializing both art and science rather than creating a powerful cultural union. For Riley, who rejected the notion, it may have presented the risk that her work would be considered formulaic rather than the product of a unique artistic sensibility. Hence an impassioned debate was inevitable; there was no neutral ground.

Chapter 2 Painting the Doors of Perception

In late 1998, an exhibition of Bridget Riley's work from 1961 onwards was mounted at the Abbot Hall Art Gallery, Kendal, Cumbria. More than thirty years after her earlier paintings had first attracted public attention, one aspect of their original reception was still of interest to two critics. Laura Cumming commented in the *Observer*:

> *Looking at those early black and whites, for example, you can see why* [Riley] *was so irritated that people liked dropping acid in front of them. The paintings glare at you with elegant aggression, their optical blaze so meticulously calculated, so sharp and austere, it's hard to imagine their talismanic appeal to doped out psychedelics.*[1]

Alfred Hickling, writing in the *Guardian*, disagreed:

> *In aesthetic terms* [these paintings] *are a linear development from Post-Impressionist enquiries into optical perception; in sensory terms, they're like getting stoned.*[2]

As Cumming's comment implies, the notion that Op paintings related in some way to the experiences produced by psychotropic drugs had also been expressed in the early 1960s. At that time, a phenomenon that was to create increasing public interest and concern as the decade progressed was the use of drugs such as LSD to explore altered states of consciousness and perception.[3] By 1965 increasing public familiarity with the effects of psychotropic drugs created what Bridget Riley, whose Op art works were by then known internationally, later called

> *a collision between my intentions as an artist and the cultural context in which I found myself. I remember being told, as though it were some sort of compliment, that it was the greatest kick to go down and smoke*[4] *in front of my painting* Fall.[5]

In this chapter, I wish to examine more closely the nature of this collision between Riley's artistic intentions and certain aspects of the cultural context in which the artist 'found [her]self'. A 'collision' suggests a violent impact and even the threatened destruction of one or both of the colliding bodies, something very much 'there', although Riley seems to suggest that the work itself existed somewhat to one side of this event. I suggest that Riley's works themselves mark points of collision for many ideas current in the early 1960s, whether or not these were in any way connected with the artist's intentions.

In particular, there was a collision between those who thought that science and technology would be the source of a better future for humanity, and those who rejected this in favour of a more 'people-centred', less materialistic future. For one set of ideals to triumph, the other must be vanquished. A key word here is 'perception'. What did this term mean in the 1960s? How did it relate to both the technocracy discussed in Chapter 1 and the emergence, during this decade, of a 'hippy'/drug counter-culture? 'Perception' is a word with both physiological and socio-political connotations: perceptions as products of stimulation of the eye-brain system (perception as a physical process), and perceptions in the sense of ideas, here specifically those about art's social role and social impact and its status in a changing society. Riley has said:

> *even the word perception, which had hitherto had such a precise meaning both in the development of painting and in its criticism, suddenly became, thanks to the popularity of Aldous Huxley's* The Doors of Perception, *linked with the drug culture of the sixties.*[6]

If indeed the word 'perception' once had a precise meaning, this precision had been undermined in a culture where newer associations derived from Huxley and from a nascent drug culture existed alongside older usages in the fine arts and in science, where perceptual phenomena were being investigated.[7] The term perception suggested the objective, scientific study of the natural world. At the same time it was linked to Aldous Huxley's exploration of the possibilities of enhancing, or even transcending, subjective, personal experience of the world through the use of psychotropic drugs.[8] These different associations of the term 'perception' may be seen in attitudes towards Op art in the 1960s and continue to influence how it is interpreted today.

There were a variety of ways in which Riley's contemporaries could connect differing notions of perception to her work. Previously separate ideas – relating to philosophies of perception, philosophies regarding hallucinogenic drug use and aesthetic philosophies associated with modernism – now collided for viewers of these paintings. Cultural contexts are not merely the setting for such collisions: they both produce them and are produced by them. If the colliding 'objects' are two very different ideas of what society is now and should be in future, any collision may be seen as especially destructive and threatening. This notion of cultural confrontation was described by Christopher Booker, a writer and a founder of the satirical magazine *Private Eye*.

> *Essentially, the twentieth century dream has had two components, closely related. On the one hand there has been the technological dream, whereby man would achieve a golden age of power, freedom and silent efficiency ... and a complete scientific mastery of his environment. On the other, ... has been the libertarian dream, whereby man would be freed from the conventions, inhibitions, repressions, superstitions, imperialism and authoritarianism which had restricted him in the past ... through the sweeping away of social and political barriers and hierarchies, through a complete understanding of his own psychology and through the pursuit of a new and total freedom in the arts and social relationships.*[9]

Booker suggested that destruction of past values was desired by those seeking 'a golden age' and that such destruction was something to be feared and avoided. As I shall discuss later in this chapter, earlier in the twentieth century the French philosopher Georges Bataille had explored the idea that destruction (or 'expenditure') as an end in itself was a deep impulse in the human unconscious. He argued that as the whiteness of a piece of paper had to be destroyed in the act of drawing, all art was in fact based on destructive impulses.[10] The notion that Op art was 'aggressive' and therefore destructive can be seen as an aspect of contemporary desires to destroy the 'old order' so as to create a new one. It may also be interpreted in relation to a theorized human need for pure destruction that has attracted the attention of philosophers from Marcel Mauss and Bataille to Jean Baudrillard and Julia Kristeva. I shall explore further, below, these notions of destruction in relation to Op art.

Technocracy and perception

In the 1960s there were two imagined alternative futures, one dominated by 'technology/technocracy' and the other rejecting this in favour of more 'people-centred' ideas of social organization. As we saw in the last chapter, that Op was regarded as 'scientific' by some critics encouraged its association with notions of the 'technocracy' or the 'space age'.

By the early 1960s, the phenomena of visual perception had come under considerable scientific and philosophical scrutiny. Perception can be regarded as having two components: *exteroception*, whereby one obtains information about one's environment and is able to interact with it, and *proprioception*, whereby one is aware of one's own body – for example, its orientation or speed of movement. In looking at any painting, exteroception is obviously involved. Viewing many of Riley's paintings arguably also involves elements of proprioception: contemporary commentators agreed that looking at her paintings gave rise to physical sensations in the body other than purely visual ones. In other words, in looking at these paintings the viewer became more aware of his or her own body. As with the use of psychotropic drugs, the notion that mind and body are separate was challenged by Riley's work. To postulate that mind and body are unified might appear to support a materialistic, and therefore technocracy-orientated view of life, or alternatively it could mean that spiritual aspects of existence should permeate the social, as well as the physical, body.

The language of movement: technology and the body

When artist and journalist Lil Picard[11] reviewed 'The Responsive Eye' for the July 1965 issue of *Kunstwerk*, she compared the effects generated by Op paintings to those experienced when driving through a modern city at night, watching the moving reflections of light on cars and buildings. Her remarks prefigure the later claims of Reyner Banham,[12] that the modern city could only be 'read' through a car windscreen, with history viewed metaphorically as reflections in the rear-view mirror. For Banham, Los Angeles, the quintessential modern city, could only be experienced through technology. This experience was not a matter for the eyes alone: the whole body was involved in the act of driving the car, for the body's movement was seen as central to perception. Here, technology was not alien to the body; car and body combined to allow perception of the city, and the body was enhanced by technology.[13] The body and technology could work together, rather than being intrinsically separated by a 'nature/anti-nature' dichotomy.[14] Here, technology enables the body to experience and interrelate with the world in new and exciting ways. Banham's enthusiasm for the empowering might of technology, apparently echoing Futurist interests from before the First World War, was foreshadowed in Canaday's desire for an art 'that can compete with launching pads and industrial machinery'.[15] Where Baudelaire's *flâneur* strolled at a leisurely pace, detachedly observing the nineteenth-century city, Banham described a distinctly twentieth-century flâneurial mode, combining physical leisure (the *seated* driver) with speed.

The notion that the body can be at rest and yet experience movement is expressed by various critics writing on Bridget Riley's work. As a phenomenon of twentieth-century life, speed had been connected with modernity at least since the Futurists. High speed as a contemporary phenomenon was also associated with Riley's work: 'Miss Riley's paintings ... are geometrical approximations of the frenzied rhythms of contemporary life' as an American critic put it.[16] British art historian and critic Norbert Lynton compared the experience of looking at a Riley painting to the plunge of 'sky diving'.[17] The sensations of movement that viewers experienced when looking at these paintings aligned Riley's art with experiences of speed otherwise associated with technology: like Banham's driver, the viewer of the painting was stationary but still experienced movement.

American critic Harold Rosenberg wrote in the mid-1960s that 'The proponents of [Op art] ... claim that they alone represent a "machine age aesthetic"'.[18] Despite the celebration of such ideas in the work of, say, Fernand Léger, by the 1960s the notion of a 'machine age aesthetic' may have been problematic, a form of cultural heresy associating art with notions of industry and technology. As the twentieth century progressed, artistic modernism and scientific, technical modernity had moved apart, and were not associated by writers such as Fry and Greenberg.[19] Now, perhaps, modernity and modernism could re-unite; scientific associations meant that, for those who wanted this, Op could be a fitting art for the new technological utopia that they imagined lay ahead, an urban art for the space age. For these people, the perceptions generated by Riley's work could be associated in a positive way with technology.

Art as destruction and creation

For those who rejected the technocracy, Riley's art nonetheless had a powerful appeal and, unlike the critics quoted above, they did not associate it with cars and rocket launches. Through associations with drug use, these people saw Riley's work as evocative of a very different utopia, where individual subjectivity and experience would be paramount. The creation of one of these futures implied the destruction of the other, and notions of aggression and destruction crop up repeatedly in the cultural debates of the time.

Riley's work showed that all visual response is mediated by the body. It is this aspect, I suggest, that attracted the interest of those, such as the viewer who wanted to smoke cannabis in front of *Fall* (1963) [Fig. 13], who sought a different kind of engagement with art objects from the 'pure' aesthetic engagement conventionally encouraged by museums and art galleries. Both art that drew attention to the physicality of looking, *and* the act of taking drugs in an art gallery could be said to be 'destructive' of aesthetic and social values. To smoke at all in a gallery, with the potential damage that smoke and fumes might do to the works of art, raises questions of 'appropriate' behaviour. The fact that a psychotropic drug altered perception evinced the ultimately physical nature of perception. To use such drugs with the aim of enhancing the experience of looking at (perceiving) a work of art, emphasized the physicality of that experience and raised questions about what was 'appropriate' in this respect as well. This has implications for certain modernist theories regarding what constituted an appropriate response to art, which I shall consider further below.

Arguments could be made that either the use of drugs such as LSD and mescaline was likely to destroy one's sanity, or alternatively (as Huxley had argued) such use could improve one's perceptions of reality and thus enhance sanity. For Bataille the notion of destruction is always present for every spectator of art, regardless of the various interpretations made of individual works.[20] The painter 'destroys' the white canvas, and the sculptor the block of stone, in the act of creating the work of art. The use of drugs has long been directly associated with madness: cases of ergot poisoning-induced insanity were common in the Middle Ages and occurred in France as recently as 1951,[21] while from the early 1950s, British psychiatrists had experimented with psychotropic drugs in attempts both to replicate 'insane' mental states (with a view to understanding them better) and to find cures for conditions such as schizophrenia.[22] Like Bataille's notion of artistic creation, drug use could be presented as both constructive and destructive. The painstakingly constructed surface of a painting such as *Fall* – its evident 'constructiveness' – was countered by the feelings of physical disorientation, of lack of self-control of the spectator's own response to the work, which could be seen as 'destructive'.

The notion of art as destructive runs counter to perceptions of the act of creation as *constructive*. Although in the twentieth century *science* became increasingly associated with destruction,[23] destruction has periodically been associated with art, for instance with Futurism and Dada around the time of the First World War. In the 1960s the concept of destruction as a component of art was again being promoted and explored. In 1962, artist Gustav Metzger gave a series of lectures on auto-destructive

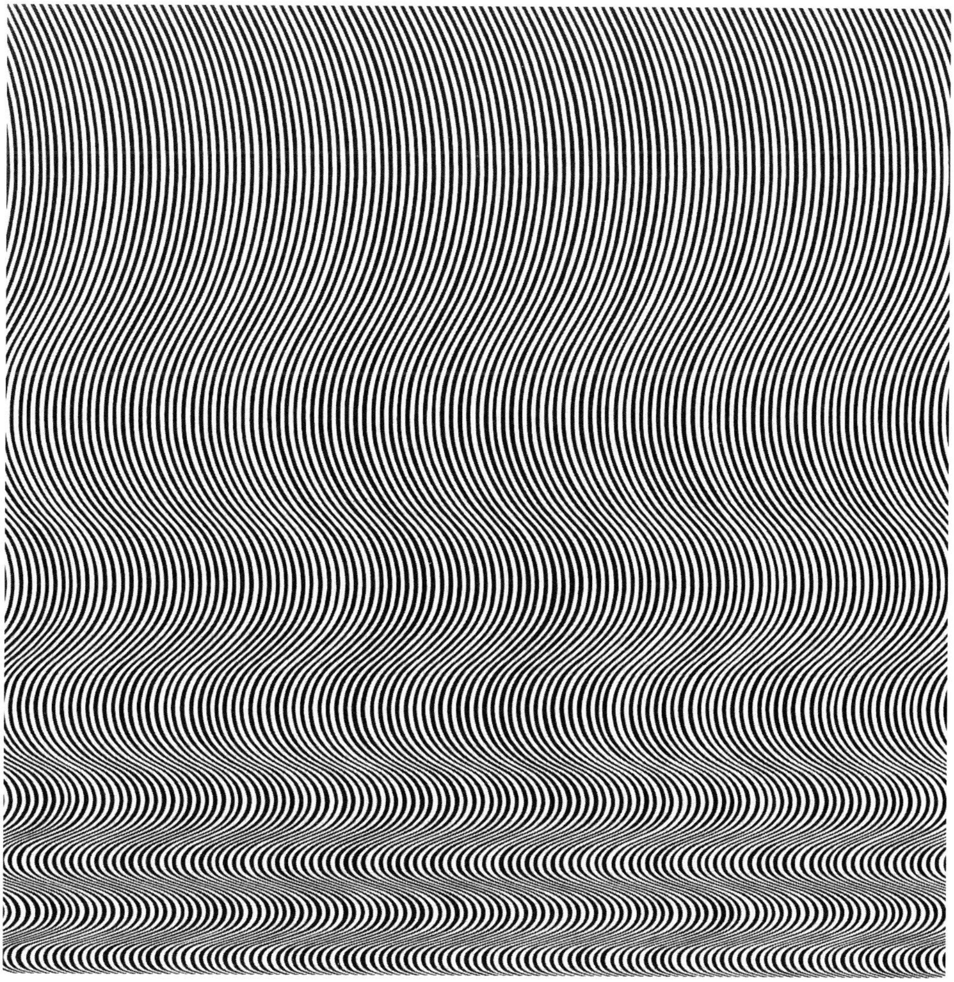

13. **Fall** 1963

art at Ealing School of Art.[24] In the same year, writer, sculptor and founder member of the Situationist International, Alexander Trocchi, declared at the Edinburgh Festival that 'Modern art begins with the destruction of the object. All vital creation is at the other side of Nihilism'.[25] In 1964, Yoko Ono performed *Cut Piece* in Kyoto, Japan, in which members of her audience were invited to cut the clothes from her body with scissors. By 1966, The Who were destroying their instruments on stage; artist John Latham was building 'Skoob Towers' (piles of books that were then set alight); and The Beatles had created (and suppressed) their notorious 'Butchers' album cover (featuring the group posed with broken dolls and pieces of meat). In this period, therefore, the concept of destruction (even to the point of death) was associated not just with science, but also with art and popular culture. Op art was associated with notions of 'the scientific' as well as notions of 'aggression', all of which connoted 'destruction', in certain contexts.

The psychotropic connection

A sensation of LSD

As we have seen, by 1965 Op art had attracted speculation about possible connections with psychotropic drugs. Indeed, the language of some critics and commentators discussing Op encouraged such associations. Both William Seitz and Anton Ehrenzweig, a psychologist specializing in aural and visual perception, who wrote several pieces about Riley's work, made comments that may have encouraged readers to connect Riley's work with psychotropic drugs. Discussing the effects of black and white Op paintings in the catalogue of 'The Responsive Eye', Seitz cited Riley's work as an example of the phenomenon of the illusion of light, movement and colour produced by black and white Op paintings. He was also concerned with the pictures as sources of 'energy', a term which held negative as well as positive connotations: the energy of the atomic bomb, the energy of those acts of 'vandalism', carried out as art, apparently advocated by Metzger and Trocchi:

> *the impression of brightness and pulsation can reach a startling intensity. The eyes seem to be bombarded with pure energy, as they are by Bridget Riley's* Current. *Even effects of colour can result – usually pale pink, gold or blue.*[26]

These effects were frequently commented on in writings on Op art, but Seitz's next sentence made a dramatic connection with the psychotropic drugs, the use of which had been so graphically described by Huxley.

They are increased, Gerald Oster[27] has determined, under the influence of the drugs mescaline and LSD.[28]

Here we have one of Riley's paintings cited in close proximity to the claim that such effects were enhanced by the use of psychotropic drugs, with the implication that viewing Riley's work was enhanced likewise. Hence, one may suppose, the conversation cited earlier in this chapter, with the person who had smoked cannabis in front of *Fall*.[29]

Seitz's description of the painting as emitting energy, the 'startling intensity' with which the eyes were 'bombarded', suggests an experience of brilliant, even explosive light making a violent impact on the nervous system. The associations triggered by Seitz are twofold: that Op paintings were actually 'enhanced' by viewing them under the influence of drugs and that the act of looking at them was potentially traumatic, a theme echoed in Bataille's concern with the light of the sun as burning, blinding and destructive:

the sun for Bataille is the most elevated of conceptions ... Because of our incapacity to look at the sun, which elicits horror and which blinds, such elevation is always and unavoidably combined with a sudden fall from grace.[30]

A 'fall from grace' might also suggest the drug user who has sought to experience a higher plane of existence but may be destroyed in the attempt. Given the associations of drug use with an 'anti-social' stance, Seitz's words may have implied that Op was potentially socially traumatizing as well as physically so.

Akin to an hallucination?

Seitz's comments were not the first that may have encouraged readers to connect Riley's work with psychotropic drugs. Writing on Riley's work in 1963, Anton Ehrenzweig described the effects of her paintings in the introduction to the catalogue of her second one-person show at Gallery One, London. Ehrenzweig rejected the term 'illusion' (a term associated with painting since classical times). He replaced the notion of 'optical illusions', and their connotations of 'scientific' diagrams and children's encyclopædias, with a more profound interpretation of the experience of looking at what he considered a 'good' Op painting, such as one by Riley. The term he preferred was 'hallucination', a word which may also have religious connotations, in the sense of 'a vision'.[31] Whilst it is not necessary to take drugs to experience an hallucination, in the early 1960s, public concern about the power of drugs to engender hallucinations was increasing as the use of drugs such as LSD grew.[32] Ehrenzweig gave a detailed description of his experience of viewing one of Riley's paintings.

> *A perilous balance is achieved as in a moving but stable living organism. As we feel this balance the whole experience can turn inward to a new invigorating awareness of the structure of our own body. When the moment of transformation arrives the single elements will cease straining and pulling at each other. A new total vision comes through that is akin to a true hallucination (it is misleading to talk of 'optical illusion' which lacks all important feeling of revelation).*
>
> *As an outer sign of the delicate balance achieved, strangely disembodied iridescent colours, like St Elmo's fires, may begin to play around the centres of maximum tension. This effect may be only incidental, but we must be grateful to the sensuous richness it imparts to the total scene of transfiguration.*[33]

Like Seitz, Ehrenzweig referred to colours that were not actually present in the works. He later attributed his use of the term 'hallucination' to Riley herself, describing how she developed a painting on the canvas until:

> *the final unpredictable transformation takes place to which Riley looks forward with impatience. A 'presence' comes through which she likes to compare to an hallucination.*[34]

The use of terms such as 'transformation', 'vision', 'revelation', 'disembodied' and 'transfiguration' suggest both religious experience and the psychological effects produced by psychotropic drugs (which Huxley described as having a religious dimension[35]). Ehrenzweig echoes the language used by Huxley in describing his mescaline experiences: 'Words like Grace and Transfiguration came to my mind'; 'the sacramental vision of reality seen apocalypses of flowers and flannel'; 'renewals of transcendental otherness, hints of the morning's heaven'; and 'The Revelation dawned and was gone again.[36]

On the other hand, Huxley did not describe his experiences under the influence of mescaline as hallucinations. He emphasized the way the drug heightened the experience of (mainly)visual phenomena in the real world. He also noted that while under the influence of the drug 'my awareness of the transfigured outer world was no longer accompanied by an awareness of my physical organism',[37] a very different sensation to Ehrenzweig's 'new invigorating awareness of the structure of our own body'. For Huxley, the mescaline experience was a way of transcending the body, whereas for Ehrenzweig the experience of viewing one of Riley's paintings was centred in the body itself.

The notion of the body as central to the experience of art had not been a strong theme in previous modernist discourse, other than in the work of Bataille. Clive Bell, writing in 1914, stressed the notion of the 'aesthetic emotion' claiming that:

> *Art transports us from the world of man's activity to a world of aesthetic exaltation. For a moment we are shut off from human interests; our anticipations and memories are arrested; we are lifted above the stream of life.*[38]

Alfred Barr, modernist theorist, art historian and director of MoMA since the 1930s, stressed formal considerations in his assessments and classifications of twentieth-century art. He produced an 'evolutionary tree', 'The Development of Abstract Art' which literally charted the supposed lines of influence from one form of art to another, from the 1890s to the 1930s, culminating in two forms of abstraction: geometrical and non-geometrical. A feast of diversity was hence channelled, somewhat tortuously, into two main streams. Clement Greenberg, since the late 1940s, had used a Kantian philosophical framework for defining and evaluating modernist art. Greenberg wanted to 'edit out all [criticism/evaluation] which is not relevant to value judgements and aesthetic questions'.[39] Michael Fried considered that in modernist art at its best there was a 'continuous and entire presentness, amounting, as it were, to the perpetual creation of itself'. Fried wanted 'to see everything, to experience the work in all its depth and fullness, to be forever convinced by it'.[40]

T.J. Clark describes this quasi-religious language of transcendence and conversion as 'sounding like old time religion'.[41] Such approaches suggested an emphasis on a spiritual state in which the nature of the body has little relevance. In this connection, Huxley's description of the mescaline experience did not resemble Ehrenzweig's description of the experience of Op art, but rather suggested the 'idealized' experience of art advocated by Bell and Fried:

> *The experience by which art is in the end recognised and defined in Modernist criticism is the intuitive and supposedly disinterested experience of an emotional or spiritual value.*[42]
>
> *Michael Fried's Modernist 'beholder'* [the viewer of a work of art] *was essentially located outside space and time, in 'grace'.*[43]

One could argue that the 'transfigured and transfiguring mind'[44] admired by Huxley is 'essentially located outside space and time, in "grace"'. By this argument, it was Fried's notional 'beholder' whose experience on viewing, say, an Abstract Expressionist work, seems to have resembled a drug experience of the kind advocated by Huxley. The body-centred perception experienced by the viewer of an Op painting (as described by Ehrenzweig) was actually less like a drug-induced experience. So while, superficially, Ehrenzweig's description of Riley's paintings may appear to connect them with the experience of psychotropic drug use, his emphasis on the body conflicts both with Huxley's description, and with contemporary notions of the experience of modernist art, as expressed by critics such as Fried. Instead, we may relate Fried's views (if somewhat mischievously) to ideas connected with psychotropic drug experiences.

Fried's descriptions of what the experience of modernist art should be ('in all its depth and fullness'[45]), suggest Huxley's 'sacramental vision of reality'. Huxley also uses the word 'Grace' with its connotations of a divine gift. The language of both Fried and Huxley has religious connotations, presumably deliberately in Huxley's case, not necessarily so, of course, in Fried's. In the 1950s and 1960s, with conventional religion in decline, people such as Huxley and Fried were looking in different places for the same thing: an experience that transcended the quotidian trivialities of modern life.

To return to Riley's comment about the young man who had smoked cannabis in front of her painting *Fall*, it is possible to imagine that, in some way, both Huxley's views on psychotropic drugs and Fried's views on the 'ideal' experience of art were colliding in that act of drug use. The drug user wanted either to intensify the physical experience of looking at the painting or to transcend the body through a combined act of drug use and aesthetic contemplation. It may seem ironic that the art chosen for the latter exercise should have been one that Ehrenzweig and others saw as rooted in physical experience, and doubly ironic when one considers that the 'spiritual' effects of drug use had an entirely physiological origin. Whatever the actual intentions of writers such as Ehrenzweig and Seitz, they provided material that suggested such a connection with Op art, and specifically with Riley's work.

Nonetheless, critics in the 1960s did not make connections between the modernist experience of art as envisioned by Fried and the developing fashion for psychotropic drugs. The notion that the perception of art and perceptions mediated by psychotropic drugs might be related became attached only to Op art (and subsequently, the so-called 'psychedelic art' of the late 1960s[46]) as if by a process of 'transference' (to borrow the psychoanalytic term), even though Ehrenzweig, for example, would have argued that this was inappropriate and Riley certainly rejected the connection.

Drugs and commodification

The notion of commodification of experience could also be associated with drug use. I will discuss in Chapter 6 how Op art was exploited commercially by the makers of, for example, wallpaper and clothing and the outrage at this felt by Riley and supportive critics. Founder-member of the Situationist International, Guy Debord, argued in *The Society of the Spectacle* (1967) that contemporary society absorbed opposition by commodifying it. Drugs such as alcohol and tobacco had long since become commodities and it was possible, as Thomas Hess' review of 'The Responsive Eye' showed, to think of more controversial drugs in much the same way.

> *Op is the art that the public flocks to see and critic Jack Kroll reports that they 'bob and weave' in front of the exhibits, shake their heads back and forth, make little jumps, like penguins at a mating dance, to get the biggest retinal kicks. (Perhaps this peripateticism is due to one Op theorist – moiré variety – who was widely misquoted in the press as saying certain optical illusions give a sensation of LSD, so hundreds of people innocently sway in front of laminated black-and-white constructions, convinced that they are getting a cheap jag. This writer admits to feeling queasy after a long look at Op, but William Seitz assures him that it is a passing reaction, 'like your first cigarette').*[47]

The connections made here for Op art are interesting. In this lengthy review of the MoMA show, Hess used humour to attack Op art: the Op spectators were 'like penguins at a mating dance' – funny, not sexy. Hess reinforced the supposed connection between Op and LSD by publicizing it even as he dismissed it, relating Op instead to the less controversial drug, nicotine. Hess was not a supporter of Op art, so a trivialized connection with a commodified notion of drug use was a way of attacking what he saw as a public over-valuation of Op.

The social consequences of involvement with drugs were becoming serious.[48] In 1963, Drs Alpert and Leary, authors of a guide to using LSD, were sacked from Harvard for involving their students in experiments with this drug. Even cigarettes were causing concern: in February 1965 the television advertising of these was banned in the UK.[49] By 1965, when LSD was made illegal in the USA, around four million Americans were estimated to have tried it.[50] Some of them presumably attended 'The Responsive Eye' while many more visitors would have been curious about the drug's effects. While Ehrenzweig's use of terms such as 'hallucination'

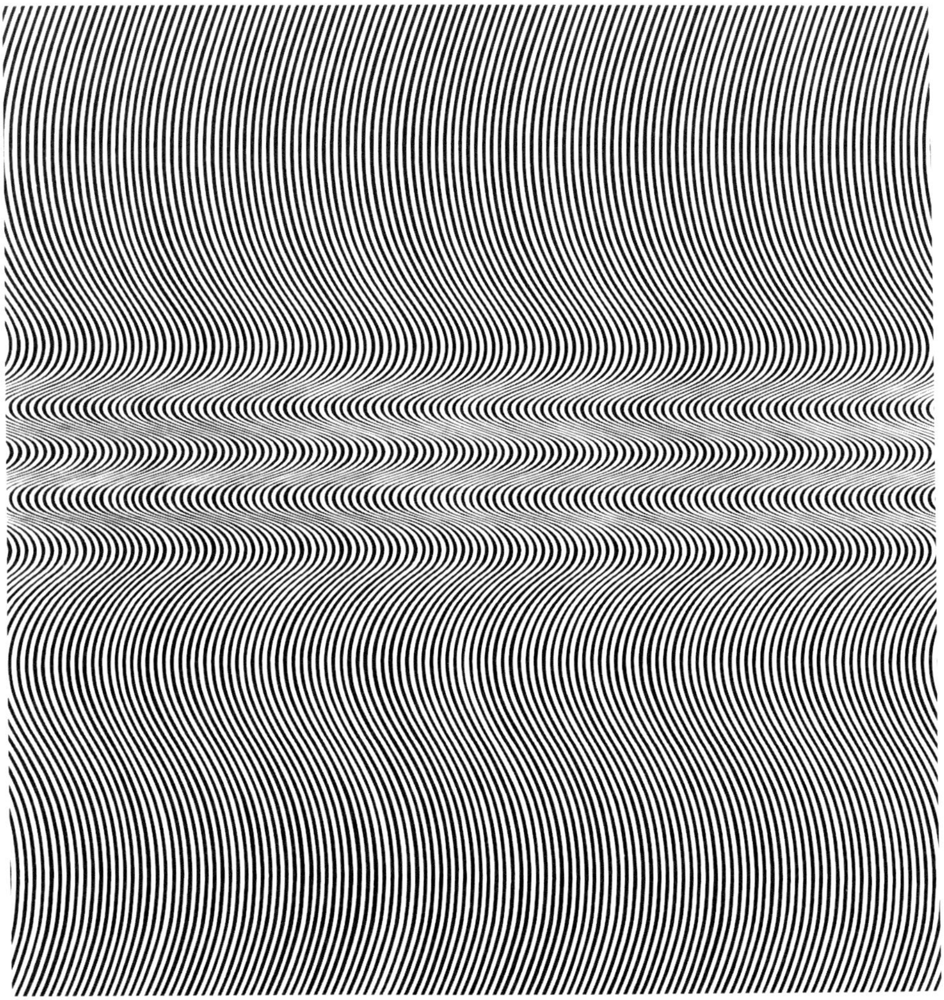

14. **Current** 1964

and 'revelation', made no overt allusion to drug use, nonetheless, this sort of language[51] – and Seitz's allusion to Oster's work with mescaline and LSD – inadvertently invited comments such as those by Hess, quoted earlier.

Although he apparently dismissed the suggestion that Op paintings 'give a sensation of LSD', Hess substituted one drug for another by likening the sensation induced to a first experience of tobacco. The notion of the teenager trying his/her first cigarette suggests immaturity, as though LSD were for adults but Op's thrills were only for teenagers. It was as though the experience of looking at the paintings in 'The Responsive Eye' must be likened to some kind of drug experience; Hess picked the mundane, ubiquitous cigarette rather than the more exotic and exciting LSD. He implied that the experience of looking at Op art was not terribly exciting either. The dismissive reference to the unnamed 'op theorist' (presumably Oster) as 'moiré variety' may also have been another allusion to Riley's work. Her painting *Current* (1964), featured on the front cover of the exhibition catalogue [Fig. 14] and which Seitz apparently connected with Oster's work, had been greatly distorted by the odd placement of the exhibition title over the image, perhaps suggesting to Hess the moiré effect he condemned. Riley's paintings had been plagiarized by dress designers so in this context, the use of the word moiré, suggesting fabric, looks like a further attempt to trivialize Op by hinting that it was merely a fashion commodity.

Later in his article, Hess again used language suggesting both a link between Op art and psychotropic drug use, and the commodification of both:

> *Op becomes a commodity which can be used at will to produce a predictable (and once habituated, probably enjoyable) feeling. … I see no reason why collectors should not keep Op in racks, like wine in cellars*.[52]

So according to Hess the viewer would in time be able to enjoy the feeling generated by Op – a feeling that had been reduced to a commodity.[53] The word 'habituated' then suggests the experienced drug user, for whom a 'trip' holds no surprises. In practice, LSD did not produce a 'predictable' effect, even for experienced users; rather, the idea of a commodified, predictable drug suggests the Soma of Huxley's *Brave New World*, a 'perfect' drug providing an artificial release from the pressures of the real world.[54] The reference to wine also echoes this idea of a commodified (although socially acceptable) drug. This was in sharp contrast to Ehrenzweig's 'new invigorating awareness of the structure of our own body', where the mental state of one viewing a Riley painting was alert, not drugged.

At home in the body: Rejecting technocracy

Drug use was linked by some people to dreams or fears about the future of Western societies. In his book *The Making of a Counter Culture* (1970), American writer Theodore Roszak examined what he claimed was the disaffection of young people in the 1960s with the materialistic, cold war-dominated society in which they had grown up. He argued that fear of war and a desire for prosperity had resulted in 'an awe-stricken public reverence for science' which some young people were now rebelling against.[55] Unlike Banham, Roszak did not believe that technology could be reconciled with the human mind and body. The increasing use of psychotropic drugs during the 1960s was part of a rejection of 'the technocracy' and its attendant materialism. Albert Hofmann, the chemist who had discovered the psychotropic properties of LSD in the 1930s, shared this view. Hofmann later wrote of the drug culture that:

> *it had deep-seated sociological causes: materialism, alienation from nature through industrialisation and increasing urbanisation ... and lack of a religious, nurturing and meaningful philosophical foundation to life.*[56]

In the 1950s, Huxley had emphasized the spiritual and religious aspects of mescaline use and its tendency to make the user uninterested in practical affairs; implicitly, the mescaline user is not interested in servicing the technocracy. Then, in the early 1960s, Timothy Leary and Ken Kesey had promoted an anti-technocracy view of psychotropic drugs, with Leary claiming a religious dimension in the drug's use.[57] An art form associated with such drugs, therefore, could be associated with the counter-cultural dream of a Utopia in which technology would be superseded by a return to the perceived 'wisdom' of earlier, non-technological cultures, the mythical golden age before 'the Fall'.[58] Roszak believed that:

> *the fascination of the young for exotic religions and narcotics is a symptom of their quest for some new foundation that can support a program of radical social change.*[59]

Given that Huxley's and Leary's publications were widely read, 'exotic religions and narcotics' may well have been connected in the minds of many people. 'Exotic' suggests 'foreign', 'alien': Hofmann's 'alienation from nature'. Roszak suggested that the search for the ultimate 'exotic' country, Utopia, was a response to alienation. The 'new foundation' could only be built on a new attitude towards perception and knowledge.

Roszak was influenced by the work of the Gestalt psychologists, a school that had originated before the Second World War but had become increasingly influential since the 1950s. He argued that, since the technological society had alienated people from their 'natural' mode of perception and concomitant sense of place in the natural and social worlds, drug use was an attempt to restore perceptual innocence.[60] The Gestaltists saw perceptions as the result of the interaction of perceiver and object, rather than as passive experiences, so that life itself becomes:

> *a purposive give and take between every organism and its environment which has the same inexplicable spontaneity and self-regulation as the process of perception. Just as visual figures are co-operatively drawn against a ground by the seer and the seen, so, within their field, organism and environment are understood to be in a constant natural dialogue, an ongoing series of 'creative adjustments' which make man at home in his body, his community, his natural habitat.*[61]

Anton Ehrenzweig argued that Op art did not allow the brain to produce a gestalt. For him, the brain itself had psychological needs (rather than psychology being a product of the brain) and the eye was decidedly separate from the brain, a passive receptacle of the 'retinal image', having no 'need' to organize the images it registered.

> *Gestalt psychology has investigated the psychological need of the brain (not of the eye) for organising the chaotic mosaic of coloured blobs contained in the retinal image. It is this need of the brain for gestalt which 'optical' art frustrates so effectively. There is a constant tug-of-war between shifting and crumbling gestalt patterns.*[62]

Ehrenzweig argued here that Op art did not allow a single gestalt to be produced. The viewer was denied the 'psychological' need for wholeness and stability. Nonetheless, Ehrenzweig then went on to describe a subsequent stage of the experience – a 'total vision' (or gestalt 'whole') created by the brain from the 'single units of the composition' which at first seemed in 'a constant tug-of-war'.

> *But at a certain point in our experience this relentless attack on our normal viewing habits can peel our eyes into a new crystal clear sensibility which has none of the cold aggressiveness of the first phase. To achieve this transformation we have to submit to the initial attack in the way in which we have learned to enjoy a cold shower bath. There comes the voluptuous moment when the senses and skin tingle with a new warmth and sharpened awareness of the body and the world around. When this moment of*

> *transformation arrives the single units of the composition cease straining and pulling at each other. A total vision comes through that is akin to a true hallucination ... .*[63]

So notwithstanding his belief that Op prevented the formation of a gestalt, Ehrenzweig in fact described the triumph of the brain in creating a 'gestalt' that is more than a visual image because it includes non-visual sensations. This recalls Roszak's description of the ideal gestalt perception: 'a constant natural dialogue, an ongoing series of "creative adjustments" which make man at home in his body, his community, his natural habitat'.

So for both Roszak and Ehrenzweig, true perception was experienced through the body. A notion of the body as the centre of the most profound experience lies at the heart of these men's views on two very different phenomena: psychotropic drug use and fine art. While Ehrenzweig's views on Op apparently conflict with, say, Huxley's description of the experience of psychotropic drug use, his descriptions of Riley's work do find parallels with Roszak's notion of the gestalt, which Roszak implied was connected to drug use. As when looking at a Riley painting, when considering the relationship between Op art and drugs, the focus constantly shifts and wavers; a fixed focus (a single interpretation) is impossible; the steady gaze is evaded.

Intertwining vision and movement

The differing factions in the interpretation of Riley's work agreed on one thing: that it dealt, in some fundamental way not found in previous art, with the bodily experience of visual perception. This bodily character of optical experience had interested artists and philosophers for many years before the upsurge of artistic and public interest in Op art in the early 1960s. Gino Severini, one of the original signatories of the 'Technical Manifesto' of Futurist painting (1910), had once written, in a passage familiar to Bridget Riley, that:

> *All philosophies tending to separate the body from the mind are anti-scientific and seem to me to be absurd. The job that we artists have to accomplish today is to establish an equilibrium between intelligence and sensibility.*[64]

In 1960, the French philosopher Maurice Merleau-Ponty wrote about the relationship between the bodily nature of perception and the nature of art.[65] Whereas in earlier, Cartesian philosophy the body is subordinate, and inferior, to the mind, it is central in Merleau-Ponty's philosophy, where consciousness is not separate from the body but part of it. His philosophy constitutes a version of Gestalt theory. In his view all vision is, to some extent, an illusion, a 'delirium' of the waking mind, where to see a painting gives the illusion of 'hav(ing it) at a distance' but it also involves being 'had' by the painting, as the being of the beholder 'enter(s) into the work of art':

> *Painting awakens and carries to its highest pitch a delirium which is vision itself, for to see is to have at a distance; painting extends this strange possession to all aspects of Being, which must somehow become visible in order to enter into the work of art.*[66]

For Merleau-Ponty, it was the artist's bodily, physical experience of the world that had to be translated into the medium of paint. He used the term 'transubstantiations', imparting a sense of the religious or spiritual; the world is changed into paintings, the better to be ingested by the body of the viewer, a body that is not merely a physiological machine but both product and expression of its own vision and movement. The eye is not merely a subordinate physical link between the outside world and the mind: 'eye and mind' constitute an inseparable unity, parts of one system.

> *It is by lending his body to the world that the artist changes the world into paintings. To understand these transubstantiations we must go back to the working, actual body – not the body as a chunk of space or a bundle of functions but that body which is an intertwining of vision and movement.*[67]

This account of the experience of painting is echoed by Ehrenzweig's claims of sensations of 'transformation', 'revelation', 'transfiguration' and the 'new invigorating awareness of the structure of our own body'. It can also be related to the Gestaltist mode of perception that Roszak suggested users of LSD sought to recover.

Such ideas found echoes in criticism of Riley's work in the art press. Writing in April 1964, critic and painter Guy Burn described Riley's and John Hoyland's contributions to the Whitechapel's 'New Generation' exhibition of that year. His language has resonances of Huxley and Merleau-Ponty, emphasizing the physicality of the act of looking at the paintings while insisting on the importance of the notion of 'spiritual experience'.

> *Their* [Riley's and Hoyland's] *pictures really act, for they both set off optical illusions which worm their way into the brain, attack the sense of balance, produce colour echoes like mirages and generally invoke mixed feelings of nausea, bewilderment and delight which must bid fair to rival the effects of mescalin. If you feel that there is no spiritual experience, no message to move one nor any human communication then the point is lost. For there is no attempt at any internal tension between forces opposing each*

other in the picture, but an external tension, an alchemy between picture and spectator. You move on feeling that you have not been a spectator but a participant.[68]

Here again Riley's work is compared to the use of mescaline. Burn referred to 'mirages' (suggesting a physically derived illusion, an objective phenomenon) rather than Ehrenzweig's 'hallucinations' (a word that suggests subjective experience) and 'alchemy', which like Merleau-Ponty's 'transubstantiations' suggests a miraculous transformation of one substance into another.[69] Burn argued that the point of such art was to induce a 'spiritual experience' (notwithstanding the nausea he claimed the spectator could expect). This spiritual experience was clearly mediated by the body: the attack on one's sense of balance and the nausea were the distinctly bodily accompaniments to the sensations of bewilderment and delight that the spectator could expect.

These works transformed the spectator into a 'participant' in the work. If we recall Merleau-Ponty's description of viewing art: 'to see is to have at a distance', we are here faced with the notion of 'having' the art while apparently eliminating the distance; the spectator becomes a participant in the work. Where the artist '[lends] his body to the world' in creating the painting, the spectator must now lend his/her ('working, actual') body to the painting in order to participate in it. Merleau-Ponty also wrote that 'to look at an object is to inhabit it', further emphasizing the participatory nature of the experience of viewing art.[70] For Merleau-Ponty, we have direct access to the world only through the body; perception, which is dependent on the physical senses, is our primary source of knowledge. This view was shared by gestalt psychologists such as Rudolf Arnheim, whose book *Art and Visual Perception* appeared in 1954. Arnheim argued that lines and shapes on paper set up visual 'forces': 'Psychologically, our visual forces are as real as anything else we perceive or think or feel'.[71] Arnheim dismissed the idea that these visual forces are illusions and appears to provide support for Ehrenzweig's later assertion (in 1962) that 'optical illusion' is a misleading term to apply to Riley's art (and by extension to other Op art):

the term illusion is useful only when a difference arising between the physical and psychological world makes us commit a mistake in dealing with physical things – for example, walking into a mirror.[72]

As nobody makes any mistake in dealing with the physical reality of an Op painting – one knows it is a painting and treats it as such – we might presume that Arnheim, who did not mention Vasarely's work in his book and who was writing well before the more widespread development of Op in the early 1960s, would not have applied the term 'illusion' to Riley's paintings. Seen in the context of Merleau-Ponty's writing, and the research of psychologists such as Arnheim, Ehrenzweig's interpretation of Riley's work is that it constituted a successful attempt to produce an art that recognized and exploited an understanding of perception as a product of a physically located mind: a mind that is a product and part of the body.

Perception, art and the body

Hence, in the early 1960s philosophy and psychological science both produced arguments that perception was a *bodily* experience: thus *everything* experienced when looking at any painting was a *physical* sensation. Op's challenge to some contemporary, modernist notions of art lay not in any narrowly defined 'scientific' connections, nor in any counter-cultural associations, but in its insistence on the bodily character of perception and therefore of aesthetic appreciation.

Nevertheless, there had been earlier challenges to notions that aesthetic appreciation in some way transcended the body. Rosalind Krauss has argued that Marcel Duchamp made an attack on this idea in the *Rotoreliefs* that he produced in the 1930s, well before Greenberg and Fried achieved their influential positions as critics. These spinning discs bore spiral-based patterns that appeared to 'beat' or pulsate when the disc was spun. It was the physical sensation of the 'beat', with its connotations of popular music, 'that the modernist artist senses all too well as the enemy of his craft. For that pulse is devolutionary, destructive, dissolving the very coherence and stability of form'.[73] We may compare this to Briony Fer's reading of Bataille, where the destruction and 'decomposition of forms'[74] is central to the creation of art. Max Ernst also experimented with optical devices such as the zoetrope, where rotating slits produced both an illusion of movement and a physical 'beat', as in Duchamp's *Rotoreliefs*, with its erotic associations, again relating the perception of art to the body.[75] The erotic, according to Freud, was central to the 'life instinct' that he argued counterbalanced the 'death instinct' in the human psyche. If death is the ultimate destruction, then Duchamp's Rotoreliefs, Ernst's zoetropes and by extension, Riley's Op art paintings could be argued to carry within them, simultaneously, physical associations of creation (Eros/life) and destruction (Thanatos/death).

In this context, note that the painting that was especially associated with drug use was called *Fall*. The word connotes 'ending': the Biblical Fall, Autumn (the end of the summer), a 'fall from grace', even the 'fall' of a hero in battle or of Icarus from his over-ambitious flight: all instances where 'the end' also involves some form of destruction (of a golden age, of the vulnerable plants of summer, of reputation, death). It recalls Bataille's interest in the destructive element in modern art: 'The fall, of course, restores things to ground level and to the base material of dust and dirt'.[76] Theologically, the Fall is the moment when death enters human experience and 'dust and dirt' also have the ultimate connotation of death, as in the ritual formula of the Christian funeral: 'ashes to ashes, dust to dust'. So in a number of ways the title, *Fall*, connotes ideas of death and destruction. In May 1964, Riley was quoted as saying 'I wish somebody would give me a big wall to destroy. I mean, to make it no longer seem a wall'.[77] This foreshadows Fer's reading of Bataille that:

> *[d]oing violence to representation forms the basis, for Bataille, of any representative act*
>
> *[i]n the act of drawing, a clean piece of paper or a bare wall is in effect 'spoilt' and so transformed into something else*

and

> *the impulse within modernism is to do violence to the text, by obliterating the text.*[78]

Fer links Bataille's interest in destruction with both death and art, and particularly with the production of modernist art, including that of Miró and Picasso – so this was not a new phenomenon in the 1960s.

The notion of the destructiveness of Op art itself has wider relevance. Riley's work can be seen as a threat to contemporary notions of value in modernist art[79]– as an attempt to renegotiate certain modernist ideals by grounding the experience of art within the body. This is art not as a means of transcending the physical but as exploring the heights of experience that the physical – the body – can attain. Hence, Riley's work represented the potential destruction of a particular modernist aesthetic, by its insistence on the physical basis of visual perception. Thomas Crow's view is worth quoting at length because it sums up the point so clearly.

> *Riley's work called the bluff of much vague and unspecific talk of 'expressive content' in Modernist painting. For a critic like Fried, the exact character of the psychological transformation induced in the viewer by a suitably serious and ambitious painting lay beyond articulation, in large part because no precise description*

could ever equal the enormous moral importance placed on the consummation of the experience. Riley filled in the psychological component and it turned out to be neither trivial nor transcendent, but rather some interesting place in between. She had the temerity to exercise a certain control over the viewer's mental state, to trigger palpable physical experiences of heightened alertness: she meant the viewer's involuntary cognitive responses to recall sensations, in her words, of 'running ... early morning ... cold water ... fresh things, slightly astringent'. For taking that reasonable measure of the powers of abstract painting, as well as for recognising the inherently physical, bodily character of optical perception, the Modernists could never forgive her.[80]

Crow presents modernism as a monolithic philosophy, its adherents united in their beliefs and artistic ideals. Agreement between different authorities such as Fry, Barr and Greenberg was far from complete, however, and divisions continued in the 1960s as, for example, Fried's views diverged from Greenberg's as the decade progressed. The essential richness and diversity of modernist art was reflected in critical debate.[81]

It has been suggested that Greenberg's account of modernism maintained itself by 'repressing' conflicting ideas.[82] This account is complicated by the fact that Riley herself and her supporters regarded her work as modernist; if Riley's Op painting threatened any modernist ideals it did so as an act of subversion from within, not as an attack from without.[83] If it were part of the brief of modernist art to be self-referential and self-critical, Riley's work may be seen as extending this ideal to the concept of modernism itself, challenging the notion that modernism could or ought to be monolithic.

The autonomy and self-referencing of modernist art was supposed to induce, in Roger Fry's words, 'that clear, disinterested contemplation that is characteristic of the aesthetic attitude'.[84] Associations with either science or an emerging counter-culture would be as much anathema to modernists such as Fried and Greenberg as literary content in a painting, which they had long decried. As a modernist, Riley rejected such associations for her own work but, in making manifest the 'bodily character of optical perception', it challenged 'the enormous moral importance placed on the consummation of the experience' of looking at a work of art. Ultimately, the insistence on locating this experience within the body forces a questioning of what is meant by the 'spiritual' in art and whether such a concept has any meaning that can be separated from the concept of the body itself.

Perceptions of art

Crow's claim that 'the Modernists could never forgive' Riley may seem sweeping, but in the context of the 1960s it raises another point relating to the notion of perception. So far I have discussed 'visual perception' but we also use the term 'perception' in the sense of the knowledge or beliefs we have gained as a consequence of our examination of the world. We have a 'perception' that some objects are 'art' but others are not. The 'perception' of modernist art held by a Fried or a Greenberg might not coincide with that held by those who promoted Op's claims to be recognized as modernist. Thomas Hess argued that for a painting to be 'art' it should be 'difficult, serious, remote, aristocratic' and Op did not, he argued, meet these requirements.[85] The large numbers of people attending 'The Responsive Eye' and many concurrent Op art shows in New York seem to have been evidence, for Hess, that Op was not 'difficult' enough: Op was attracting attention from the 'wrong' people. His use of the term 'aristocratic' suggested that painting was not for the majority. Some Op artists believed that Op could and should be enjoyed by a wider public. In the style of early modernist avant-garde groups, the French Op art collective GRAV produced a manifesto proclaiming:

> *There must be no more productions exclusively for:*
> *the cultivated eye,*
> *the sensitive eye,*
> *the intellectual eye,*
> *the aesthetic eye,*
> *the dilettante eye.*
> *The HUMAN EYE is our point of departure.*[86]

Here, GRAV rejected the idealized viewer, or 'beholder' assumed in the writing of Fry, Fried and Greenberg, in favour of a wider, less elite, audience. Hess recognized this audience with some contempt:

> *Op enjoys* [some critical success] *among the art-reporters of the mass mediums* [sic] *who have always felt that the function of Art is to teach, or at least divert, the People. They are exasperated by the aloofness of Abstract-Expressionism (which they interpret as snobbism and slyly diagnose as paranoia). In Op they sense that art, at long last, is not only meeting the audience half way ... Op will actually come down off the walls and shake your hand.*[87]

Only 'art-reporters' (not 'critics') from the 'mass mediums' (not including such august journals as *Art News*) gave critical support to Op. They interpreted the 'aloofness' of 'remote, aristocratic' Abstract Expressionism as 'snobbism', a charge that might plausibly be laid on Hess' critique of Op. Hess presented the bodily nature of experiencing Op as trivial, whereas for Ehrenzweig, for example, it was profound: a 'sharpened awareness of the body and the world around'.[88]

Other writers have noted the appeal of Op art beyond what was considered, in the 1960s, to be the usual (and, for some perhaps, desirable) audience for art. Just as Hess claimed that 'Op is the art that the public flocks to see',[89] another critic, Cyril Barrett, in his account of the development of Op, claimed that:

> [Op] *was in a sense proletarian. ... Wherever these exhibitions have gone, they have drawn spectators far in excess of anything the gallery had previously known.*[90]

Barrett implied that Op art had a mass audience but his only evidence that Op was 'proletarian' was that very large numbers of people visited Op exhibitions. He presumed that such large audiences could only be achieved if the 'lower' social classes were making up the numbers. Such comments must be seen in the light of Greenberg's denunciations of 'middle brow culture', from the 1950s onwards, reflected in Hess' views on the 'aloofness' of 'remote, aristocratic' art.[91] None of these commentators presented any actual evidence of the socio-economic positions of audiences for Op or any other art. The notion of widening access to the arts was not on the agenda in the 1960s. At a time when an academic at a provincial university might feel a failure compared with one at Oxford or Cambridge,[92] however, ideas of what constituted the 'proletariat' need to be formulated cautiously.

A 'social' art

Reviewing 'London, The New Scene',[93] an exhibition in Washington DC that included work by Riley, Canadian critic Kenneth Coutts-Smith commented on the change in emphasis in art and its criticism since the emergence of new art that had challenged the pre-eminence of Abstract Expressionism. He presented the new art as breaking decisively with a long-standing valuation of art as the unique expression of the inner life of a gifted individual, and presented it as a new kind of 'social' art. The audience for Abstract Expressionism were expected to 'read' the paintings as personal artistic expressions, a private language that excluded many people, whereas Pop art had apparently eliminated the need to understand such a language. As one wealthy collector said of Pop art 'Here was a timely and aggressive image that spoke to me directly about things I understood'.[94]

Barrett's comments quoted above suggest that Op exhibitions attracted more visitors than Pop exhibitions; Op's 'proletarian' appeal was implicitly greater than that of Pop. Was the public perception of Op that it spoke more directly about things people understood than even Pop art? I will quote Coutts-Smith at length because this passage relates to Barrett's comment on the 'proletarian' appeal of Op art. Coutts-Smith focused on points that were often commented on in relation to Op art, as well as Pop art: the anonymity of surface of the Op work (Riley's use of assistants in executing her works; her admiration for Seurat, who also claimed anonymity of facture), and the collective production of some Op (for example by GRAV in France, Group Zero in Germany[95]).

> *It seems obvious that the central point of the current mental climate is a rejection of expressionism. The personal visionary element in art, the intense individual commitment and solitary exploration seems no longer to be operative in the wider field of acceptability. Romanticism is clearly out ... Is it perhaps that art has become a search for a collective, fluid and temporary iconography, and that the artist is moving round to a position where he is objectifying the collective fantasies of the whole of society rather than exploring his own, rather than examining the peculiar and particular fantasies of the solitary individual?*
>
> *The quality of* anonymity *in much contemporary work seems to support this suggestion. The machine made or craftsman constructed quality of much painting and sculpture is the antithesis of that personal signature embedded in the very paint and gesture of expressionism. This anonymity is the reverse of the special and unique touch of the solitary individual; it suggests more the mark of the socially adjusted collective man.*[96]

Coutts-Smith questioned whether such an art had arisen from needs within society or been imposed upon it by 'highly professional promotional machinery' and wondered if 'the art of the future will be collective and public and anonymous?' The claim that the typical artist in this show was 'objectifying the collective fantasies of the whole of society' was probably intended more as a comment on the Pop art element of the show. Nevertheless, it also relates to the 'objective' nature of Op, where a painting was thought to have the same effect on every viewer, independent of any subjective readings or responses. The works in 'London, The New Scene' were presented as the works of individual artists (Op collectives being more a European phenomenon), and Pop artists (e.g. David Hockney,

Allen Jones, Joe Tilson) outnumbered the Op artists (apparently just Riley and Jeremy Moon). Coutts-Smith's comments read as applicable to both groups.

The Pop debate

To understand the concerns that some critics may have had in relation to Op's status, it is useful to look at the related debate around Pop art. In the USA, creators and promoters of Pop art were anxious for it to be accepted as a high art practice, despite its use of images familiar from sources such as advertising and comic books. They sought to present it in terms familiar from critiques of Abstract Expressionism and its successors, such as Post-Painterly Abstraction. Such arguments linked Pop to the values of the elite audience for the earlier works and implied that specialist knowledge was necessary to understand the work of the Pop artists. Without this, Pop risked being relegated to 'mass culture' rather than avant-garde 'high art'.

> *To reclaim Lichtenstein's paintings as high art, critics insisted that his works transformed their sources and addressed strictly formalist issues. Indeed, these critics defended Lichtenstein's paintings on the formalist grounds staked out by Clement Greenberg's analysis of Colour-field painting and Post-Painterly Abstraction.*[97]

This debate may have caused confusion. Did Pop art really mean more than met the eye? How was one supposed to 'appreciate' it? Anxieties about Pop art were reflected in an article in *Life* magazine in 1964 about New York's Bianchini Gallery, which was temporarily fitted out as a small supermarket. Among real cans and packets of food, wax replica food and authentic-looking signage, the gallery interspersed 'Brillo boxes by Warhol, chrome fruits and vegetables by Robert Watts, and a painted bronze slice of watermelon by Billy Apple'.[98] *Life* showed a (posed) photograph of a middle-aged woman intently studying a can of soup as if wondering whether to buy it or not. *Life*'s readers were supposed to feel superior to the ignorant 'shopper', as they would see the gallery for what it was.[99] *Life* made fun of the shopper's ignorance but, while it raised issues concerning the difference between the art and the non-art in the gallery, did readers learn much from the article? They may have felt some anxiety about their own ability to distinguish art from non-art at the Bianchini and, by extension, wherever Pop art might be encountered. The article's author, Clive Tomkins had a didactic approach, but praised some works and dismissed others without explanation.

He asserted that only artworks could raise the question of what defined art and what constituted reality, even though he did not unveil precisely how art addressed such weighty issues.[100]

The 'aloofness' and 'snobbism' that Hess argued were associated with Abstract Expressionism by the mass media may also have become associated with Pop by readers of articles such as Tomkins'. Barratt's claim that Op attracted larger audiences than other kinds of art[101] suggests its apparent lack of 'aloofness'.

Riley's Op: A special position

The large audiences for Op art partly arose from the heavy media coverage it received, which emphasized the physical effects of the works and the power of the 'optical illusions' commonly experienced when viewing them. These were phenomena that, it was claimed, no one could miss. As critic Robert Melville put it in 1964 'it's very easy to tell the failures – their surfaces don't heave or twitch or quiver or oscillate'.[102] If a work did not produce the 'advertised' effect, it was the artist's fault, not the viewer's. The coverage of Op within a wide range of media, not just specialist art journals or the 'quality' newspapers, suggests that a large public were aware of Op and the effects such art was supposed to induce in the viewer. In particular, the coverage of Bridget Riley's participation in 'The Responsive Eye' apparently brought her work to very widespread attention in both Britain and the USA. This encouraged people outside the usual audience for contemporary art to attend Op art shows, so enlarging their audiences as Barratt noted. This may have engendered concerns, among both supporters and detractors of Op, that such large audiences threatened distinctions between high art and mass culture. As with Pop, if no specialist knowledge were required to appreciate Op, its status as high art could potentially be undermined.

Among the critics and specialist press commentators, controversy characterized the debate about Op art, with every connection or association made for Op being subject to interpretation in favour of both the defence and the prosecution. Hence, associations with notions of the scientific could be used to praise Op for its evocation of the technology that characterized the age or to attack it as being simple-minded derivations from basic diagrams illustrating the laws of visual perception. In turn, the connections between Op and the study of the phenomena of visual perception could be used to incorporate it in serious debate about the bodily nature of perception or to attempt to trivialize it as a poor man's LSD. As I have argued above, the association with LSD was not necessarily a trivial one, given the profound social changes that some users of such drugs apparently hoped to bring about and the rejection of a materialistic, technology-based culture that commentators such as Roszak interpreted as the core of the 'drug culture' of the period.

Lil Picard complained that by 1965 a large number of artists were working in styles characterized by the media as Op, many of them evidently trying to exploit the market. In both the USA and Britain, however, Riley's work was often singled out by commentators as being of exceptional quality.

> *Bridget Riley is still in a special position because people seemed to recognise from the outset that her work explored moods, sensations, experiences which could be different with each visual image. With most Op art, different visual images all seemed to boil down to the same sensation.*[103]

This strength and variety in Riley's work can be seen as the elements that attracted particular attention, when so many art works that could broadly be described as 'Op' were all competing for media, critical and public attention. The support for the high art status of Riley's work by many respected critics, on the one hand, and concerns with its apparent 'popularity', on the other, created a conflict similar to that which the promoters of Pop art had sought to avoid by positioning Pop firmly in relation to modernist values. As we have seen, Crow has argued that there were modernist critics who could never forgive Riley for exploring the physical aspects of the perception of art.[104] It may be that another part of Riley's 'crime' lay in creating an art that was difficult to deny as art but which may have found favour with an audience not previously attracted to avant-garde art.[105] Popularity in itself provoked anxiety among those who believed that avant-garde art must necessarily have a small public, fearful that a large public was associated with products of 'mass culture'. Just as Riley's paintings refused a constant, steady visual focus, so they evaded a single conceptual, critical focus. With the perspective of time, even jibes meant to trivialize have taken on meanings unintended by their makers. If, as Merleau-Ponty claimed, 'to look at an object is to inhabit it',[106] the viewer who inhabits a Bridget Riley painting is not standing in one secure and solid place.

Chapter 3 A Modern English Art

To talk of a modern English art would normally be to convey a kind of double approval: to suggest that the work in question is at one and the same time modern in a culturally specific fashion, and representative of the national culture at its most progressive. It is also to imply that no contradiction is involved in this. But the evidence of history is that this last implication is by no means always a secure one ... the meanings of modernism cannot always or often be made to coincide with the particular values generally associated with English culture.[1]

In this passage, from his study of modernist art in England before the Second World War, Charles Harrison suggests that it is accepted as a 'given' that art may be recognizably 'English' (or, by implication, of any other nationality) – that art reflects or expresses the nationality of its producers. Further, if the term 'modern English art' conveys a 'double approval', it follows that 'English art' by itself is a term of approbation – to create something evocative of the nation itself is 'good'.

A 'nation' has been defined as:

an imagined political community ... imagined *because the members of even the smallest nation will never know most of their fellow members ... yet in the minds of each lives the image of their communion.*[2]

Cultural products such as works of art lend a sense of tangibility and continuity to notions of national culture and national identity. They can give material expression to feelings of patriotism.[3]

Yet these arts must be recognizably the products of *a particular* nation – not those of another nation. There may be a very large number of national styles but clearly they cannot be limitless. If some styles are associated with 'our' nation, there must be others associated with 'foreign' nations. Can there be a style which will not only be recognized by the members of our nation as expressive of our nationhood, but also recognized abroad as being ours and not theirs? Might the same style appear to some British observers as truly British while appearing foreign to others? This question of the national identity of art goes back at least to the nineteenth century, with John Ruskin and Heinrich Wölfflin claiming 'racial' characteristics for art.[4] Such ideas were explored by Nikolaus Pevsner in *The Englishness of English Art* (1956), but Pevsner associated particular styles with places (countries) rather than races: for Pevsner, author of the 46-volume, county-based *Buildings of England*, 'place' was paramount:

> *he saw 'Englishness' ... as being the product of a communal culture developed by all the peoples of Britain ... Furthermore he saw national identity as being something that changes according to situation rather than ... some endemic characteristic that would constantly reassert itself in new situations. Pevsner was talking about what Englishness was and had been.*[5]

In reflecting on what Englishness was in 1956, Pevsner claimed: 'None of the other nations of Europe has so abject an inferiority complex about its own aesthetic capabilities as England'.[6] He argued that this was because art was then 'violent' (the later 1940s and the 1950s saw the rise of Pollock, De Kooning and other Abstract Expressionists) and the English rejected this in favour of 'evolution'.[7] Such statements still have resonance when one considers comments made about Riley and her contemporaries in the 1960s.[8]

How were Bridget Riley's Op paintings, in particular, viewed in relation to 'the particular values generally associated with English culture', and to notions of 'Britishness' or 'Englishness' (or conversely to notions of internationalism and even 'foreignness') in modern art during the period 1961–65? The concept of English/British national identity as a product of an 'imagined community' is useful in considering how perceptions of Op art might impinge on the image of the nation, especially that image as it was promoted and manipulated in the contemporary media. What associations did Op evoke that could be used to enhance or undermine this image?

A new generation

Op art began to impinge on British public awareness in the early 1960s, the same period in which not only various forms of abstract art but also the new figurative styles of Pop art were associated with a 'younger generation' of artists now rebelling against the kinds of art previously thought of as 'British'. For *The Times* critic David Thompson, this new generation had:

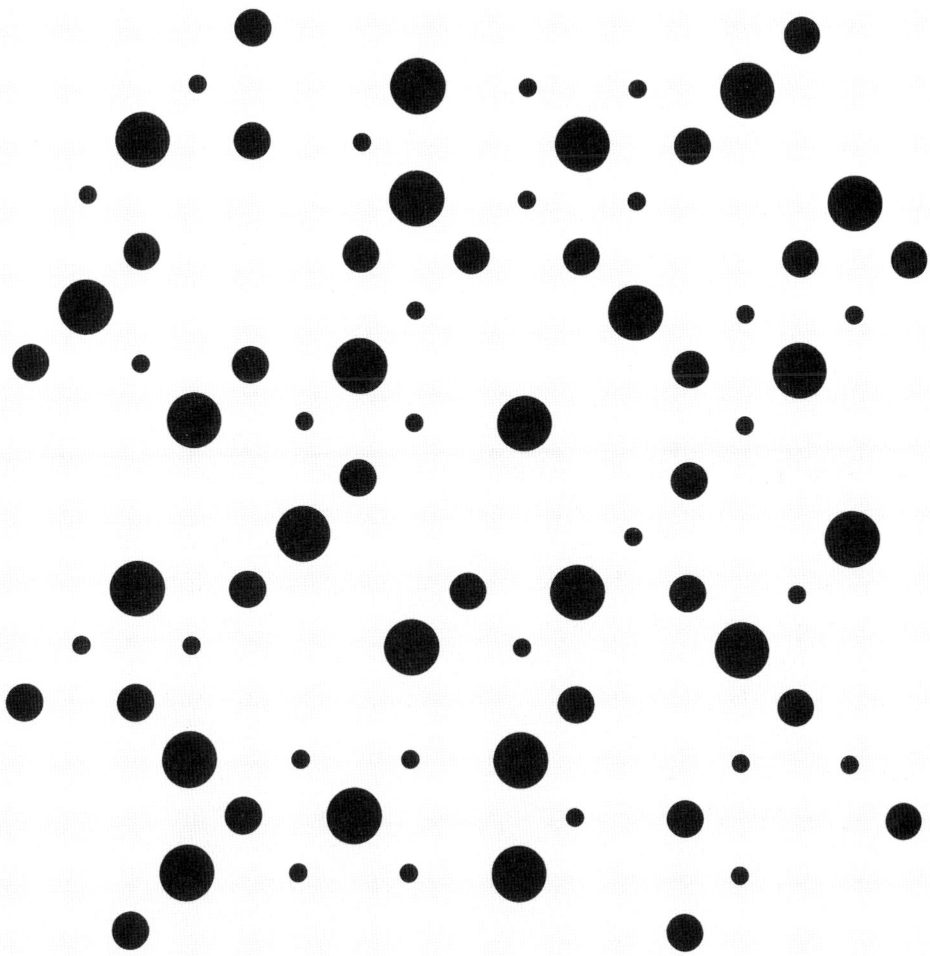

15. **White Disks 1** 1964

come roaring into prominence, versed in the international art of the day as by right and not content to be judged by narrower standards.[9]

As Bryan Robertson, Director of London's Whitechapel Gallery, wrote in 1965:

> *A younger generation has turned its back, in recent years, on the English landscape tradition, believing that the very nature of typically English landscape painting is evocative of a dated nostalgia, a digression from the basic problems of modern art.*[10]

What were 'the basic problems of modern art' and could there be acceptably 'English' ways for an artist such as Riley to solve them that did not involve the application of 'narrower standards'? Could there be solutions in keeping with the national self-image that would not seem parochial? Contemporary press commentaries and reviews reveal a concern with a number of issues that relate (expressly or implicitly) to English or British national identity. These included notions of a national art-historical tradition, in which landscape art was important; notions of professionalism versus amateurism; associations perceived or created between Op and 'foreign' art forms; and concerns that British art was intrinsically 'provincial' and unable to achieve the 'greatness' of French or American art. In this chapter I will discuss the insecurity and ambivalence displayed towards British art and its ability to compete with the art of continental Europe, particularly France. The question of how Riley's work was received in the USA, where its 'national' characteristics were viewed from a different perspective, will be considered in the next chapter.

Bridget Riley was prominent among the younger generation so forcibly seizing the attention of critics such as Robertson and Thompson in the early 1960s. Thompson mentions her as an 'established' name among his 'younger generation'. Her work was included in the 1964 exhibition of works purchased by the Peter Stuyvesant Foundation, entitled 'The New Generation: 1964', at the Whitechapel Gallery, London [Figs. 15, 16, 17].[11] The title of this exhibition reflects the contemporary emphasis on the reconstruction of the identity of the British artist as, above all, young. This also has implications for contemporary notions of national identity – was Britain a 'young' country in the sense of being dominated by the energy and enthusiasm of youth? Or was a mythologized historical narrative, with its associations of heritage, empire and tradition, a 'true' (or more widely acceptable) expression of national identity? Was 'new Britain' or 'old Britain' the central ideal of the imagined community of the nation? Could

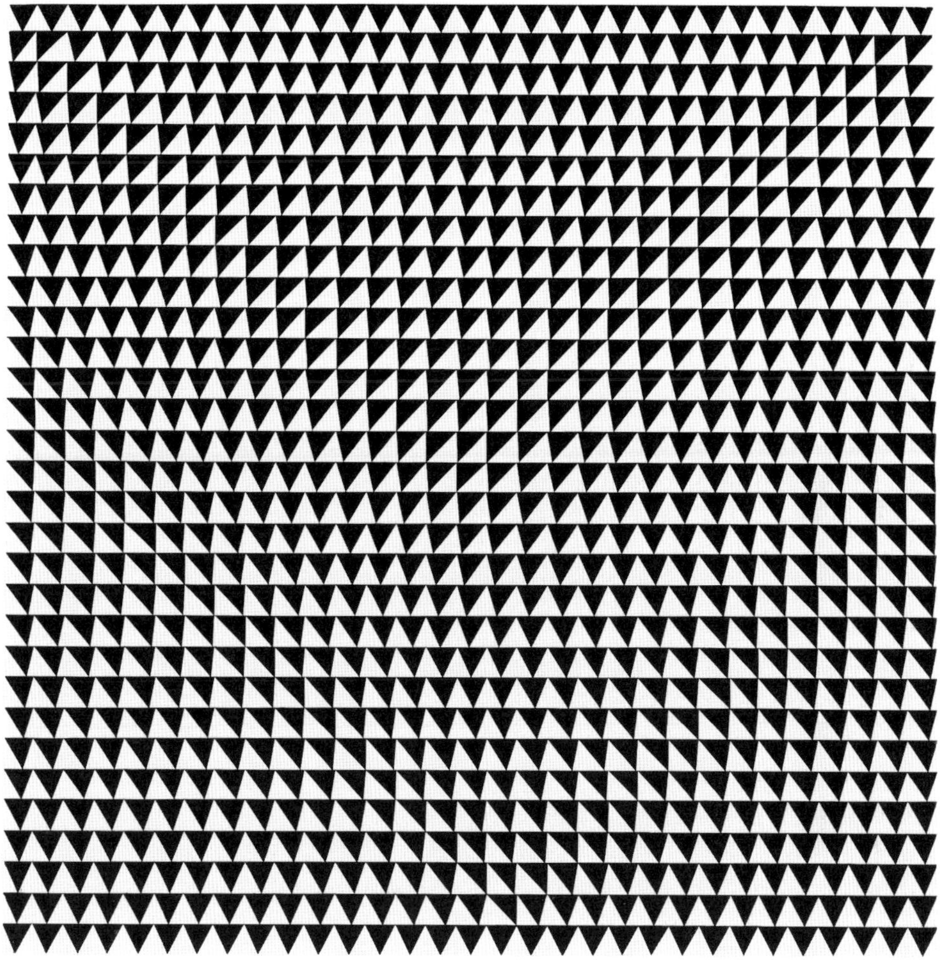

16. **Shiver** 1964

these two imagined communities co-exist? Where was Riley's work positioned in these debates? The discussion of her work in the general and art press of the early 1960s reflects wider concerns with Op's identity in nationalistic terms and the implications of this for its reception in both Britain and the United States.

The English landscape tradition

As Robertson's reference to the English landscape tradition indicates, this type of art had long been promoted as typically English. This went much deeper than an aesthetic preference for such art. Riley's work could not, in any obvious way, be accommodated within such a tradition.[12] As we have seen, Op art connoted 'futuristic' notions, in opposition to the English rural myth. Hence, when Edward Lucie-Smith curated an exhibition of recent British art at Arthur Tooth & Son's London gallery in January 1962, he included one of Riley's paintings, *Blaze 1* [Fig. 12], in a selection of works that he considered showed: 'what British art looks like now ... things which seemed to contain the seeds for the future'.[13] In sowing such seeds, Riley's work came into conflict with certain notions of what constituted Englishness (or Britishness) and did so at a time when such ideas were already challenged by rapid social changes. The retinal 'blaze' of her work seems to presage the 'white heat' of Wilson's scientific revolution, proclaimed the following year.

If Riley's work lacked connotations of the rural landscape, what did that environment itself connote to the British people? In the 1960s many still regarded Britain as an essentially rural nation, even though most people lived in urban locations.[14] This attitude had persisted for decades. One early wartime opinion poll revealed that a widespread national image was: 'predominantly of landscape, village life, country churches and thatched cottages'.[15] The notion that the fertile, farmed, and specifically English countryside (whose ownership lay in the hands of a small percentage of the population) was itself the most essential expression of national identity was a political idea as well as a cultural one.[16] After the relative agricultural self-sufficiency of the war years:

> [Jacquetta] *Hawkes*[17] *was surprisingly confident that the current form of government, a centralised State Socialism, was the expression of the 'consciousness of the land' itself.*[18]

In this context, it is not surprising that landscape art should be particularly identified as an 'English' art in the immediate post-war period.[19] In the 1950s, artists of the St Ives Group either painted landscape directly (Ivon

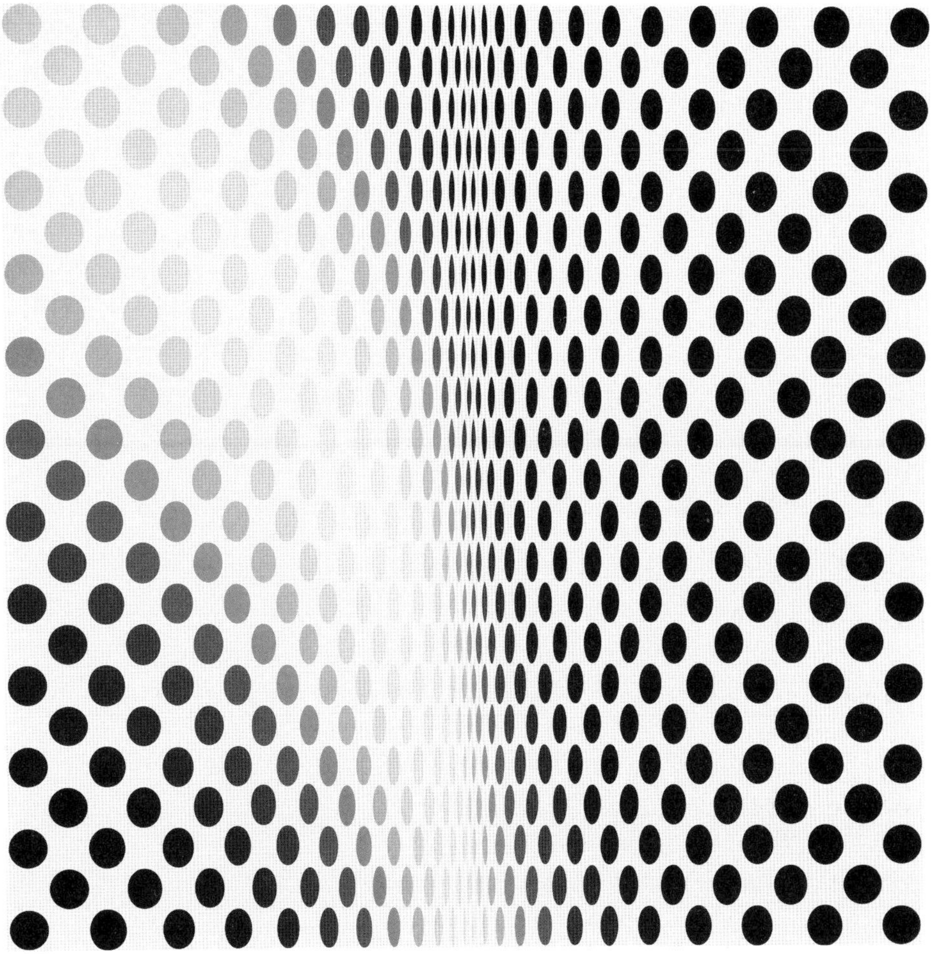

17. **Loss** 1964

Hitchens), or were recognized as incorporating elements of it into more abstract work (Ben Nicholson). The modernism of Henry Moore's sculpture, for instance, was made 'English' by what the critic David Sylvester described as 'the suggestion of landscape that is almost ever-present in Moore's more complex pieces'.[20] The idea that England was fundamentally rural persisted through the 1960s:

> *A literary reviewer remarked in 1969 (as he could have any time in this century) that 'a foreigner reading some recent English verse might imagine that we spend most of our time behind the plough or tickling trout, and that the town is still alien to us'.*[21]

Critical reactions to Riley's work, on the other hand, did not link it with notions of landscape and the rural life. One review of a 1964 group exhibition featuring her work was headed 'Painters of the Urban World', and in another Lil Picard associated Op with the urban environment.[22] Yet the town or city was apparently not a habitat regarded as really 'British' by many people. Urban associations actively conflicted with the image of Britain associated with the work of artists such as Hitchens and Moore.

'Banishing provincial timidity'

One of the concerns of British critics was that British art was provincial, not really up to the international competition. This attitude had dogged the British art world since the introduction of modernism to Britain earlier in the century. Writing in 1965 on the contemporary British art scene, Bryan Robertson and John Russell commented on Fry and Bell's enduring influence:

> *... for forty years the London artworld was dominated by the influence of Roger Fry. ... Fry imposed his views in his own writing and lectures, ... and through friends as influential as Samuel Courtauld, Maynard Keynes and Clive Bell. ... Taste was something to be cultivated by looking at French painting. Mondrian, Malevich, Brancusi, Klee, Kandinsky and Max Ernst might as well not have existed.*[23]

Robertson's and Russell's list of non-French artists of importance notably lacks any British examples. That any British artist of the earlier twentieth century might have made a significant contribution to modern art was, apparently, no more credible in 1965 than it had been thirty or forty years earlier. In 1932, for instance, the painter Paul Nash had published an article on 'Going Modern and being British' and questioned whether it were possible to achieve both. Again, he saw the roots of modern art as European.[24]

After the Second World War, Britain, along with her Commonwealth, could claim to have had a crucial role, alongside the USA, in the liberation of Europe and the defeat of Fascism. Britain's single-minded determination to win was widely recognized and within Europe her influence and prestige were increased.[25] Yet whereas the USA exploited a similar rise in influence and prestige to achieve a position of recognized cultural dominance, in particular through the success of Abstract Expressionist art, in Britain there was little sign of any parallel attempt. 'Between 1945 and 1950, then, the country lay in a crepuscular zone with the shadows of night as firm upon the landscape as the heartening hints of the rising sun'.[26]

In Britain during the war years, the value of the pound fell by over 40%, the national debt tripled and per capita expenditure on consumer goods and services fell by 16%, whereas in the USA such spending rose by about the same amount and continued to grow rapidly after the war. Britain's estimated losses over the course of the war amounted to a quarter of the country's total wealth – around £7000 million. Despite her comparative wealth, the United States was reluctant to grant loans or aid to Britain and the rest of Europe after the war (until the Marshall plan was launched in 1948); such funding as was forthcoming was inadequate and carried a high rate of interest. Rationing of food and consumer goods became even more stringent after the war than it had been during it, and did not cease completely until 1954. A fuel shortage in the winter of 1947 compounded these problems.[27] If Britain spent the latter half of the 1940s in a twilight zone, the parlous state of the economy would seem sufficient explanation. The nation's attention was absorbed by these economic problems and by efforts to create a more just society symbolized by the Welfare State: little was done in this period by British organizations to promote British art abroad. Despite both lack of funds and the fact that Picasso, based in France, dominated perceptions of European art, the British Council wanted to establish an international reputation for British 'Neo-Romantic' painting ('the product of the soil and a Celtic past') as 'the summit of contemporary art'.[28] In spite of the Council's success in supporting the work of Moore, however, British artists in general received little help. As late as 1967 the Beeley Report[29] showed that less than 2.5% of the Council's budget was spent on presenting British painting, sculpture, drama, music and ballet to foreign audiences. Lacking substantial funding, British art failed to achieve a strong international reputation after the war. British artists still looked to Europe for inspiration and, unlike US artists, remained in much the same peripheral position they had occupied before the war.

In the 1960s, then, younger artists were rejecting not only a particular kind of painting – landscape – but also a long-standing myth of the nature of British national identity and inherent inferiority of British art. To what extent this rejection was successful and a new paradigm for indigenous art was established, was a matter of contemporary debate. If Britain were *not* a rural idyll, a land of timeless stasis, then an alternative was an urban environment of technology, rapid transport, constant change, advertising – a world now most readily associated with Pop art. Op also connoted this urban world, but had the advantage of lacking the overtones of American-style commercialism with which Pop art had been associated since the activities of the Independent Group in the early 1950s.

For many critics, a central question was whether contemporary art was managing to escape from what they saw as a long-standing provincialism, which was held to be at the heart of Britain's failure to produce art worthy of international recognition. Characteristics perceived to be British in the 1960s included 'literary' qualities, 'good taste' and even 'linearity',[30] which were seen as the products of British inhibition and provincialism and which some critics detected in the work of even the most progressive of the younger generation. For some, British art was characterized by its perceived limitations. The distrust of the literary can be traced back to Clive Bell's dismissal of 'descriptive painting' and 'illustration',[31] and may also have reflected a Greenbergian view of modernist art, where each form of art should be discrete, self-contained and self-referential. At a time when New York dominated international artistic practice and values, any hint of the literary in a painting would necessarily appear provincial. On the other hand, the Neo-Romantic movement, replete with literary connotations, had been the most recognizably 'British' new development of the immediate post-war years.[32] The view that literariness, provinciality and Britishness were inextricably bound together was expressed by *The Times*' critic, David Thompson. In December 1963, when Thompson looked back on a year of 'International recognition for British Painting', Bridget Riley was cited with Ron Kitaj and David Hockney as an established name, one of a small élite who were breaking with a stereotyped image of British art as inhibited, timid and provincial. Various exhibitions had: 'set the seal of official recognition on the fact that British painting as a whole had acquired a new standing in the world'.[33] For Thompson, who saw earlier generations of British artists as 'hampered by their isolated position', this followed a period of several years in which:

it has been increasingly evident that a new spirit and confidence were doing something unprecedented to British painters: they were banishing a collective provincial timidity.[34]

Nonetheless, Thompson cautioned that:

The best of the new British painting, for all its confident internationalism, has not lost all its British characteristics – what some would call its typical limitations. It is often a little thin blooded, linear, bodiless, governed more by good taste than strong feeling. It is generally cautious about colour and relies on fantasy or allusive reference more than it does on the sensuous, material, physical aspects of art.[35]

Terms such as 'fantasy' and 'allusive reference' suggest the idea of storytelling – the basis of literature and therefore not, by modernist standards, a suitable basis for painting. British art could achieve a position of high, if not equal, standing with foreign art but only by shedding its 'typical [British] limitations'. Young artists were familiar with international art – like Nash, Thompson promoted engagement with this as essential, and he had sufficient confidence in his 'new generation' to see them as plausible competition for their foreign counterparts.

A year, then, of encouraging recognition that the centres of creative activity are not necessarily all located in foreign capitals. It can, and does, happen here.[36]

Thompson's article raises a number of issues. Why should Britain always lag behind its neighbours abroad in terms of artistic excellence? Although the Channel could easily be crossed by 'plane and boat, Britain was seen as isolated from its neighbours. In what sense was art produced in Britain – even in London – 'provincial'? Despite his optimism, Thompson still conveyed a sense of national inferiority with regard to the visual arts and implied that this sense was universally shared.

British post-war confidence

In the late 1950s and early 1960s, Britain was beginning to enjoy the sort of material wealth that had been associated with the USA in the immediate post-war years.[37] Art reviews in the early 1960s suggest that, only then, was any confidence in indigenous art at last being felt among those concerned with producing or evaluating it. Thompson's view that British painting had acquired a new standing reflected the belief that outside Britain there was a new respect for British art. This view was shared by G.S. Whittet, editor of *The Studio*, who made much of the unusual nature of this phenomenon. 'The welcome acceptance of modern British painters as important contributors to the art of the twentieth century has about it an air of the incredible'.[38] Whittet had visited Zurich, the sophistication of whose art lovers he was keen to emphasize before relating his apparently credulity-stretching experiences there.

> *From conversations with critics, dealers and gallery directors, I gained the opinions, freely vouchsafed, and not out of courtesy to me, that British painting is regarded as representing one of the most potent forces in modern art ... one or two people ... in fact, regarded the paintings of British artists as comparing in vitality and imagination with* [sic] *the works of painters of the post-war New York school.*[39]

The *New Statesman's* art critic, the artist Andrew Forge, was also impressed by what he perceived as a widespread enthusiasm for new British art.

> *Everybody agrees that something is happening to painting in England at the moment, and that there is an unprecedented drive among younger painters and new talents are swelling in a favourable climate.*[40]

Forge went on to review 'The New Generation' show featuring Riley, David Boshier, Anthony Donaldson, David Hockney and Allen Jones. Riley's work was not singled out but presented as part of an upsurge of artistic activity. The show's catalogue was introduced by David Thompson, who used this opportunity to reaffirm his belief in young British artists.

> *They are starting their careers in a boom period for modern art. British art in particular has suddenly woken up out of a long provincial doze, is seriously entering the international lists and winning prestige for itself. The atmosphere is one of self-confidence, but also of competition.*[41]

The belief that modern British artists must look to continental models was certainly not extinguished, however; not only was the new British art influenced by foreign developments, but this was a prerequisite of international success. By the 1960s the foreign developments that had to be taken into account included, prominently, New York's Abstract Expressionist movement. Barbara Hepworth's son-in-law, the critic Alan Bowness, writing in 1967, looked back on how, partly inspired by American developments:

> *Feelings of an innate national inferiority vanished overnight; though it may be more accurate to say that they were replaced by a suspicion of American superiority.*[42]

Yet in the early 1960s there is a sense in the writings of the critics and commentators that British artists such as Riley were not merely seen as attempting to assimilate the work of Parisian or New York artists, but as actually competing – 'entering the international lists' as Thompson combatively expressed it – with their contemporaries abroad.

Going modern and being British

If Riley and her contemporaries were seen to have lost the 'provincial timidity' that had prevented their recent predecessors from actively competing for international recognition and leadership, this did not mean that they had won these prizes. In entering such a competition there was a danger that in becoming international, British art would cease to be recognized as truly 'British'. For many British critics in the early 1960s, British contemporary art was engaged in a struggle not only to achieve parity with international art but also to do this in a way that would be distinctively British. The question raised by Paul Nash thirty years earlier, as to whether it was possible to 'go modern' *and* 'be British', was still unresolved in the early 1960s. Riley's work was a candidate for criticism for lack of Britishness because Op art was seen, by critics in both Britain and the USA, as having origins in Constructivism. Constructivism was primarily associated with Russia (Vladimir Tatlin, Naum Gabo and his brother Antoine Pevsner) and subsequently with Germany (the Bauhaus). On the other hand, British artists had been assimilating the principles of Constructivism since Gabo's visit to Britain in the 1930s.[43] Gabo and Pevsner had influenced the work of Ben Nicholson, and the early work of Barbara Hepworth and Moore, none of which was seen as lacking in 'Britishness'.[44]

In 1962, Norbert Lynton commented on Riley's first one-person show:

> *in spite of British constructivist activities and our 'Situation' painters, one thinks of this quasi-scientific art as something outside Britain's range. So Bridget Riley's first one-man show comes as something of a surprise (Gallery One): she uses the grammar of black squares, bands and segments with a cool economy that makes her French counterparts (except perhaps Yvaral) look fussy and extravagant.*[45]

This writer was surprised to find a British artist producing competent Op art. There is a suggestion here, however, that in bringing Op within 'Britain's range', Riley had in fact made this art British by means of a rejection of foreign 'extravagance'. 'Cool economy' can be read as a signal of a nationalist claim: a specifically British sangfroid; only grudgingly could the French be admitted to exhibit such a characteristic. Any question as to the 'Britishness' of Riley's art was immediately answered by the assertion of British 'cool' – with a stiff upper lip, Britain could take on the foreign competition and win. In producing Op art, Riley had not succumbed to foreign fussiness and extravagance. This passage suggests an underlying anxiety about the Britishness of Op that was to surface in other commentaries. The American critic Max Kozloff commented in 1964: 'The pre-eminent critical issue so far raised about British art centres around its possible loss of 'Britishness', as if the latter was some burdensome form of virginity'.[46]

In his review of the exhibition 'A Year of British Art', John Russell was much concerned with the attempts of 'English' artists to achieve 'greatness', which he asserted had eluded them since Turner's death more than a century previously.

> *An entirely adult English painting has something miraculous about it, for it takes a Turner to survive the characteristic climate ('that demi-paradise of euphemism' as Sickert called it) of the English art world. English art has always seemed to be on the edge of greatness ... Since Turner died the ideal of grown-up greatness has, if anything, receded. Promise has been killed by kindness, nine times out of ten, but if Mr Lucie-Smith is right about the ruthlessness of his varied team, the tenth man may just turn up when we need him.*[47]

As press reviews of Riley's work at this time often stressed its supposed aggressiveness and ability to induce feelings such as seasickness and vertigo, we may suppose it did not lack the desired 'ruthlessness'. Russell implied that even the work of Francis Bacon, for example, was not 'grown-up', not 'ruthless' enough, too 'kind'. Other critics complained that British art was genteel and overly tasteful.[48] Russell noted approvingly Lucie-Smith's comparison of English contemporary and European seventeenth-century art but made no mention of contemporary European art – an art against which one might expect contemporary British art to be measured. The English art world, both past and present, was presented as small-minded, even childish and rarely able to produce 'an entirely adult' painting.

Although Russell suggested that one of the artists[49] selected by Lucie-Smith for the Tooth Gallery show might be able to achieve this 'grown-up greatness', he did not suggest which one. Whoever it was would need 'ruthlessness' if they were to succeed. Lucie-Smith's introduction to the exhibition catalogue emphasized this quality:

[The selected artists] *have a ruthlessness I admire, a determination in pursuing a given end which seems to me a basic necessity of art, and which has until recently been somewhat lacking in British painting.*[50]

Despite acknowledging this need for ruthlessness, Russell believed that only 'a private and inward revolution' could achieve great results. There was an implication here that looking to contemporary Europe was of no use to the British artist – he or she had somehow to find the necessary greatness internally.

Every generation believes itself to be on the point of producing the great English Picture. Some hope to achieve it by opening a quarrel between the present and the past, others by pertinacious borrowing. But history shows that those borrowings are most successful when they are the least obvious – as when Gainsborough lifted from Rubens in the Birmingham Harvest Wagon*; and that the quarrel is most effective when it is a matter not of thumping the table but of a private and inward revolution such as occurred when Francis Towne pulled the fluff off the tradition of landscape painting in watercolour'.*[51]

These critics were willing to cite Europe as a source for British art provided such sources were historical (such as Rubens), well removed from the present. Russell displayed a tension between his frustration with the history and development of British (or specifically 'English') art and his unwillingness to embrace contemporary influences from elsewhere. 'Private and inward' suggests not just private to the artist but confined within the boundaries of a certain concept of Englishness. 'Grown-up' English painting was rare but he gave no examples of foreign cultures where it occurred more frequently, there was simply an implication that it was regularly produced abroad. The British art world was not directly compared with foreign models; modern European painting remained an undefined 'other'. Unlike Thompson, Russell seems to have been unable to confront the notion of a contemporary foreign art world against which British art must compete and be judged.

The forms of art taking on this competition were diverse – Riley's Op art was one possibility among several, and neither Thompson nor Russell picked it out at this stage as a candidate for the substantial international success it was later to enjoy. Both men regarded it as part of a wider renaissance of British art, which was restoring confidence in the latter's value, vigour and future after a period in which it had seemed to have little merit outside the work of a small coterie of older artists.

Later that year, however, Russell gave a more confident assessment of Riley's work.

> *In any anthology of British painting since the war a place should forthwith be reserved for two pictures, at least, from Bridget Riley's new show at Gallery One.* Fall *and* Ascending and Descending (Hero)[sic] [52]

By July of 1964, Russell's enthusiasm had grown. Not only was Riley's painting outstanding among British art but 'the three new Rileys are major inventions which could hang with credit in international company'.[53]

For some critics, however, even the best British art failed to stand up to foreign competition. In October 1964, while the *New Statesman*'s art critic, Robert Melville, noted that at the 'Seven '64' exhibition at the McRoberts and Tunnard gallery in London, Bridget Riley showed 'a brilliant panel in which over 300 black ovals dilate and contract like the eyes of a cat',[54] he nevertheless moved on to comment that:

> *the American painter, Frank Stella, exhibiting at the Kasmin Gallery, has worked out a kind of abstract illusionism*[55] *that makes the English varieties look somewhat fussy and provincial.*

This is significant in the context of the concern expressed by commentators in the 1960s that British art was provincial. For other British critics, however, there was a danger that in ridding their art of 'provincial' characteristics, Riley and other Op artists would not produce truly 'British' work. Such a concern may be detected in Norbert Lynton's comment that Op was 'outside Britain's range' and distinguishing Riley's 'cool' painting from that of the 'fussy and extravagant' French.[56] Not everyone, however, perceived this 'Englishness' in Riley's work. In July 1964 *The Times* declared that:

> *we can account for the brashness and assertiveness of many of our young painters and sculptors, and the inflexible and rather obscure slogans that go with it* [sic], *as an attempt to get with a single lunge into the forefront of the international art scene.*[57]

There is a hint here of the American comic-strip: 'with a single bound our hero was free' – suggesting that, for this writer, it was America that formed the front-line competition at 'the forefront of the international art scene'. *The Times* argued that the emphasis on terms such as 'professional', 'uncompromising' and 'hard-hitting', frequently used in the press to describe the work of Riley and her contemporaries, indicated:

> *the presence of a certain morale-boosting bravado to cover up a nagging uncertainty, not only on the part of the critics but of the*

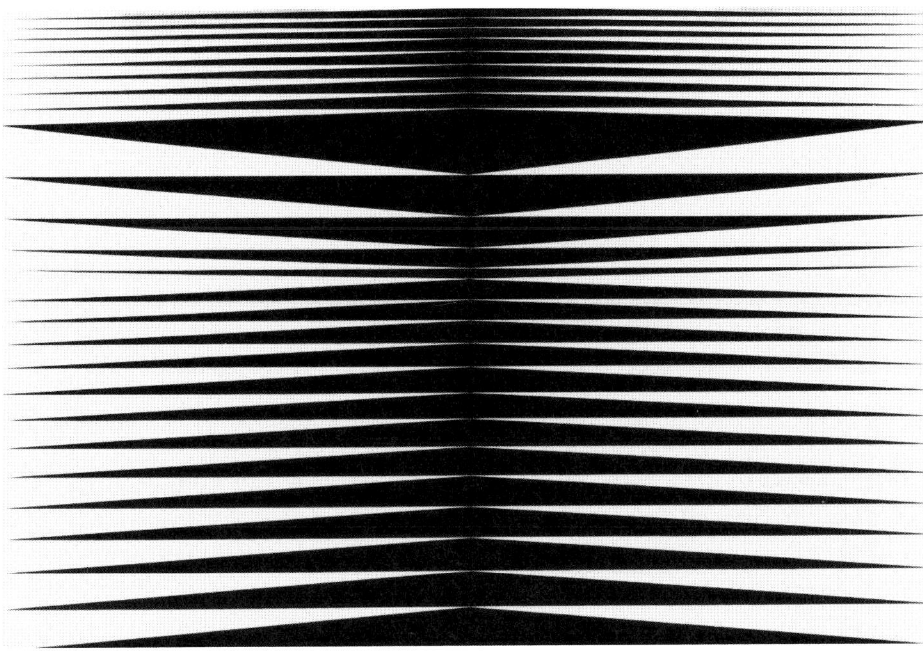

18. **Ascending and Descending Hero** 1963

artists as well, about the role English artists should play in coping with modes of artistic expression whose centres of activity lie outside our shores.

There is a suggestion here that 'good taste' was not a wholly reprehensible quality in art. Where others saw boldness, daring and professionalism, this correspondent saw British artists as attempting 'a gesture' towards the international art scene and:

we have had to borrow someone else's megaphone to make such a gesture – American Pop and Situationist art, European kinetics – and we have probably succeeded in crushing the life out of gentility.[58]

Op artists Derek Boshier and Bridget Riley had been named, at the start of the article, as part of the group alleged to be attracting the kind of comments the author deplored. Op could not be accused of 'gentility' but it was not truly British: it was a foreign import used to sidestep the inherent provincialism and gentility of British art. If the centre of activity for Op was Europe, British Op was merely imitating a foreign style. 'Provincialism' was still a problem but *The Times* considered that 'the only thing that can combat that is real originality'. This brings us back to Benedict Anderson's view that love for the nation is expressed through its arts. Styles of art derived from foreign sources, or believed to be so derived, risk devaluing the home nation by implying that indigenous art is inherently inferior to foreign art. In this case, foreign influences were to be feared as destroying those qualities that, although not presented as laudable, were at least perceived as genuinely British. Foreign influences were a barrier to real originality whereby, presumably, a new and 'British' art, untainted by foreign associations, could emerge.

Coming to terms with the future

The Times' correspondent implicitly denied that British artists could take foreign influences and make something 'British' from them, although that had been the project of earlier British artists such as Nicholson. The comments of British critics in this period present a paradox: qualities that were widely regarded as truly British were the antitheses of those perceived as necessary for contemporary international art, yet avoiding these characteristics in favour of a perceived bold, internationalist professionalism invited the criticism that the artists concerned were copying foreign art and not being original. For *The Times*, the need to make 'gestures' had prevented 'a work of real profundity, and Englishness if you like, emerging slowly in its own time'. This call for the slow development of some truly profound artistic statement echoes John Russell's desire for 'a private and inward revolution'.[59]

The Times made a connection between Englishness and profundity, and implied one between the (superficial) gesture and foreign art, suggesting that British art *could* be superior to the foreign competition, given the 'right' kind of development. The nature of the desired development was far from clear, however. While Thompson had claimed that British art did not sufficiently emphasize 'the sensuous, material, physical aspects of art',[60] *The Times* criticized Bridget Riley as 'yet to get beyond the physical powers of her medium'.[61]

While *The Times* argued that art such as Riley's was not British enough, an alternative view was that recent British art still did not break decisively enough with the past. The artist Robyn Denny, reviewing 'The New Generation', wrote of his disappointment with the show, exempting only Riley, David Hockney and Patrick Caulfield from the charges that:

> *the New Generation is bedevilled by plagiarism, parody, guileful make-believe, and the absence of any kind of risk, and it is a combination of just these things which, handed gift-wrapped from one generation to another, has doomed in English art all attempts, in the past, to come to terms with the future, and which makes the new generation so like the old.*[62]

Denny did not make it clear just who or what was being plagiarized or parodied. A plausible interpretation is that it was foreign art. Where Riley was clearly implicated in *The Times* as 'borrowing' 'European kinetics', however, for Denny she was one of the few who had *not* succumbed to plagiarism, demonstrating that a single art form may have connotations of both 'our' and 'foreign' national identity, depending on who is making the interpretation. Bryan Robertson was of the opinion that no artist from any country would be happy to have his or her work associated too closely with a particular nation.

> *The truth is that national characteristics in art are undeniable and should be understood and cherished; nationalism, on the contrary, is a degenerative sign of provincial insecurity.*[63]

Here, any question that assigning specific 'undeniable' national characteristics to a work of art might be problematic was ignored. While nationalism was a sign of provincial insecurity, one may infer from this passage that in practice provincial insecurity could be induced in any artist by the suggestion that his or her work had any national identity at all. Robertson commented, for instance, that Eduardo Paolozzi's work showed 'an exceptional awareness of aesthetic issues in the air outside England and a refusal to be circumscribed by native parochialism'.[64] This suggests that provincial insecurity, expressed as a concern with Britain's 'native (= inherent?) parochialism', was still a problem for British critics, even if the artists themselves were free of it.

To complicate matters further, at least one critic sought to validate Riley's Op work by placing it in a context of earlier, European, avant-garde art. This *Times* critic wrote at length about the optical qualities of Monet's *Waterlilies*,[65] which had first been publicly displayed in London's National Gallery two months earlier, and related the Monet to later developments in American Abstract Expressionism. This was by way of preparing the reader for an account of a more recent, British, artistic practice.

> *The curious thing is that the one abstract work in London at present that has a comparable effect is not an abstract expressionist type of painting at all. It is the 'environmental' work called* Continuum *in Bridget Riley's show at Gallery One.*
> ..... *many people will be understandably inclined to dismiss as 'art' anything so limited to exploiting pure sensation. Cézanne almost implied as much when he called Monet 'only an eye'.*[66]

Here, an Op painting, which the writer clearly felt was at risk of being excluded from the category of 'art' (let alone avant-garde art), was validated by reference to Monet. Moreover, the correspondent declared that Riley's painting was *not* 'abstract expressionist' – but derived from the European avant-garde of which Monet was a part, by-passing Abstract Expressionism. This foreshadowed later American concerns that European Op art was continuing a pre-war European avant-garde project which had no place for Abstract Expressionism. *The Times* placed Riley in a clearly (even defiantly) European tradition, but without suggesting she had plagiarized European art. Indeed, she was taking it forward.

The cult of the professional

Another major concern in this period was the concept of professionalism and how this related to 'Britishness'. There was an emphasis on the emergence of 'professional' attitudes and standards in British life. The notion of professionalism was a complex one and had particular connotations, in a British context, that made it problematic for artists. Riley's professionalism was commented on favourably by a number of critics so it is worth examining the meanings attaching to this attribute and how the notion of professionalism related to the image of 'new Britain'. Since the nineteenth century, 'the professions' and 'trade' had been regarded as quite separate, as various groups (civil engineers and pharmacists, as well as doctors and lawyers) had distanced themselves from the notion that they sold their services in a marketplace.[67] The English poet Matthew Arnold declared in 1868 that 'in no country ... do the professions so naturally and generally share the cast of the ideas of the aristocracy as in England'.[68]

'Professional' as a label of status implied both 'aloofness from the struggle for income'[69] *and*, notwithstanding this, the ability to command a high price for one's services. In a class system that places at the top those perceived to be financially independent, with no need to sell their labour, the term 'professional' both indicates and disguises the connection between the labour of an intellectual, skilled élite – and money. To be professional is to earn money as far as possible without *appearing* to do so. Long before the 1960s, therefore, the term 'professional' had associations of high social class, expertise in matters outside most people's grasp, and distance from the practical aspects of making money. Commentators on British art in this period demonstrated considerable concern with the notion of professionalism. It was a word that could connote 'upper class-ness' but now also connoted a new meaning, the 'classlessness' of a meritocracy based purely on skill and talent; or its meaning might slide uneasily between the two.

Ambivalence about the meanings and consequences of professionalism can be detected, for example, in the writing of the critic Bryan Robertson. Thus, of the Royal College of Art (where Bridget Riley studied), Robertson wrote 'The students from the college certainly seem to be more professional in their attitude to work, patrons, dealers, career in general, than students elsewhere'.[70] He attributed this to '[Robin] Darwin's [the principal] alignment of it more directly with the professional worlds of industry and design in general'.[71] After strongly supporting the notion of professionalism, however, Robertson also expressed an implicitly *negative* view of it in his comments on the Venice Biennale: 'it has degenerated over the years to an international trade fair and mostly degrades everyone who participates'.[72] Here, the alternative meanings of the word 'professional' come into conflict: it was possible to value professionalism, in the sense of possessing, and knowing the worth of, a relatively rare, respect-worthy skill, while deriding the lower-class associations of a 'trade fair'. The logical consequence of 'professionalism' in art might seem to be that art fairs would become trade fairs where artists, dependent on selling their work (as autonomous professionals not working to the specific commissions of individual patrons), would find a market.

In practice, very few artists could afford to dissociate themselves from 'trade' in some respect; besides selling their works, many needed to sell their labour in other ways in order to make an acceptable income. According to Robertson, many artists supplemented the inadequate income from the sale of their works by teaching.[73] The large number of artists working as teachers was partly the result of financial necessity but also stemmed from the belief that teaching was socially valuable, and gave English artists a sense of community. Teachers occupy an ambivalent position in relation to the question of social class, however, tending to claim the status of professionals but without the financial rewards of say, medicine or law. Teaching (as opposed to working in a commercial art studio) provided a limited income but allowed the artist to maintain a professional identity even when not directly engaged in the production of art. It was also reasonably easy to obtain part time work as a teacher and the status of being a professional (i.e. practising) artist would have helped secure such work. Thus teaching was the commonest way in which artists supplemented their income, even though they might have earned more money for less work (and hence would have had more time for their art) if they had engaged in the more obvious 'money grubbing' of commercial art.

New-style professionalism

The post-war period saw new service industries emerging, such as broadcasting and advertising, which 'by the mid-fifties ... had become classic refuges for the upper class'[74] (or, one presumes, those members of it who had to earn a living). This class association gave an air of professionalism to these new areas of work and by the 1960s they had become both glamorous and respectable. If teaching was the 'classic refuge' for artists, Bridget Riley stands out as unusual in that for several years she worked as a commercial artist for the advertising agency, J. Walter Thompson. As a graduate of the Royal College of Art, praised by Robertson for its 'alignment ... with the professional worlds of industry and design' she may have been better prepared to combine a commercial art 'day job' with a fine art career than were the 'students [from] elsewhere' mentioned by Robertson as being generally less 'professional' than those from the RCA (though it is perhaps unlikely that this is what Robertson had in mind).

Riley's connection with advertising was well known and alluded to by journalists. The advertising industry connoted the new professionalism that some elements of the media were promoting as an expression of a renewed and youthful Britain. The white-collar, middle-class and somewhat glamorous advertising industry fits well into Robertson's conception of the 'professional worlds of industry and design'. Advertising was a profession appropriate to the Beatle era. The new professionalism attributed to Riley as an artist was thus linked to her life outside her role of fine artist, connecting all aspects of her working life to those notions of national identity that foregrounded the image of the young meritocrat gaining success in 'new' professions such as advertising and art. In the USA, since at least the 1930s, it had been more common for 'fine' artists to work in commercial art.[75] Andy Warhol is probably the most famous example but Hess' review of MoMA's 'Responsive Eye' show claimed that a number of the artists showing there had also had careers in commercial art.[76]

Professionals v. amateurs

The term 'professional' had connotations of both the old class system, which was now dismissed as 'dead' by some people, and the new, youthful Britain characterized by professional footballers and television presenters. Christopher Booker's extremely pessimistic account of the period 1956–68 cites frequent use of the claim that certain people were 'professional', used in ways that implied that this was not the norm. 'Amateurism' was detected everywhere and was derided. In the examples Booker quoted, professionalism was often implicitly associated with youth.

> *[T]he message of the 'What's Wrong with Britain' journalists* [in 1961] *was clear enough. Britain was being 'strangled' and 'suffocated' by 'complacency', 'inefficiency', 'outworn attitudes', 'archaic institutions' and 'amateurism'. The remedies, only too obvious, were 'dynamism', 'professionalism', 'ruthless competition', 'tough mindedness' ... more tough ruthless professionalism in every direction.*[77]
>
> *[I]t was the pattern of that same collective 'dream image' – 'young', 'classless', 'irreverent', 'crisp', 'superbly professional' – that gilded the New Aristocracy and the heroes of 'Swinging London'.*[78]

Professionalism was equated with 'toughness' and 'ruthlessness', echoing John Russell's demand for 'ruthlessness' among British painters.[79] Some artists also joined the debate. In June 1963 a group of artists, including Peter Blake, Anthony Caro and Eduardo Paolozzi, wrote to *The Times* complaining about what they claimed was the British glorification of amateurism.

> *Make no mistake, amateurism has been strangling British art just as it has been strangling our economy and our government*

system. ... Mr [David] *Sylvester seeks to drag British Art back to the suffocating club atmosphere of amateurism and dilettantism at a moment when, for the first time in this century, a generation of artists has deliberately taken up position outside it and against it. We believe that any painting which will not stand on equal terms with the best painting produced anywhere in the world is not worth bothering about.*[80]

Here, Blake and his associates promoted the idea that professionalism among British artists was a completely new phenomenon (at least in the twentieth century). In this they echoed Booker, insisting that professionalism was a new phenomenon in all aspects of public life, implicitly denying that artists such as Moore, Hepworth, Nicholson and Bacon were 'professional'. The letter conveys the sense that the notion of professionalism was problematic and, while being widely celebrated, excited opposition as well. The concept of the artist as professional implied that art was something done to earn money whereas the term 'amateur' signalled a degree of financial independence – implying artistic freedom without regard for the art market. Blake et al.'s reference to 'the suffocating club atmosphere of amateurism and dilettantism' hints at the class associations of such financial independence, with the implication that the amateur is a member of a gentleman's club (there is a gender as well as a class implication). As an artist, Riley could not belong to such a 'club' – her sex and the 'professionalism' that others commented on positioned her outside and against any such establishment.

The new meaning of 'professionalism' may also have connoted 'American-ness'. The 'old' meaning with its connotations of superior social class was well established as a recognizably British phenomenon, but the newer sense of the word, with its implications of classlessness, might be construed as a foreign import. In his article summing up British artistic achievement in 1963, Thompson was of the opinion that:

Not unnaturally, there tends to be some wariness about all this activity, this 'getting in on the international act'. ... by and large it has become a settled conviction that modern art is for the professionals *and that this, somehow, does not mean quite for us. There has been justification enough in the past for such a view and it cannot be reversed overnight'.*[81] [My emphasis]

Well before the term became so widely used in the 1960s, there was a concern that 'professionalism' was incompatible with a truly British landscape-inspired art. As early as 1933 the artist Paul Nash and Professor

Tonks of the Slade art school had conducted an open correspondence in *The Times*, in which Tonks had lamented the development of a 'new type of professionalism in the arts' and the way that it detracted from a traditional 'study of nature'.[82] So even in the 1930s professionalism had not been seen as new in itself but as appearing in a new form that actively discouraged the 'study of nature'. At that time, abstraction and Surrealism were becoming the dominant forces in British avant-garde art and may have been components of Tonks' 'new type of professionalism'. Both had strong European associations, so there is a suggestion here that the new type of professionalism in art was not truly British. In addition, it had been achieved at the expense of the genuinely British 'study of nature' – a term that refers back to the English tradition of landscape art discussed earlier in this chapter.

With these conflicting connotations of professionalism in mind, one notes John Russell's comments on Bridget Riley's work in 1963.

> Fall *and* Ascending and Descending (Hero) [sic] *are pictures which nobody else in England would have thought of and nobody else, quite certainly, could have carried out with Miss Riley's particular brand of armoured professionalism.*[83]

Riley's work was thus seen as very far from the productions of the stereotypic genteel, amateur, British painter. Russell was to use the same language again, in 1965, in a contribution to the book *Private View*: 'Bridget Riley's paintings ... exemplify an armoured professionalism of a kind that has always been thought to be rather bad form in this country'.[84] 'Armoured' suggests the ability to combat those who saw professionalism as 'bad form', a term connoting outmoded upper-class disapproval. Riley's professionalism was not the old-style professionalism of the barrister or career army officer (who, like the landed gentry, the one-time patrons of British landscape art, might use terms such as 'bad form') but rather that of the new, young meritocrat who is tough enough to ignore such criticism.

Russell's concern with 'professionalism' emerged again in July 1964, in his article, 'Downright professional', where he asserted that Riley's work was now as good as the foreign competition.[85] This article created a link between the concepts of 'professionalism' and 'internationalism'. Riley's work was valued as transcending the provincial limitations so often attributed to British art. Its abstraction, in particular the link between Op and Constructivism, relates it to Tonks' concern, thirty years earlier, that there was a new type of professionalism whose connotations were not British. The contrasting uses of the terms 'professional'/'professionalism' in the 1960s suggest that the class system itself was now regarded as outdated. One's view on whether the old establishment or the new meritocrats really dominated society had clear implications for the 'imagined community' of the nation. The connections made between Riley's work and the new form of professionalism again place her and her art on the side of the 'new Britain' notion of the nation's identity.

Swinging Britain

Although some people may have experienced nostalgia for a real or imagined pre-war Britain, by the 1960s it was not only in the art world that a younger generation had come 'roaring into prominence'. Riley was promoted as a 'young' artist at a time of increasing social prominence for young people. Greater affluence[86] and the rise of an American-style consumer culture gave young people more economic power than ever before, increasing their social influence and initiating what would come to be known as 'youth culture'. New media emerged that promoted the interests and values of this age group: magazines such as *Nova* (launched 1965), pirate radio stations (from 1964) and youth-orientated programmes on television (e.g. *Ready Steady Go!* 1963), while pop music became increasingly a product of the young for the young, marketed by established corporations that recognized the value of the new youth market. Many areas of culture were now dominated by much younger people than had been the case up to the mid-1950s.

> *The 'angry young men'*[87] *were certainly not youths. But their writings, and the publicity which surrounded them, helped none the less to create the notion of a culture led by individuals of a rather younger age than had hitherto been usual: ... intellectuals were now fifteen or twenty years younger than they used to be, so the age of popular entertainers and fashion setters, too, was shunted back by fifteen or twenty years.*[88]

Examples of this phenomenon included musicians such as the Beatles (whose oldest members, Starr and Lennon, were only 25 in 1965); fashion designer Mary Quant (who opened her first boutique in 1955 at the age of 21); playwright Harold Pinter (27 when *The Birthday Party* was produced on the London stage in 1957); satirist Peter Cook (23 when he co-wrote and performed in *Beyond the Fringe* in 1960); and television presenter David Frost (23, presenter of the satirical review programme *That Was the Week that Was* in 1962). The mass media, in particular television, rendered such personalities much more prominent than would have been possible in earlier decades, creating an image of a culture led and dominated by youth.

Without such an image, it is doubtful that the US magazine, *Time*, would have declared 'Swinging London' to be the 'City of the Decade' in 1966.[89]

As older images of a pre-war imperial Britain or a post-war economically diminished Britain ceased to dominate the 'imagined community' of the 1960s, the image of youth became part of a renewed English/British national identity. The Whitechapel exhibition, in 1964, 'The New Generation' emphasized this notion of youthfulness, as did the annual touring exhibitions organized by the Arts Council – 'Young Contemporaries' (in which Riley had shown some pre-Op art work in 1955). Lucie-Smith claimed of the artists he had selected for 'One Year of British Art' in 1962 that 'the average age of the artists exhibiting here is hopefully low'. The title of John Russell's article (quoted above), reviewing this show, 'Towards grown-up greatness' and its reference to 'entirely adult English painting' indicates some concern about this contemporary emphasis on youth. Generally, however, youthfulness was presented as a desirable attribute. In his introduction to the Contemporary Art Society's 1963 exhibition 'British Painting in the Sixties', John Sainsbury, the Society's chairman[90] claimed the show included 'some of the youngest as well as the oldest painters working in Britain today'.[91] In *The Sunday Times* in July 1964, dealer Robert Fraser was praised for having 'come up with as good a younger British list [of artists] as any in town',[92] Riley being included in this list. The image of the young British artist was promoted abroad. In Spring 1965, the British Council sponsored an exhibition of work by British artists 'mostly under thirty'[93] which travelled throughout the USA, Riley being among the artists represented. Riley's 'youthfulness' was frequently implied by her inclusion in lists of artists described as young, and sometimes directly commented on. In 1965 the *Guardian* described her as 'a slight, dark haired girl [*sic*], unassuming and unspoilt',[94] giving the impression of a teenager, though Riley was then 34.

Youthfulness was an important component of an image of national identity that had a powerful appeal. The British artists most associated with Op art – Riley, Boshier, Michael Kidner and Jeffrey Steele – were all young, or young enough to be presented as such by dealers, exhibition organizers and the press. There was considerable plagiarizing of Op paintings by the fashion industry, for clothes aimed primarily at the youth market, which reinforced this connection. These factors connected both Riley and Op itself to a particular image of Britain as a youthful country, which conflicted with those images that emphasized concepts such as 'tradition', 'history' and the continuing existence of a supposedly static, rural life. As an Op artist, Riley was part of 'new Britain' along with the Beatles, Mary Quant and David Frost, her art aligned with the urban, scientific, socially progressive face of a new, young national identity.

An art for New Britain

Anderson's concept of the nation as an 'imagined political community' suggests that there is a common ideal of what the nation is and what it means to belong to it. Mass Observation's wartime poll, and later analysis by an anthropologist, Geoffrey Gorer,[95] of a mid-1950s poll, both indicated that an image, or ideal, of a rural, apparently pre-urban landscape and way of life was commonly held in Britain at least as late as 1955. On the other hand, as we have seen, rising prosperity and the development of the media through the 1950s allowed a younger generation to acquire a degree of social prominence that would have been difficult or impossible before the war. Social changes both resulted in, and were expressed in, the rise of the new meritocrats. The image of Britain as a rural, agricultural nation – an image that might seem to come from a Constable painting – was not, however, extinguished by these social changes. Indeed, the literary reviewer who wrote in 1969 of the imaginary foreigner who 'might imagine ... that the town is still alien to us' indicates that the ideal of rural Britain was still very much alive at the end of the 1960s. The image of rural Britain co-existed with the Britain of Swinging London, of the Beatles, of affluent urban youth who appeared nightly on the television screens to which most of the population now had access. These two images could not coincide without tension, without raising the question 'which is the real Britain?'

The concerns of the art critics, curators and commentators at this time reveal the ways that the tensions and contradictions between contemporary notions of Englishness/Britishness affected attitudes towards and evaluations of contemporary British art. As we shall see in the next chapter, both the genuine interest and media furore that Riley's work inspired in New York in 1965 led to much more widespread interest in her work in Britain than had existed prior to 'The Responsive Eye', suggesting that Pevsner's observation of the national 'inferiority complex' in relation to art still had some relevance: only foreign acclaim could confirm the worth of a British artist's work. The complex relationship between perceptions of Riley's work and notions of national identity was to be further affected by reactions to Riley's work in the United States and the ways in which these were reported at home.

There was pride in Britain at Riley's achievement in gaining recognition in the USA, 'where few English artists have been so well received', as *The Times* recorded on Riley's return home after 'The Responsive Eye'.[96] Despite having exhibited in many one-person, group and competition shows in Britain during the previous four years, Riley's name was still unfamiliar to many people until this MoMA show. Within three years, however, her stature was such that she was chosen to represent Britain at the 1968 Venice Biennale, where she became the first contemporary British painter and the first woman to win the International Prize for painting. Her selection suggests that concerns about the 'Britishness' of Op (or lack of it) became less prominent as international acclaim gave Riley a status in Britain attained by few other artists. In 1967 a magazine poll named her as one of the three most famous women in Britain, after the Queen, along with Twiggy and Mary Quant.[97] The art produced by such a widely-recognized British artist had now to be perceived as itself British. As if resolving any remaining doubts, Edward Lucie-Smith, commenting on Riley's success in Venice in 1968, declared that

> *Her paintings have an absoluteness which seems alien to the historic tradition in British art, though perhaps one might say that she is a classicist of a kind that Stubbs might have recognised.*[98]

Here, Lucie-Smith transmuted 'foreign' classicism into the thoroughly British work of George Stubbs and placed Riley's work in this context: as Stubbs had adopted the foreignness of the classical style and made something indisputably British from it so, while Riley may have started from European material, she had made of it something that could now be regarded as 'British'. With this review Lucie-Smith sought to close the door on the debate over Op's national identity. Riley's work had been given decisive foreign endorsement in New York in 1965 and Venice in 1968: for her work, at least, Britishness does not seem to have remained 'a burdensome form of virginity'.

Chapter 4 Un-American Activities

The Reception of Riley's Work in America

How many people in New York, or for that matter in London, where she lives, had heard of Bridget Riley six months ago? Yet now, one of her works is reproduced on the cover of 'The Responsive Eye' catalogue and another on the cover of a recent issue of Art International*; she is having a one-man show at the Feigen Gallery that has been completely bought up by purchasers whose names read like the Burke's of* avant-garde *collecting; she was interviewed on the Sunday art page of the* New York Times*; and so on.*[1]

Many of the exhibitors in 'The Responsive Eye' were not American artists. Riley's painting, *Current* (a title variously suggesting electricity, water and contemporaneity) appeared on the cover of the catalogue [Fig. 14], rather than one by an American artist. The choice of a work by an artist from abroad then little-known in the USA indicates that the curator, Seitz, had chosen it in spite of its obscurity, that is, as being particularly appropriate to the theme of the exhibition: an exemplary work. A work by one of the well-known American painters who contributed to the show might have seemed a safer choice, in terms of attracting domestic gallery-goers and press. Despite these marketing considerations, Seitz selected Riley's painting for this key role in the promotion of the show, indicating his considerable confidence that this work would attract favourable attention. Riley's work was indeed to make a significant impact in the USA, and her reception there was somewhat different from the British situation explored in the last chapter. Her reputation at home was to grow as a result of British reactions to her American achievements.

The post-war cultural settlement

Before the Second World War, American artists had, like their British counterparts, worked peripherally to, and at a greater physical distance from, the centre of the art world, Paris. Both countries had held a common position as marginal territories, as far as artistic production was concerned. Their combined military success in the First World War did not give either country any advantage in terms of recognition for cultural achievements, and certainly not in the field of the visual arts. Nonetheless, both countries had highly active art communities, some of whose members were influenced by movements originating in Paris (Cubism and Surrealism), or in Russia (Constructivism) or Italy (Futurism). In America there was still a sense in which the country seemed culturally youthful and provincial, and artists such as Grant Wood and Thomas Hart Benton emphasized this in their work.[2]

This sense of 'provinciality', which so dogged British commentators' perception of their own national art, was not to last in the USA. Literary theorist Nigel Wheale has argued that the USA was, in effect, to claim a pre-eminent cultural position, which it had never previously held, as a 'settlement' in return for the military and financial help it had extended to Europe during and after the Second World War.[3] During the war, France had capitulated (in 1940) and was later liberated largely by British and American troops. Art historian Serge Guilbaut has explored the apparent demoralization and lack of energy among French artists in the post-war years and contrasted it with the situation in America.[4] The USA – especially New York – seems to have exploited the cultural opportunities available and Guilbaut essentially agrees with Wheale as to the significance of this. From the beginning of the war the USA perceived that its own economic strength would not only allow it to intervene decisively in the military conflict, but also to dominate the West culturally afterwards. The role that art would play was not clear, but there was a widespread belief that it would be important.[5]

Although not all historians agree with this picture of an opportunistic American state carefully planning future dominance,[6] in the post-war period the USA was certainly to assume a dominant position. The development of the cold war provided another incentive for the USA to promote its own culture abroad, with cold war politics being instrumental in the rise of Abstract Expressionism to international prominence in the post war years.[7] MoMA was to a great extent founded and controlled by the Rockefeller family, a highly influential political dynasty, Nelson

Rockefeller holding MoMA's presidency in two periods preceding and following the war, but also taking various important government posts during and after the war.[8] The Rockefellers used MoMA to promote American culture, and in particular Abstract Expressionism, abroad.[9] In addition, the domestic market for contemporary art was expanding as affluence increased and New York artists became increasingly well known (because of MoMA's efforts and those of interested dealers).[10]

Guilbaut and Charles Harrison both suggest parallel experiences of artists who, before the war, had looked to continental Europe, and especially Paris, as the centre of excellence for modernist art practices. Whereas after the war, Britain was economically depleted, America boomed.[11] The average American citizen was better rather than worse off and the state looked outwards, consolidating power and entering the long cold war with the Soviet Union in the process.[12] Britain, divesting itself of imperial possessions which it could no longer afford, lacked the energy for cultural conquest. By contrast, in the USA, the 'New York School' and its supporters, including the privately funded MoMA, energetically developed Abstract Expressionist painting and promoted it internationally.

Op's challenge to the post-war settlement

All this may give the impression that by 1965 the USA stood secure in her position as leader of the visual arts, with her neighbours all looking to Abstract Expressionism as the paradigm of modernist art practice. Some American critics may have felt this to be the case. Reviewing a group show 'New British Painters' at Los Angeles' Feigen-Palmer Gallery in December 1964, critic Nancy Marmer asserted that American artists had much more influence over European and British artists than vice versa. She implied that what she called 'optics' was an American art form, which she described as one of 'various post-abstract expressionist stances'. She described Derek Boshier's work as 'romantic' and declared that 'these paintings neither seek nor achieve the formal clarity and presence of the best American optical painting'. Marmer described Riley's contributions to the show as 'more purely optical. One thinks of Bauhaus and Vasarely ... Though Miss Riley's aspirations are modest, her paintings, within the formal limitations she sets, are highly satisfying'. Overall, Marmer's view of the work on show was that 'The excitement of experimentation is too often tempered with imitativeness and a lack of virtuosity'.[13] Her claim of imitativeness echoes the views of Denny and *The Times*, with their concern about plagiarism, although unlike Denny she was not specific in her criticisms. She made a

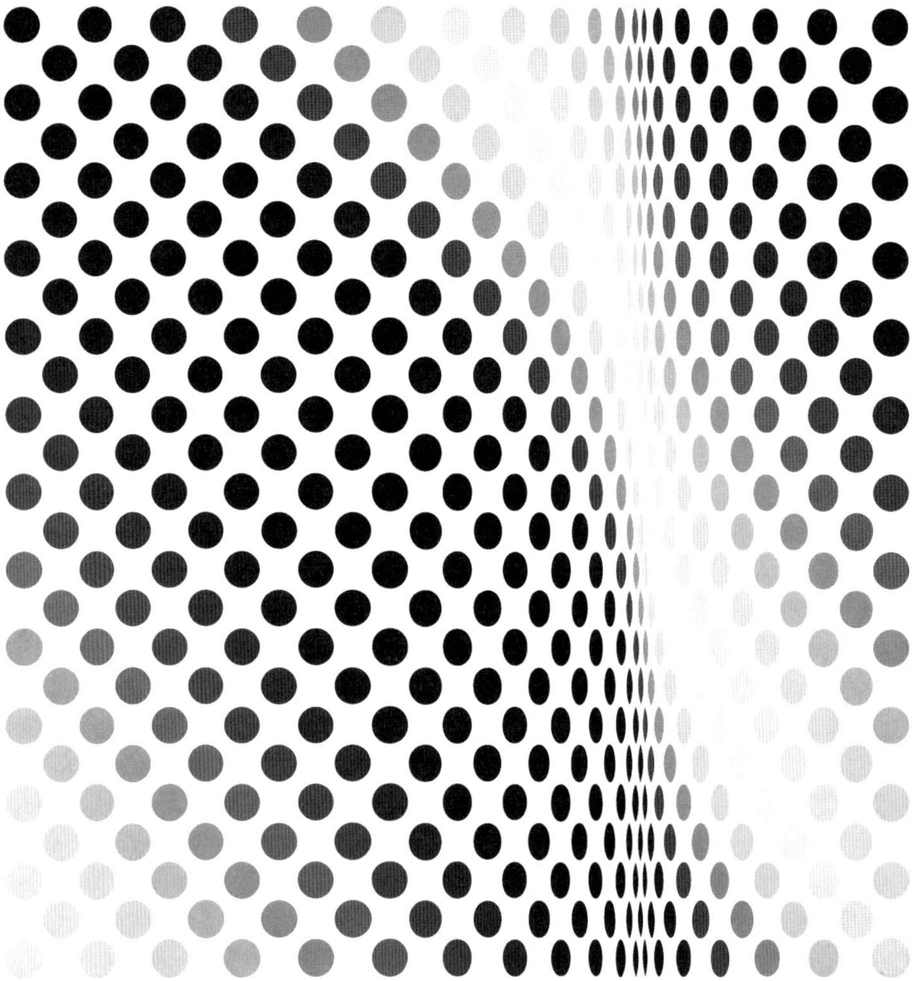

19. **Pause** 1964

clear connection between Riley's work and pre-Abstract Expressionist, European art, but her work was described in terms of 'modest aspirations' and 'limitations', as if relegating it to a corner where its lack of overt American influence could be regarded as unimportant.

Writing about the show 'London: The New Scene' in *Art News* in April 1965, Sidney Simon declared that this British art, exhibited in Washington DC (and previously at a variety of venues across America), was 'still strongly in debt to American prototypes'. The work shown included Riley's *Pause* (1964) [Fig. 19]. He particularly commented on her work's 'dancing surfaces [which] despite the optical discipline, are continuously radiant in their formal transformations', but nonetheless claimed that they gave 'no hint of radical premises strenuously pursued'. Simon argued that unlike American art 'the new British art seems not to be impelled toward the point (literally) of no return'.[14] This echoes British concerns about the 'cautious' nature of British art and its need for 'ruthlessness', but whereas some British critics were finding an answer to these problems in Riley's art by 1965, Simon detected only 'the possibility that we are encountering the first signs of changes in the making'. Riley's work was attracting massive attention in New York at this time, but Simon's article does not mention the MoMA show drawing to an end there as his article was published.

'The Responsive Eye' was covered elsewhere in that issue, however. In his review, Thomas Hess seemed concerned to distance the American art at the show from the 'Op art' tag attached to it by *Time* magazine the previous year.[15] He argued that the wide variety of work made the show a 'mish-mash' and while he did not discuss the works in terms of national origins or characteristics, he argued that 'rugged individualist visionaries, like Albers and Reinhardt', and 'New York painters' Ludwig Sander, Paul Brach, Morris Louis and Kenneth Noland were inappropriate artists to include in this show. With the exception of Albers, who was German but had worked in the USA since the 1930s, all these painters were American artists. Hess' disparagement of Op art[16] can therefore be read partly as an attack on non-American art, which was invading New York and winning far too much attention. Meanwhile, Frank Stella's contributions were described by Hess as 'positively anti-Op'. A year later, Stella was jointly interviewed with Donald Judd by *Art News*; by then the Op art tag gave both artists some concern, and this was apparently tied to its European connections. Stella admitted:

> *that members of the Groupe de Recherche de l'Art Visuel 'actually painted all the patterns before I did – all the basic designs that are*

> *in my painting...' but, he went on, 'it still doesn't have anything to do with my painting. I find all that European geometric painting – sort of post-Max Bill school – a kind of curiosity – very dreary.' Asked why he wanted to avoid symmetry and compositional effects, Donald Judd replied 'Well, those effects tend to carry with them all the structures, values, feelings of the whole European tradition. It suits me fine if that's all down the drain... Vasarely's composition has the effect of order and quality that traditional European painting had, which I find pretty objectionable...'*[17]

The 'European tradition' was presented here as an enemy of American art, as though this should have another, independent basis.

Nonetheless, in 1965 the MoMA show was the culmination of a widespread enthusiasm for Op art among both American artists and the public, with Hess claiming that some 40,000 exhibitions had been shown in the period 1963–65.[18] Before 'The Responsive Eye' opened, *Art in America*'s 'New York: Gallery notes' column was subheaded 'Nan Rosenthal previews the op art explosion', reflecting the effect of Op on New York.[19] Rosenthal claimed that Seitz had been assembling the exhibition for 'several years', involving 'seventy-five artists from ten countries'. She noted that the art on display would be very diverse and claimed that 'no one has come up with a handy, all-purpose misnomer that quite covers' all the art shown, despite the use of *Time*'s 'op art' tag in her article's subhead. Rosenthal noted the prominence the exhibition would give to European artists: Vasarely and Albers would have a room devoted to their work. Rosenthal went on to cover Op art shows at various galleries in New York, mentioning that the best-known foreign artist to show was an Italian, Piero Dorazio. Nonetheless, she suggested that 'The artist who may best symbolize the museum's exhibit to the public is Bridget Riley ... whose black, gray and white paintings are ... impossible to focus on for more than moments'. She compared Riley's work to Vasarely's but commented that it acted on the eye 'more aggressively'. She also noted that scale was important and the effect of the works was diminished by reproduction.

Although Riley's work was compared to Vasarely's, and Rosenthal made much of the different nationalities of artists showing in New York at this time (Italian, Hungarian, French, Swiss, Japanese, Venezuelan, as well as British and American), the review did not discuss the significance of the foreign origins of much of this work. Unlike Marmer and Simon, Rosenthal made no nationalist claims for influences and origins, asserting that the works on show were an international selection of the latest 'direction' in art; any question of their position in relation to earlier developments was left out of the discussion.

So here we have perhaps the first hint of the impact Riley's work was to make when 'The Responsive Eye' opened on 25 February, closely followed by her opening at the New York branch of the Richard Feigen Gallery on 2 March. The Feigen gallery had made its reputation showing the work of many European modern masters from Monet and van Gogh onwards. While Rosenthal did not dwell on the European origins of the works she reviewed, other commentators could not ignore this aspect of Op art. Op was not derived from (American) Abstract Expressionism; it was arguably a European movement and, from the American side of the Atlantic, British art was as European as that of France or Germany. Despite the confidence of Marmer and Simon that such art was influenced by American art, and inferior to it, and notwithstanding Rosenthal's apparent indifference to such matters, other critics writing in the American press revealed considerable insecurity at the impact that European Op art was making on the New York art scene, in terms of both the public response to the MoMA show and that of the art market there. Op paintings by European artists, and by British artists Michael Kidner, Jeffrey Steele and Riley, were shown alongside American work at 'The Responsive Eye', which travelled subsequently to St Louis, Pasadena, Seattle and Baltimore. With her concurrent show at the Feigen Gallery Bridget Riley was a notable presence in both these contexts. By April she was being described as the 'leading Optress from London'.[20] Some of the American critics who promoted Abstract Expressionism as the modernist paradigm reacted strongly against this European onslaught; again, Op's European origin coloured its reception. Harold Rosenberg noted in the mid-1960s that 'Europe ... to all appearances has taken the lead over the United States in this category [i.e. Op art] of painting and sculpture'.[21] Concern about the possibility of a 'counter-coup', in which Europe might seize back the modernist initiative, informed a discussion, by American critic Sidney Tillim in a leading American art journal,§ of how Op had originated and developed.[22] Writing before the MoMA show opened, Tillim argued that Op was divided into 'American-type' and 'European-type', although in theory either type could be produced anywhere; he specifically denied any partisanship:

> *and to qualify in advance what might seem to be chauvinistic arrogance, it is necessary to distinguish between two broad types of optical art – American-type and European-type. By 'type'*

> *I mean that it can happen anywhere, that it is not confined to national boundaries.* (p.16)

Tillim claimed that there was a growing influence of 'European-type' Op in the USA but little 'American-type' in Europe. In the USA, Op had evolved as a form of 'post-Abstract Expressionist abstraction' (p. 18) – Tillim found it less obviously 'optical' than European Op.

> *European abstractionist art, on the other hand, has not had, at least until now, an equivalent 'hard edge' reaction of such clarity partly because that need has been partially filled by the greater tolerance on the continent for traditional geometric art, partly because painterly abstraction never achieved the violence and the pervasive influence there that it achieved here and consequently did not require as clean-cut a reaction, and, finally, partly because of the persistence of doctrinaire habits implied in the first two reasons.*
>
> *It follows then that there would be a considerable difference between the overt hard-core opticality of the European brand and the more covert American kind which reflects the passage of Abstract Expressionism across its perceptual and conceptual horizon.*[23]

Tillim asserted the superiority of 'American-type' Op, which he argued was little practised outside America despite his earlier statement that it was not, in principle, restricted to America. European artists had a 'tolerance' for 'traditional geometric art' but this was not because they were broad-minded but rather because they persisted in 'doctrinaire habits'. Tillim went on to say that European Op (or 'European-type neo-formalism'[24]), was 'inhibited by its traditional geometric orientation'.[25] European Op apparently failed to display 'the expansiveness and sense of style that are among the valuable and elegant heirlooms of Abstract Expressionism'[26] because European Op was:

> *essentially a post-Cubist rather than post-Abstract Expressionist art, opaque, restrictive rather than reductive, and highly programmatic, ... a latter day version of geometric art in its Bauhaus formulation with overtones in certain constructions of Constructivism. It is* purisme *in search of its baroque.*[27]

This passage is loaded with references to art from Europe and beyond. Even the term 'geometric art', which might appear neutral, has strongly European connections, recalling Cézanne's injunction to 'treat nature by means of the cylinder, the sphere, the cone'[28] and the promotion of geometry by Purist painter Amedée Ozenfant, in the 1920s, as an expression of nature.[29] In pronounced contrast, when the American art historian and critic, Rosalind Krauss (an adherent of Greenberg's earlier in her career) reviewed a show of Riley's work in 1966, she seemed in no doubt that in Riley's earlier work her 'pictorial notions [were] derived unquestionably from the canons of all-overness established by the advanced American art of the 1950s'.[30] The importance of Abstract Expressionism is asserted here once more, its practices now 'canons' – dogma for the succeeding generation. Although she placed Riley's work firmly in a line of descent from the 'richly shifting spatiality' developed at the Bauhaus in the 1920s, it was for Krauss 'unquestionable' that the most important influence must be Abstract Expressionism. In 1965, however, Tillim found no way of positioning European-type Op among the progeny of American high modernism. To add a further twist, Riley herself was to assert that she had indeed been influenced by American art, in particular in relation to the way her pictorial space was constructed:

> *open space, shallow space, a multi-focal space, as for example in Jackson Pollock, and I feel more in sympathy with this than with centralised European space, the focally centred situation of the European tradition.*[31]

Riley added, however, that this American space originated in the work of the European artist Mondrian earlier in the twentieth century – a view which in itself suggests that even the most radical and 'American' aspects of US art were derived from European precursors.

In line with the theories of American modernist critics from Alfred Barr to Greenberg,[32] Tillim implied that art *should* develop and progress and, while he admitted that Abstract Expressionism was derived from European sources, he promoted it as a development beyond anything achieved previously by European art. Hence a truly progressive, modernist art must be derived from Abstract Expressionism or at least respond directly to it. Tillim saw European Op artists as ignoring Abstract Expressionism: by deriving inspiration from Cubism or Constructivism they could be seen as asserting the superiority of earlier European art movements over subsequent American developments. It was as if they were casting Abstract Expressionism aside as irrelevant to the modernist project. Just as a *Times* correspondent had related Riley's work to that of Monet and asserted the work's lack of indebtedness to Abstract Expressionism,[33] so, for Tillim, European-type Op was an attempt to re-establish European primacy in painting, a move which would negate the USA's crowning artistic and cultural achievement.

Although Britain had never enjoyed the artistic prominence established by the USA since the war, this concern over the national origin of art is reminiscent of the concerns expressed by the anonymous *Times* critic discussed in the previous chapter, who was so concerned about British artists' attempt 'to get with a single lunge into the forefront of the international art scene'.[34] For Tillim, as for this *Times* critic, the national art of his country should uncompromisingly express qualities associated with that country and no other. Hence, if Op had any future as a movement in the USA, only the 'American-type', with its Abstract Expressionist influences, would be important, even though (or because) he believed that this was less overtly 'optical' than its European counterpart. Given that Tillim considered that 'European-type Op' was having far more influence on American artists than 'American-type Op' had on Europeans, one may infer an underlying plea to American artists to return to their own artistic 'roots' and resist foreign influences. The perceived prevalence of European-type Op influences may have stemmed from a belief that 'European-type' Op was attracting more public and critical attention than the 'American-type'. Nan Rosenthal's enthusiastic review of foreign Op artists' work singled out Dorazio and Riley, and is evidence of the presence of numerous foreign artists in the city's galleries. Hence Tillim's article may also have represented a call to the American public to support Abstract Expressionism – presented here as an authentic American artistic style – and subsequent American art derived from it, and resist handing back the laurels of modernism to Europe. This article appeared only two months before 'The Responsive Eye' opened at MoMA. As Rosenthal's article shows, New York admitted an influx of European artists both for that show and for numerous Op art shows held by New York dealers in their own galleries. For Tillim's American audience, there may have been an implicit reminder that New York's primacy in the visual arts was of recent origin and possibly not immune to a European counter-revolution.

Tillim's concerns were shared by Barbara Rose, another American critic and follower of Greenberg,[35] who also found European Op wanting, and approvingly mentioned Tillim's critique in her own review of 'The Responsive Eye'.

> *In many ways the European art seemed like a showcase for the American work which by contrast shone like so many diamonds in a field of synthetic brilliants. ... Sidney Tillim ... has already done such an adequate job of demonstrating that optical art is the last wing of the Bauhaus.*[36]

Rose was particularly concerned that by organizing 'The Responsive Eye' MoMA was giving an endorsement of Op that would give this art a status she did not believe it merited. 'In this context the current exhibition, for example, becomes irresponsible and dangerous'. She even suggested that MoMA should stop showing contemporary art and confine itself to 'historical exhibitions and surveys'. As MoMA promoted a particular modernist aesthetic influenced by the Bauhaus, Rose may have been using the Op show as a reason to attack the museum more generally.

Riley's work appeared on the front of the catalogue and, by the time Rose wrote her review, she was no longer an unknown foreign artist but a star of the New York art scene. She had won the support of artists who were already prominent in America, such as Barnett Newman, Ad Reinhardt and Josef Albers.[37] Yet Rose does not mention her anywhere in this review. This seems an odd omission, perhaps suggesting that to tackle Riley's work would itself be problematic for Rose. MoMA's construction of modernism was broader and more inclusive than Greenbergians such as Rose and Tillim were prepared to accept. Both referred disparagingly to the Bauhaus, a formative influence on the MoMA modernist aesthetic. In his diagram charting the 'evolution' of abstract art, MoMA's director, Alfred Barr, had also related the Bauhaus to the development of geometrical abstract art, but unlike Tillim he had cast this in a positive light.[38] Hence attacks on the Bauhaus contained an implicit attack on MoMA itself and can be construed as an attempt to narrow the accepted boundaries of modernism to those defined by Greenberg and his followers. Greenberg himself never wrote on Riley's art, despite its prominence in New York at this time, and this raises the same question: was he wary of addressing the issues raised by her work?[39]

The historical primacy of Abstract Expressionism was under threat, even in the USA. According to John Canaday, Op artists

> *are dealing with a kind of vision, a relationship between object and observer, that shows Abstract Expressionism to have been the poor, tired tag end of a great tradition .... and makes clear that Pop art is now dying of the prostitute's occupational disease, exhaustion through corruption.*[40]

Like Abstract Expressionism, Pop art was strongly identified with the USA. The language used here expresses weariness and even disgust with two forms of art very strongly identified with New York. The association between Pop art and prostitution suggests that Pop was now debased through commercialism: it had become primarily a saleable product.

Canaday castigated 'The sloppiness, the shoddiness, the amateurism posing as esthetic sensibility, that has marked avant-garde art for so long', preferring instead the 'immaculate precision' of Op art. The concern with amateurism echoes contemporary British concerns and suggests that a desire for 'professionalism' in art, as in other aspects of life, was not a purely British phenomenon. Canaday also claimed that Op art was 'potentially the most important development in several decades', implying that Op might be more important than anything that had happened in art since well before the advent of Abstract Expressionism. No one would have argued that pre-Second World War American art occupied an international avant-garde position so, if Op were perceived as a predominantly European art form, this implied a return to the pre-war position, where Europe held international leadership.

Despite the deep reservations of some American critics, there was great enthusiasm for Riley's work among collectors and the wider public. The latter formed the target audience of *Time* magazine, which like some of its British counterparts took a somewhat sensationalist stance. *Time* had begun to get excited about Op in May 1964, almost a year before 'The Responsive Eye' opened in New York, when it noted Riley's 'visual torments ... on view at London's Whitechapel art gallery' [Fig. 20].[41] In October of that year it published an article headed 'Op art: pictures that attack the eye',[42] which looked ahead to the MoMA show. The author saw Op as 'preying and playing on the fallibility in [*sic*] vision' and complained that 'Op art is made tantalizing, eye-teasing, even eye-smarting by visual researchers using all the ingredients of an optometrist's nightmare'. The article again picked Riley out as an artist whose work would make an impact, though presumably not in a way that the artist had in mind, going so far as to say that Riley's 'stark black and white patterns have made viewers physically sick'. The magazine continued to promote this theme after 'The Responsive Eye' had opened:

> *Since word drifted across the Atlantic last year that Bridget Riley's stark, vertiginous optical art made many Londoner's retch, New York art buffs have had a nervous hankering to see if their stomachs were any stronger. It's easy to get queasy, all right. The paintings force the viewer to ride high on black and white herringbone waves, squint through a maze of snaggle-toothed triangles, zig round lopsided circles until reels the eye.*[43]

Later that month, the magazine returned to this topic in another short review.

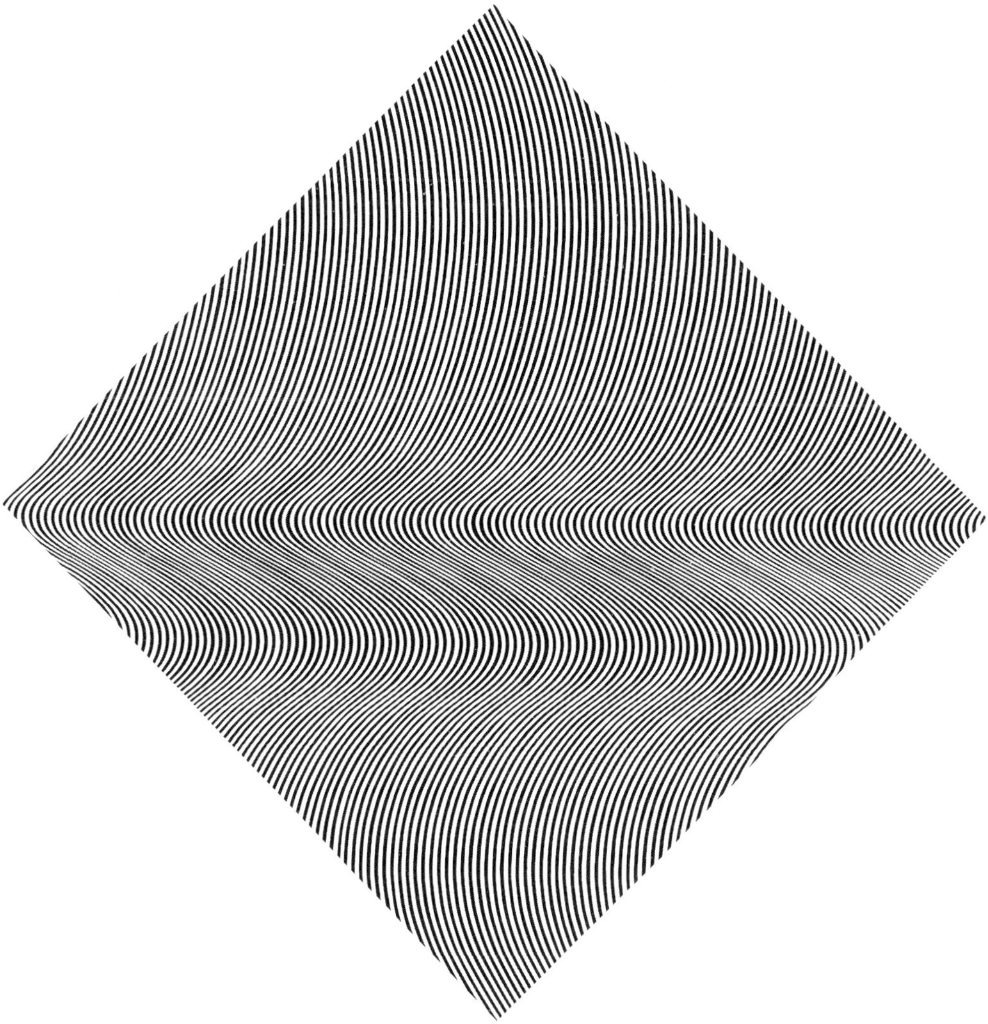

20. **Crest** 1964

A lot of surprises are in store for viewers accustomed to paintings that just hang there. In the Modern's 'Responsive Eye' exhibition, lines slither and slalom, colors clobber the eye, lights juggle, forms change. The viewer responds all right – with everything from afterimages to vertigo.[44]

This kind of coverage was bound to attract attention – and controversy – on both sides of the Atlantic.

Un-British enthusiasm

Although American critics had initially played down the importance of Riley's work, with the opening of the MoMA show she went almost overnight from being little known in the USA to being famous. Her concurrent show at the Feigen Gallery sold out before it had opened and she was interviewed by newspapers and magazines. It was as though Tillim's worst fears were being realised.

The red dot meaning 'sold' was pre-attached to each of the labels on her paintings when the exhibition was installed at the Feigen Gallery on March 2. The exhibition was sold out sight unseen. In addition the gallery has a waiting list of people who want 'a Riley'. Not something they ... feel they have to have because they like it, but just 'a Riley'.[45]

And 'Bridget Riley is the optical star'.[46]

The art collectors come day after day, sighing for more, happily accepting signed poster reproductions of Bridget Riley's work and putting their names down on a waiting list for the real thing.[47]

And 'Miss Riley ... has had a noisy New York debut and suffered an avalanche of attention in the popular press.'[48]

Whereas in the 1950s the work of American artists had toured Europe, influencing many European artists,[49] now Europe was invading the USA. The attention that Riley's work attracted in New York was not unnoticed in Britain, where commentators' attitudes were in turn affected by American interest. The public reception of Riley's paintings in the USA in 1965 was so enthusiastic that many British press commentators took refuge from controversy by discussing American reactions to it rather than the work itself. By describing – usually censoriously – the way that American media and commercial interests exploited Riley's painting, the British press could trumpet her success without appearing to have an un-British degree of enthusiasm themselves. The *Financial Times* reported in

May, that during 'The Responsive Eye': 'everything from evening gowns and wall paper to Holy Bibles were being designed in Op and the craze is still in full swing'.[50] Paintings by Riley and Jeffrey Steele were among those plagiarized by the American fashion industry. Riley described her own experience of this some years later:

> *...when I arrived* [in New York] *I was driven from the airport down Madison Avenue and to my amazement I saw windows full of versions of my paintings on dresses, in window display, everywhere. My heart sank. ... the whole thing had spread everywhere even before I touched down at the airport.*[51]

As *Burlington Magazine*'s Jerrold Lanes put it in April 1965: 'the publicity has been revolting, even for New York'.[52] In the article from which the quotation that opened this chapter was taken, Lanes described, for a British readership, the furore surrounding the opening of 'The Responsive Eye' at MoMA. It was as though the American press found the idea that a British artist could achieve 'international' status easier to believe than the British themselves. Lanes, apparently ignorant of the substantial reputations of the British Op artists, which had led to their inclusion in the MoMA show, noted the strength of the British presence at 'The Responsive Eye' (Kidner, Steele and Riley). Lanes described Op as a reaction against Abstract Expressionism, especially action painting, but pointed out that:

> *Op is not merely a New York concoction ... younger artists have been doing what is now called Op at least as long in Europe as in New York ... and those artists who may be thought to exemplify Op art at its purest, were, until quite recently, all Europeans: I mean the collective enterprises represented in Spain by Equipo 57, in Italy by Gruppo T and Gruppo N, in France by Groupe de Recherche d'Art Visuel and in Germany by the Zero group.*[53]

Like Tillim, Lanes related Op to earlier European traditions: European Op artists, he claimed, tended to work collectively in groups, recalling the earlier 'great collective movements that were de Stijl, Suprematism and Constructivism, and the Bauhaus'. Whereas both critical and mass media writers on Abstract Expressionist artists tended to emphasize both the individuality of the artists and of their productions, here Lanes appeared to celebrate Europe's 'great collective movements' and specifically included the Bauhaus among these, despite its rather different, institutional, status to the various 'movements' listed. Tillim and Rose also appeared to regard the Bauhaus more as a movement than an institution but both these writers implicitly disparaged it. Possibly, for them, the Bauhaus' status as an institution gave any work connected with it associations of the 'academicism' so despised by Greenberg, whereas the 'individualism' associated with Abstract Expressionism evoked the myth of the pioneering frontiersmen credited with founding the USA. In addition, the very notion of a 'collectively produced' art may have held suggestions, in the midst of the cold war, of Communism.[54] The Bauhaus was extolled by critics such as Herbert Read, who was noted for his Communist sympathies.[55] European myths of collective endeavour – the establishment of empires, the French Revolution, the overthrow of Hitler – found an echo in the desire of groups of European artists to come together to further common artistic aims. Certainly, the notions of the 'individual pioneer' and the 'workers' collective', as paradigms for radical development within modernism, appear mutually exclusive. The importance of such myths in the formulation of notions of national identity may have contributed to the very different attitudes towards the Bauhaus expressed by Rose and Tillim on the one hand and Lanes on the other.

Lanes distinguished between continental Europe and Britain, however, Op having had a much later start in the latter, and like Tillim he asserted that 'the geometric tradition had persisted on the Continent much more continuously and pervasively than it had over here'. Lanes regarded British Op as something of an anomaly, part of a European 'geometric tradition' that he believed had had little earlier importance in British art; yet it was a British Op artist's work that was now commanding international attention in New York. Riley's work, with its connections to European Constructivism, had seemed not authentically British to one *Times* correspondent,[56] and its 'foreign' origins could hardly be ignored by critics who aimed to appear knowledgeable. At the same time, Riley's success in New York supplied a motive to position her as a specifically British artist, albeit one working on the fringes of British artistic tradition. Lanes complained at length about the publicity surrounding the MoMA show, but used as his example the lionization of Riley by the New York media, as if borrowing the Sunday tabloid technique of describing titillating activities in a tone of moral indignation. Lanes could express his disgust at a specifically American version of rampant commercialism while still letting his readers know how a British artist had trumped the competition: American *and* European.

Lanes, like Tillim, saw the origins of Op art as lying in earlier European movements and emphatically *not* in the American idiom of Abstract Expressionism. Such associations enabled the work of British artists such as Riley, Steele and Kidner to be perceived, in Britain as well as the USA, as European (or international) but, as the artists themselves were British, their work could also be positioned as British (national) *and* as constituting a serious assault on New York's post-war supremacy in modern art.

While the idea of a British artist dominating the New York scene might have been attractive for motives of national pride alone, there were other reasons for British commentators to promote a British artist and a new form of art. Canaday's presentation of Pop art, which had made a considerable impact on both sides of the Atlantic by 1965, as a 'prostituted' kind of art implies that it was too closely associated with commercialism. This was also a concern in Britain, where there was the added anxiety that the forms of commercialism Pop celebrated were specifically 'American'. When English Pop artist Richard Smith gave a lecture at the ICA in November 1962, in which he enthused on the use of advertising imagery in painting, members of the audience loudly remonstrated with him. In particular, they argued that Smith was enhancing the appeal of advertisements by promoting them through his work.[57] Although Smith had not been a member of the Independent Group, that loose association of artists and writers much enthused by American mass culture who had met at the ICA in the early 1950s, it is very likely that he had been stimulated by discussions organized by the Group, and these discussions were generally admiring of American mass culture.[58] Smith visited the USA for the first time in 1961 and used images from American advertising and consumer culture heavily in subsequent work.[59]

By this time, a younger generation was graduating from the Royal College of Art (including Hockney, Boshier, Allen Jones, and Peter Phillips). They looked to American artists such as Jasper Johns and Robert Rauschenberg for inspiration and a number of them visited the USA in the early 1960s.[60] They also dominated the 'Young Contemporaries' show in 1961.[61] For some British critics, through Pop, American influences – and commercial influences at that – were becoming all too pervasive in the work of young British artists. At the same time, the rise in importance of American art, and the relative demise of Paris, indicated that the latter did not hold a monopoly of cultural domination in the fine arts. It was clearly possible for an Anglo-Saxon culture to attain primary status in this area. In Riley, British critics now found a British artist who could be credibly presented as a competitor to both New York and European artists. Her work could clearly be separated from American influences and also avoided drawing on commercial sources for inspiration. This may have made connections with the Bauhaus and other European sources more palatable for critics such as Lanes: a small price to pay for independence from American commercialism.

Mario Amaya, writing in the *Financial Times*, specifically linked the media furore and commercialization surrounding the MoMA show to its New York location. For him, New York was 'a city which demands weekly art spectacles of every kind and which sets up baals for worship as fast as it knocks them down'.[62] Evidently matters were conducted less frenetically, more sensibly, in London. Amaya was careful to differentiate Riley's work ('an evocative eye-catching experience') from 'the razzle-dazzle assault on the eyes' of much of the MoMA show (mostly consisting of work by American and European artists). Amaya did not explain *what* Riley's work evoked, giving a general description of her work as 'a sort of lyrical play of lines that induces an attractive day dream effect; she does not tear at our eyes but hypnotises them'. Amaya suggested depths of sensation and meaning absent from any 'razzle dazzle assault on the eyes'. Riley's work was compared to that of Josef Albers, a European one-time Bauhaus teacher long based in America, whom Amaya credited with influencing such established American artists as Jasper Johns and Robert Rauschenberg. Amaya presented an image of serious, influential European Op, of which Riley was an exponent, contrasted with the 'razzle-dazzle' of a brief ('weekly') New York 'spectacle', which we may equate to Tillim's 'American-type Op'. Amaya made it clear that Riley was the British 'Op heroine of New York' while aligning her with the European Albers, creating a positive association between Britishness and European-ness: for Amaya it was apparently possible to be both truly British and European.

Op's practitioners dominated the New York art scene for much of 1965. Op was still the subject of media controversy in October of that year, when Riley published a piece in *Art News*, defending her own work from the 'hysterical sensationalism'[63] that had engulfed it since the MoMA show. Such sensationalism was perhaps inevitable considering the threat that her work potentially posed both to the USA's post-war domination of international art and to Greenberg's monolithic conception of modernism. A broader, more inclusive European understanding of modernism, stemming from Baudelaire's conception of social 'modernity' reflected in art, may be seen embodied in Riley's work, with its perceived connections to social and scientific aspects of contemporary life. This, along with Op art's links to European geometric abstraction, the Bauhaus and Constructivism – post-Cubist rather than post-Abstract Expressionist art – meant that Riley's work, in particular, must have appeared as a challenge to the post-Second World War cultural settlement. As the 1960s progressed, art continually diversified, and in the early 1970s notions of 'postmodernism' emerged, which, although (or because) it was not always easy to distinguish from modernism, further challenged monolithic conceptions of the nature of avant-garde art by turning a spotlight on a variety of international practices and practitioners. Riley's work, with its international sources and appeal, was perhaps the first hint that in future no one country could expect its art to hold a supreme position.

Chapter 5 Happenings on Canvas

Notions of 'The Theatrical' in Relation to Riley's Op Art

I feel that my paintings have some affinity with happenings where the disturbance precipitated is latent in the sociological and psychological situation. I want the disturbance or 'event' to arise naturally, in visual terms out of the inherent energies and characteristics of the elements which I use. I also want it to have a quality of inevitability. There should, that is to say, be something akin to a sense of recognition within the work, so that the spectator experiences at one and the same time something known and something unknown. I identify with this 'event'.

Bridget Riley 1965[1]

(1) The success, even the survival, of the arts has come increasingly to depend on their ability to defeat theater …
(2) Art degenerates as it approaches the condition of theater …
(3) The concepts of quality and value – and to the extent that these are central to art, the concept of art itself – are meaningful, or wholly meaningful, only within *the individual arts. What lies* between *the arts is theater.*

Michael Fried 1967[2]

Thomas Crow has interpreted Riley's Op art as challenging and subverting particular notions of modernism, including Fried's. He has suggested that this was at least partly because Riley's work recognized 'the inherently physical, bodily character of optical perception',[3] and this chapter will trace how this aspect of her work relates to the evolution of the Happening and what may be seen as a 'theatrical' element in art that went far beyond the Minimalist art with which Fried associated it. The comments quoted above, made only two years apart by a leading artist and an influential critic respectively, appear to indicate an irreconcilable difference between two views of what modernist art could or should be.

The exclusion of theatre from modernism

The notion that theatre is not a true art form, or is at best a lesser form of art than painting and sculpture, was not unique to Fried and was not a recent idea in the 1960s. The theatre's claims to be recognized as 'art' met with resistance early in modernism's development. Many proponents of modernist theory promoted the importance of the 'originality' of artistic production whereas 'acting was seen as imitative and reproductive, rather than original and productive'.[4] Furthermore, the qualities of imitativeness and reproduction have been seen as 'feminine' and within modernism there is a 'persistent gendering as feminine of that which is devalued'.[5] Notions of what may or may not be 'feminine' may be of particular interest in relation to a woman artist's work, but in this chapter the aspect I wish to emphasize is the 'inferior' position accorded to theatre, and therefore to any suggestions of theatricality, in much modernist aesthetic theory. Fried's disdain for the theatrical in art invites an examination of where the theatre was positioned in contemporary art debates, of theatre's associations with the Happening, and of how the Happening itself related to developments in modernist painting in the post-war period, particularly Riley's work.

Fried deplored the 'theatrical', that is, art that made a direct appeal to the spectator: such appeals separated 'drama', where 'the beholder ... [is not] taken into account' from 'theatre', where the work is 'addressing the audience'.[6] In his essay, 'Art and objecthood', Fried declared 'there is a war going on between theater and modernist painting, between the theatrical and the pictorial'.[7] In his attack on 'theater', Fried specifically excluded Op and Pop art. Nonetheless, he distinguished both from modernist art. In the case of Op this may seem strange in the light of his later claim that 'the modernist imperative [was] to seek to negate objecthood'[8] (i.e. the objecthood of the work of art itself). Riley's Op paintings, in particular, with their optically curving and undulating surfaces, so hard to locate exactly in space, seem to resist their own 'objecthood' with fierce energy.[9] In spite of this, like the Happening, they invite a physical engagement.

Although Fried's target was Minimalism (which he called 'literalist art' as it 'occup[ied] a position ... that can be formulated in words'[10]), in the light of Riley's comment about her paintings' affinity with Happenings, it may be fruitful here to consider Fried's remarks in relation not only to Riley's work but also to other post-war art.

Encounters and events

In what ways might Riley's work be seen as 'theatrical'? Fried believed that a painting or sculpture is theatrical if 'it is concerned with the actual circumstances in which the beholder encounters [the] work'.[11] He cited the Minimalist artist Robert Morris:

> *The better new work takes relationships out of the work and makes them a function of space, light and the viewer's field of vision. ... It is in some ways more reflexive because one's awareness of oneself existing in the same space as the work is stronger than in previous work, with its many internal relationships'.*[12]

Of course, not all these comments on Minimalist art would be applicable to Op. Nevertheless, the idea of an art that produces an 'awareness of oneself existing in the same space as the work' evokes the notion of 'awareness of one's own body' that Ehrenzweig[13] claimed for Riley's work. 'The actual circumstances in which the beholder encounters the work' may most obviously be related to the site-specificity often claimed for Minimalist work.[14] This idea might also be applied, however, to the way in which the Op painting, through its interaction with the nervous system of the beholder, could be said to have itself influenced the circumstances of encounter. It is the idea of an encounter between beholder and art object, distanced from each other in a specific space and persisting through time, that Fried identified as 'theatrical' in Minimalism. This idea of encounter arises again in relation to Happenings, in which the passage of time for the unfolding of the event is also intrinsic to the work. Fried asserted that 'The literalist preoccupation with time – more precisely with the duration of the experience – is, I suggest, paradigmatically theatrical'.[15] Fried valued what he described as the 'presentness' of modernist art.

> *It is this continuous and entire presentness, amounting, as it were, to the perpetual creation of itself, that one experiences as a kind of* instantaneousness*: as though if only one were infinitely more acute, a single infinitely brief instant would be long enough to see everything, to experience the work in all its depth and fullness ... I want to claim that it is by virtue of their presentness and instantaneousness that modernist painting and sculpture defeat theater.*[16]

Looking at comments made by Riley and her supporters, it is hard to avoid the idea that duration of experience was essential in viewing her work. Riley wrote of a 'disturbance or "event"', which suggests something unfolding over time, even if only a short time: not something that (even theoretically) has the 'instantaneousness [by which] modernist painting and sculpture defeat theater'.[17] Ehrenzweig's description of looking at Riley's work emphasized standing before it for some time, allowing a 'new total vision [to come] through': as if the work solicited this vision from the spectator.[18] Seitz remarked on the apparent movement seen when looking at many Op paintings;[19] by definition, movement cannot be 'instantaneous', it can only occur over a period of time, however short.

We can therefore relate Fried's comments in 'Art and objecthood', and the views of the Minimalist artists he quotes,[20] to Riley's work and to earlier comments made about it. In this sense, Riley may be seen as exploring an area that was to become a prominent focus of artistic enquiry later in the decade. I suggest that Crow's argument that her work undermines the prevailing modernist aesthetic of the early 1960s can be related to the connections I have posited with Fried's notion of the 'theatrical' in art. Fried described modernist painting and sculpture as 'existing in, indeed ... secreting or constituting, a continual and perpetual present' and claimed that contemporary poetry and music aspired to the same state (although it is difficult to see how either form could escape duration).[21] To consider Crow's comment again, theatre itself might be described, more than any other art form, as having an 'inherently physical, bodily character', depending as it does on the actors' use of their bodies to enact it.

Riley's claim to create works that had something of the character of Happenings and events, and Fried's denigration of theatre and the theatrical, must be considered in the context of the emergence of Performance art from the early 1950s onwards, as well as developments within theatre itself in the late 1950s and 1960s. At this time, the new 'domestic realism' of playwrights such as Joe Orton and John Osborne was widely seen as a reaction against the comfortable bourgeois values of the inter-war and early post-war periods. With films such as *Saturday Night and Sunday Morning* (1960), this new conception of what drama could encompass affected a much wider audience than the middle-class theatre-going public.[22] The emotional and physical violence depicted in the plays and films of 'the angry young men' coincided with a more widespread concern with violence, which I shall consider further below. As we have seen, Op art was perceived as being in some way 'aggressive' but also as promoting a body-centred mode of perception; these themes are relevant to a consideration of the relationship between Op and notions of the theatrical. Such an association did not necessarily separate Op from other modernist art (as Fried might have argued[23]); it is a quality shared with other art produced in this period, which also had claims to be modernist. In fact, one may trace a possible lineage for Riley's work of the early 1960s from the work of composer John Cage, through the painting of Jackson Pollock and the work of Yves Klein and Lucio Fontana, with parallels occurring in the work of Riley's contemporary, Michelangelo Pistoletto.

Although performance art can be traced back, within modernism, to the events staged by the Futurists and Dada artists before and after the First World War, 'Happenings', to which Riley related her work, date from 1952. That year, John Cage gave a 'lecture' called *Theater Piece Number 1*, a title that evokes the titles of abstract paintings such as Kandinsky's *VII* (1913) or Pollock's *Number One* (1948). This practice itself echoed the older practice of numbering musical compositions: Fifth symphony, Opus 3, and so on. Numbering emphasizes the notion of abstraction, denying narrative content and relating the paintings to the abstract quality of music. Cage's chosen title suggests that the 'performance' (of music, readings and dance) that ensued was intended as a work of art in itself. It was a 'theatre piece' – a piece of theatre but not a 'play'; theatre as pure art, and a multimedia event involving various collaborators, including choreographer Merce Cunningham, poet Charles Olsen and painter Robert Rauschenberg. The *Piece* was a performance, but not a drama in the sense of a narrative; it may be seen as an attempt at bringing abstraction into performance *and* therefore as an attempt to bring theatre into the community of modernist art forms.

The first British 'Happening' was probably one performed at the Edinburgh Festival in 1963, by a group led by American performance artist Ken Dewey.[24] A key characteristic of 'Happenings' was the involvement of the viewer, and although the 'Happening' was not an important art form in Britain, nonetheless:

> *the elision between art and onlooker at the basis of the happening is something underlying a lot of other art of the decade; the 'Situation' show's catalogue stressed the need to experience art as a total environment; Bridget Riley's work makes the viewer participate by defining shapes and movement within surfaces.*[25]

'The legacy of Jackson Pollock'

If Riley's painting seems to foreshadow what Fried regarded as the theatricality of Minimalist work, it was not the first work to do this. There are also interesting connections between Jackson Pollock's indisputably modernist abstract work and notions of the theatrical, not least the 'performances' of his painting practice in the film produced by Hans Namuth in 1950–51.

Pollock's work was to have a lasting influence on later artists, in ways that it is unlikely he would have envisaged, and it is possible to see the traces of this legacy in Riley's paintings.

Pollock's titles *Full Fathom five* and *Sea Change* (both 1947) both come from Ariel's song in Shakespeare's *Tempest*: 'one of the play's most glittering, masque-like moments' – in other words, from one of the most 'theatrical' scenes within what is, in itself, a theatrical production.[26] Such titles were often suggested by other people, so his work may have had a 'theatrical' quality for some spectators well before the Namuth film was made. American artist Alan Kaprow, who organized a number of Happenings from the late 1950s onwards, published an essay in *Art News* in 1958 ('The legacy of Jackson Pollock'), in which he traced the origins of the Happening to the supposed freedom with which Pollock had created paintings: the 'logical' next step, he claimed, was to leave the confines of the canvas altogether.[27] Kaprow positioned the Happening in the mainstream of modernist practice.

Pollock had adopted the practice of working on a large horizontal canvas in order to work 'in' the painting – it became his environment. Pollock's working method, standing over and even on top of an outstretched canvas, had a direct physicality. As Pollock stood among skeins of paint he had already applied, adding more, his body literally 'entered' the painting like an actor entering the space of the stage. This physicality invited a sexual interpretation that Pollock himself encouraged: his descriptions of the physical aspects of his working methods contain sexual connotations.[28] He actively promoted the idea of the physicality of his work via Hans Namuth's film. The film has its own sense of the theatrical: a performance is staged within it, a performance of painting. Having seen this film, the viewer who subsequently looks at a Pollock painting will see it in relation to the memory of that performance. Rather than emerging, complete, from a mysterious and invisible creative process, Pollock's art could be seen as the result of an active bodily process.

Involving the audience

Riley's work involved the participation of the viewer: 'a very explicit demand for participation is a characteristic both of major social movements in the sixties and of much sixties art'.[29] The social movements that attracted public involvement included the Campaign for Nuclear Disarmament (CND) in the UK, and student activism in the USA and Europe. In the Happenings, artists sought ways of involving their audience.

Exactly what might constitute a Happening was not precisely defined and it could take various forms.

Whereas in Pollock's work only the artist's own body actually 'entered' the painting, from 1958, the French artist Yves Klein staged events in which his models covered their naked bodies in paint and, under Klein's direction, created marks by pressing and moving their bodies against various horizontal and vertical surfaces, in the presence of an audience. Klein himself was neatly suited, emphasizing his avoidance of direct contact with the paint. The models became studio assistants, while Klein's formal dress conveyed the intellectual aspect of his work. Klein's role paralleled both that of the conductor of a musical performance and that of the choreographer of a dance. In Klein's work a number of people – the 'models' – took on a physical (but not the creative, intellectual) role. The 'models' became 'assistants' – not a role commonly associated with the modernist artist[30] and certainly not with Pollock, who cultivated a 'rugged individualist' image. Klein's audience were as much passive spectators as they were for any finished work displayed in a gallery; their subjective experience, however, might have been a far greater sense of physical involvement, given their chance (risk) of coming into contact with wet paint. They were also witnessing the creation of the work at first hand. Although the audiences for these events were small (the first was staged at a private dinner party, others took place in an art gallery and in Klein's studio), Klein also had films made of some events. The presence of an audience, however small, seems to have been important to him: musicians played during the events (a composition written by him and consisting of a single note used to create a droning sound lasting 20 minutes). This again recalls the 'intermedia' events staged by Cage and his notion that any sort of sound could constitute music. By analogy, a painting could comprise any means of applying paint to a surface. Klein was anxious to play down the erotic aspect of his work. He preferred to emphasize the changed role of the model and a notion of 'the resurrection of the flesh', which has religious connotations and suggests that religious/spiritual experience is experienced through the body.[31] His use of music and staging for his events connote both theatre and religious ritual.

This emphasis on the body again recalls the way that Op art was seen as celebrating the physical experience of engaging with art. Riley's work, like the Happening, offered a means of uniting aesthetic and physical experience. Klein's work shows that that Op was only one form of art practice that could be interpreted in this way. Klein was not the only artist who created paintings in front of an audience. By 1960 the American artist Jim Dine was giving performances at New York's Judson Gallery in which he appeared to drink jars of paint before pouring more paint over himself and then jumping through a canvas. Alan Kaprow's *18 Happenings in Six Parts* involved a number of collaborators all painting in public: 'audiences could not avoid feeling like part of the action even when not actively participating'.[32]

Inhabiting the painting

Merleau-Ponty engaged with the notion of the spectator's bodily participation in a painting as an aspect of seeing it, and devoted an essay, 'Eye and mind', to the subject in 1961. Here he 'turned to painting for evidence of the character of the body's relation to the world'.[33] He argued that painting had an inherent physicality, with the painter in some sense acting as a surrogate for the spectator, experiencing the world in a direct, physical way and then making this experience available to the viewer. He also wrote that 'to look at an object is to inhabit it'.[34] Here, the act of looking is equated with the physical movement of the body to take up the space observed; perception here is not a purely mental activity but involves the body; vision is not so much a function of the body as a part of it. Merleau-Ponty seems to suggest that 'we are what we see' and that movement is not a simple matter of transporting the body about, but is integral to the existence of the body: vision and movement 'intertwine' in a *pas de deux* in which mind and body are inseparable. 'Being' here has an essentially physical (rather than intellectual or mental) nature; only the physical – the 'visible' – can 'enter into the work of art'.[35] The 'dramatic' or 'theatrical' nature of the Happening is an attempt to bring the body into the work of art, like an actor taking the stage. Artists from Pollock to Kaprow illustrate various attempts to do this.

A precursor to Riley's work can also be seen in the series of *Ambientes spaziale (Spatial environments)*, created from 1949 by the Italian artist Lucio Fontana, which the spectator had to enter to experience. The use of ultra-violet or neon light, reflective white surfaces and restricted spaces were calculated to produce a disorientating effect. Here, as with Riley's 1963 work *Continuum* [Figs. 3, 7 and 21] discussed below, the spectator became an active participant in the work, which could be said to exist fully only when being occupied. Because the spectator of these works had to pass through them physically, experiencing them could never happen in the notional 'instant' that Fried later argued was an essential characteristic of modernist art.

A work of art that had to be entered, and moved around within, in order to be experienced fully did not meet Fried's criteria for modernist art. The act of entering one of Fontana's works, moving around within it and then leaving, was 'theatrical' in that it involved a sequential flow of beginning, middle and end, like a play, and it invited the viewer to enter it. Indeed, the work itself became a 'theatre' enclosing the 'event'. At the same time, Fontana's work actively involved the spectator, as if foreshadowing the participative[36] nature of some Happenings of the 1950s and 1960s, as well as *Continuum*.

The notion of 'inhabiting' the work of art again suggests the work of Pollock as depicted in the Hans Namuth film.[37] In *Number 1A* (1948) a line of Pollock's handprints close to the top right of the painting allude to his own presence in the work, as if the plane of the work were a sheet of glass with the painter's palms pressed against it from the inside. Merleau-Ponty conceptualized seeing as a form of possession that was available, implicitly, to both the painter and all other viewers, all of whom were potentially able 'to enter into the work of art'. This possession and entering were imaginative processes rather than the literal physical invasion of the canvas that was central to Pollock's working process. The marks of Pollock's unseen presence, left behind on the finished work, allow the vicarious penetration of the painting by subsequent viewers of the work. Namuth's film, and the related stills, also promoted the idea of the artist's physical presence in his paintings, allowing the viewer to enter the work vicariously.[38]

Images of Pollock's bodily involvement with his work were still influential for painters in the early 1960s but then attempts were made to take the viewer's sense of penetrating the painting rather further. From 1963, the Italian artist Michelangelo Pistoletto began incorporating mirrors into his paintings in an attempt to 'make the laws of objective reality enter the painting'. He felt that Pollock 'had attempted to transfer life on to canvas through action [but] did not succeed in taking possession of the work, which continued to escape him'.[39] The mirrors reflected the artist while he worked on his paintings, so that like Pollock he was 'literally ... in the painting' but once the completed work was exhibited, every viewer would see himself or herself 'inhabiting' the picture; to look at the work of art was to 'enter' it. The viewer of such a work, seeing his or her own moving image in the mirror, became an 'actor' within the painting while simultaneously being the spectator of that 'performance'. By passive reflection, the mirrors apparently 'transfer[red] life on to canvas' and allowed first the artist, then the spectator to '[take] possession of the work'. This can also be considered as an extension of Klein's work, where the models may be seen as 'standing in' for the spectator, who sits close by and watches them simultaneously creating and entering the work. In Pistoletto's work, the spectator watches him/herself entering the work – and also partially creating it, because it is incomplete without the artist's or spectator's reflection. This recalls Fried's criticism of Minimalism as theatrical because 'the literalist work depends on the beholder, it is incomplete without him'.[40]

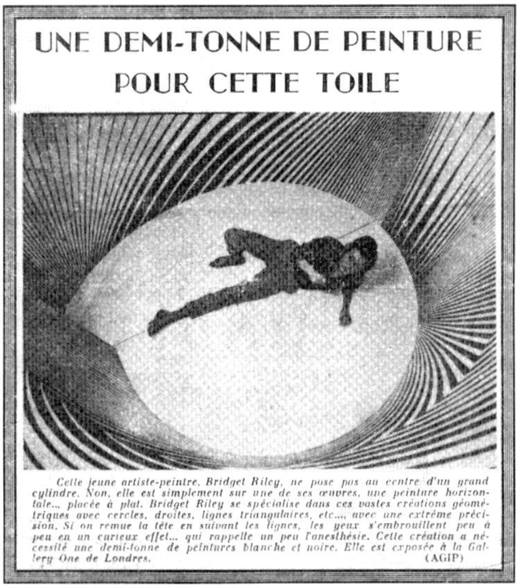

UNE DEMI-TONNE DE PEINTURE POUR CETTE TOILE

Cette jeune artiste-peintre, Bridget Riley, ne pose pas au centre d'un grand cylindre. Non, elle est simplement sur une de ses œuvres, une peinture horizontale... placée à plat. Bridget Riley se spécialise dans ces vastes créations géométriques avec cercles, droites, lignes triangulaires, etc..., avec une extrême précision. Si on remue la tête en suivant les lignes, les yeux s'embrouillent peu à peu en un curieux effet... qui rappelle un peu l'anesthésie. Cette création a nécessité une demi-tonne de peintures blanche et noire. Elle est exposée à la Gallery One de Londres. (AGIP)

21.
'Half a ton of paint for this canvas'. Bridget Riley lying in the centre of **Continuum**, *Le Provençal*, 18 November 1963

In the same year that Pistoletto began experimenting with mirrors, one work by Bridget Riley appears to have taken another, and physically extreme, approach to the idea of audience participation: *Continuum* (1963, now lost, Fig. 21). Here, Riley painted the inside of an almost circular construction into which the spectator walked to be completely surrounded by the work. A contemporary photograph, taken from above, shows Riley lying on the floor[41] in the centre of this construction, as if literally inhabiting it, as indeed the viewer had to do in order to see the work. One might relate this as much to Monet's *Grandes Décorations* (1914–26)[42] in the Orangerie in Paris as to Pollock or Fontana, but the size of Riley's construction was much smaller than the rooms of the Orangerie and more constricted than Fontana's *Environments*, while the intensity of the black and white Op painting, with which its inner wall was covered, rendered the experience unsettling for many viewers, generating a variety of responses. The very title, *Continuum*, suggests an ongoing process; it also brings to mind the notion of the 'space-time continuum' of Einstein's general theory of relativity. Where Fried's notion of 'presentness' would seem to take the work of art out of time, *Continuum* suggests a work forged from time as much as from the physical space it occupied, and necessarily experienced *in* time as well as in space. This brings us back to both the Happening and theatre, unfolding in time as well as space, and the central importance of the body, which can only experience time and space *together*; indeed, the body can be said to experience time and space as a 'continuum'.

The intense sense of enclosure and the strong optical effects of *Continuum* were interpreted as a form of violence by some commentators: either as violence against the viewer or against art itself. The *Daily Mail* suggested that it made viewers feel 'seasick' although, as I have noted, other work by Riley was accused of inducing nausea.[43] *The Times* appeared to be more impressed by the associations with Monet's late work but seemed ambivalent about the experience, writing of 'prison bars' suggesting enclosure and entrapment, on the one hand and, on the other, a 'vast geometric landscape', which might have been a utopian country in which the mind could wander. The writer described *Continuum* as 'an "environmental" work':

> *a geometrically precise, black and white pattern of compressed and expanded vertical stripes, six feet high and 28 ft. long, coiled in a circle so that you can stand in the centre of an endless surface. Here, too, focus is confounded. The optical effect of the pattern is such that only by keeping one's eye fixed on a set point can one confirm that the surface is actually within hand's reach. The second one's gaze travels, surface disappears and one might be penned in close by prison bars or surrounded by a vast geometric landscape.*[44]

There is no mention here of the 'strangely disembodied iridescent colours, like St Elmo's fires'[45] as described by Ehrenzweig in relation to Riley's black and white paintings shown at her second Gallery One show that year. The experience may have been too disorientating for such subtleties to be detected. Another commentator on Riley's work, Maurice de Sausmarez, writing in 1970, implied that this was so, giving his use of the term 'hallucinatory' (which, like Ehrenzweig, he preferred to 'illusion') the connotation of a 'bad trip':

> *the progression of lines and spacings* [was] *so dislocated that the experience of being inside was a total breakdown of one's physical orientation and capacity for estimating both distance and space, an hallucinatory experience that could be tolerated for only a few minutes without a sense of distress.*[46]

There is a suggestion here of being subjected to a violent attack but with an implicit acknowledgement that this attack was generated by the spectator's own perceptual system. It recalls Riley's own expressed desire to create works 'where the disturbance precipitated is latent in the sociological and psychological situation'. Certainly, with *Continuum*, there was no 'disturbance' until the spectator entered the work and submitted to the 'hallucinatory experience'. Both this notion of 'attack' and the enclosed, circular space within *Continuum* suggest another connection with contemporary theorizing about art: the idea of an 'arena' such as those in which the Romans had organized spectacles of violence and destruction. Art critic Harold Rosenberg and artist Michelangelo Pistoletto both used the term 'arena' in relation to contemporary art. *Continuum* can be seen as an arena where the viewer was both participant in and viewer of the 'spectacle'; the 'conflict' was generated within the spectator's nervous system, which in turn created the psychic tensions experienced as distress by de Sausmarez. This conflict was both represented by the uncompromising, all-encompassing black and white painting on the inner wall of the 'arena', and induced by it.

Rosenberg, looking back at the development of action painting, wrote in the mid-1960s that 'It had become appropriate to speak of the canvas as an arena (at length the canvas was put aside to produce "happenings")'.[47] He implied that, ultimately, artists could not achieve the physical engagement – either with the art itself or with the audience for that art, on the canvas – that the notion of the arena suggests. Only the 'Happening' could achieve this, leading to the canvas being 'put aside'. In the meantime:

> *On the white expanse a succession of champions performed feats of negation for the liberation of all. 'Jackson broke the ice for us' de Kooning has generously said of Pollock ... behind Pollock came a veritable flotilla of icebreakers.*[48]

While some artists may have put aside the 'white expanse' of the canvas, there remained others who continued to seek a more physical engagement with both their art and their audience through that very medium. In another context, Pistoletto wrote in 1967:

> *The ambiguity of art is simply a matter of putting two things in relation to each other so as to be able to observe the representation of their conflict. It's what the Romans were doing when they put the lions and the Christians in the arena to enjoy the spectacle.*[49]

In *Continuum*, the attack of the lions, the breaking of the ice, were no longer engaged in purely by the artist, with the admiring spectator looking on from a safe distance: in this instance the spectator was *in* the arena. Although sympathetic critics may have wished to see themselves joining the icebreakers when they entered this work, many felt themselves to be the victims of the lions. Nonetheless, in entering the work, the spectator could be said to be complicit in any 'attack' to which he or she was then subjected.

This is another parallel with Fried's comments on Minimalist art:

> *the presence of literalist art ... is basically a theatrical effect or quality – a kind of stage presence. It is a function, not just of the obtrusiveness and, often, even aggressiveness of literalist work, but of the special complicity which that work extorts from the beholder.*[50]

Even the term 'extorts' here suggests the threat of further aggression: the beholder faces both the aggression inherent in the work's 'stage presence' and the further aggression of being forced to be complicit in the attack. It is as though Fried were arguing that free will is bypassed, and the Minimalist (theatrical) work forces the spectator to take part in its attack on him/her – to take part in the 'performance' of the work, like an actor under duress.[51] Similarly, the viewer of *Continuum* was subjected to what many experienced as an assault on the senses, but only after they had voluntarily entered the work. It may be that reports such as those in *The Times* and the *Daily Mail* actually encouraged people to view *Continuum*. Like the audience for a horror film who have been promised that it will terrify them, they were complicit in the experience.

Op as a theatre of cruelty

The notion that Riley's work was aggressive has further connections with both the contemporary theatre and with the Happening, and all three must be seen in the context of contemporary concerns about violence in the arts. These in turn were borne of fears about the future development of a possibly technocratic and highly commercialized society. Guy Debord was to argue in *The Society of the Spectacle* (1967) that contemporary society had commodified all aspects of life and reduced them to a 'spectacle'. He believed that art could resist this, while admitting that the spectacle tended to absorb even forces that opposed it.[52] Hence any 'aggressive' qualities identified in Riley's work could be interpreted as resisting the easy viewing of a commodified art, but at the same time, the qualities that made it disturbing could be sensationalized by, for example, the *Daily Mail*, and thus render it more susceptible to commodification.

If art is an 'arena' we must recall that the ancient Roman version was a place where violent death was commodified as a staged 'spectacle' for the audience. The arena stretched the concept of theatre to its limit. In the 1960s, there were concerns that contemporary theatre was again promoting cruelty, violence and death. The ideas of the French dramatist and theorist Antonin Artaud (first published in French in the 1930s) were becoming influential in Britain, and his idea of a 'theatre of cruelty' emphasized the positive attributes of cruelty.

> *From the point of view of the mind, cruelty signifies rigour, implacable intention and decision, irreversible and absolute determination ... Cruelty is above all lucid.*[53]

In the 1960s, however, there was concern with the negative aspects of this thesis. Booker certainly failed to see any positive interpretation:

> *By and large in 1964, the new English drama was continuing its drift into the violent, sexually-obsessed and freakish fantasy world that had first become apparent in 1962.*[54]

Booker attributed this 'drift' to the influence of Artaud (whom he regarded as a 'psychopath'), whose work had influenced theatre director Peter Brook's work with the Royal Shakespeare Company.[55] A more positive interpretation of Artaud is that the Theatre of Cruelty was 'a celebration of the irrational ... [which] was a dialectical response to the increasingly materialist and technocratic society'.[56] Again, technocracy and its accompanying materialism were to engender various counter-cultural reactions – a degree of 'aggression' or 'violence' may be an appropriate reaction to negative aspects of society and such attitudes may have underlain the more positive responses to *Continuum*, such as that in *The Times*.

Artaud's work was only translated into English in 1958.[57] Hence in Britain in the early 1960s, his ideas were quite new and influenced the theatrical experimentation of Brook and playwrights such as Edward Bond.[58] Artaud emphasized the importance of movement and gesture – of the body, rather than of dialogue alone – in communicating with the audience. Artaud associated 'cruelty' and 'action' not with destruction but with rebuilding: 'Everything that acts is a cruelty. It is upon this idea of extreme action, pushed beyond all limits, that the theatre must be rebuilt' His vision could be associated with the construction of an alternative to a technocratic, materialist society.[59] The qualities he associated with 'cruelty' (a term suggestive of violence): 'rigour... decision... determination... lucid[ity]', chime with some of those used in art criticism of the period. We could add 'ruthlessness' somewhere in this sequence. Those critics who applauded Riley's apparent possession of such qualities tended to be supporters of her work, whereas much of the popular press (and some of the more 'serious' critics) saw it as being gratuitously aggressive and shocking. In his introduction to the catalogue for the 'New Generation' show, David Thompson noted that the art on display here was 'firm, decisive, hard'.[60] The notion that Riley's own work was itself aggressive or violent ('visual torments'[61] 'her cruel formula'[62]) recurs throughout contemporary commentaries. Robert Melville's comments in August 1965 are suggestive of the 1928 Buñuel/Dali film *Un Chien Andalou*, in which an eye is slashed:

> *some of her black and white optical effects have attacked the eyes of the spectator with a cold ferocity that makes some of Surrealism's efforts to take a sadistic slash at the spectator look faint-hearted ....*[63]

As we have seen, in some art criticism of this period notions of determination and ruthlessness (suggesting violence) were associated with notions of the new professionalism. This was in turn associated with a new image of 'Britishness'. To what extent the work of Bond, Brook and their contemporaries promoted the acceptance of such ideas in British culture is debatable. Certain qualities (determination, decisiveness, rigour, ruthlessness) that had been seen as 'unBritish' or at any rate 'undesirable' in the earlier post-war period became associated with the most experimental, advanced theatre of the day, with contemporary avant-garde art, especially Op, and with a new attitude towards British national identity and what it might encompass.[64] Violence and destruction are negative connotations of such terms: if not the physical destruction shown in some plays and Happenings of the period, then the destruction of certain values and ideas that might be regarded as either essential to civilized society or the root of all oppression.[65] A more positive view would be that these ideas indicated a new confidence, in both art and the rest of British culture. As so often with Riley's work, the concepts associated with it defy a precise single interpretation.

The Theatre of Cruelty can be seen as a rejection of 'technocracy'. Op was seen as either a 'natural' expression of a technocratic society (the rise of technology here being regarded as beneficial), or as a rejection of it – an attempt to re-engage the body in perceptual experience of the world. In either case, there is an implication of the present as a time that ought to be superseded by something better – a process that might be hurried on by the destruction of present evils, whether in society or the self. Jeff Nuttall, a writer, artist and CND activist who was active in 'underground' or 'counter-cultural' publishing and Happenings during the 1960s, commented on the ways in which theatre and Happenings were then experimenting with an escalating degree of violence, in which the notion of acting as 'make believe' was being replaced with a new literalism. Writing in 1968, Nuttall drew parallels between the sadistic murders perpetrated by the so-called 'Moors Murderers', Ian Brady and Myra Hindley, in the early 1960s (they were arrested in 1965) and the more extreme Happenings of the period, in which he had taken part.

> *There was a widespread rash of sado-masochism in the arts. When Brady and Hindley were carrying out their first murder plans Otto Muhl and Herman Nitsch*[66] *had already carried out their first ceremonials with entrails, flesh and smeared food. Keith Musgrave*[67] *and I were talking about publicly disembowelling a human corpse and hurling the guts at the audience. Nitsch lamented the fact that corpses were available to medical students but not to artists. So did we. Del Foley showered the audience with offal at the first Notting Hill Gate festival, and I, with Musgrave and other members of the sTigma*[68] *team, did a fake disembowelling in the Better Books basement. "I thought you'd murdered her" said Tony Godwin*[69]*. "It'll come to that," said John Calder.*[70]

This description brings to mind the excesses of the Roman arena. That longstanding avant-garde project, *épater les bourgeois*, was being taken to extremes, yet Nuttall's words suggest that his protagonists' actions were almost inevitable, springing from a society that had produced the Moors murderers. Since the emergence of new dramatic voices such as John Osborne and Joe Orton, even West End theatre sought to shock the audience, epitomized by the Royal Shakespeare Company's staging of its Artaud-inspired 'Theatre of Cruelty' season in 1964. There are parallels here with the writings of Georges Bataille, explored in Chapter 2. In *The Accursed Share* (1949) Bataille promoted the idea of 'expenditure' as essential to human societies, arguing that there were connections between sexuality, violence and death. Bataille saw destruction as an end in itself, exemplified by the sun, powered its own self-consumption.[71] The notion that Riley's work 'devoured' the viewer was made explicit by cartoonist Erich Sokol in a 1965 cartoon showing a man apparently being eaten by Riley's painting *Fission* (1963), his torso having been already sucked into the picture while his screaming wife holds on to one leg as she looks round frantically for assistance [Figs. 22, 23].

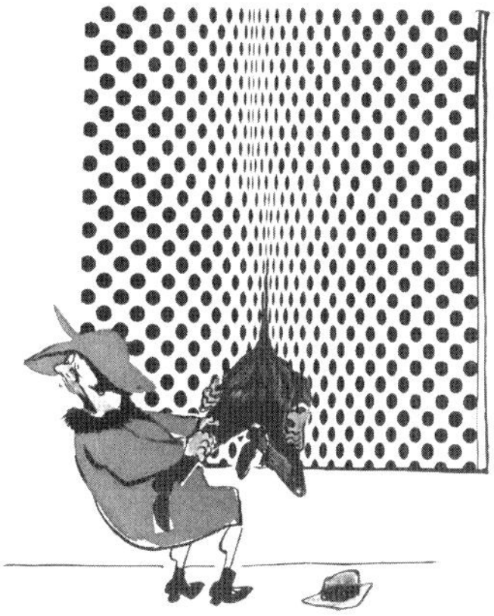

22.
Erich Sokol:
cartoon
1965

Sokol's illustration caught exactly the sense of aggression, even violence, that so many reporters found in Riley's work: here were pictures that almost literally attacked the viewer. Ehrenzweig wrote as though with this cartoon in mind, when he commented, in the same year, that:

> *It is idiomatic (not only in English but also in other languages) to speak of our eyes 'devouring' something. Here the reverse happens, our eyes are attacked and devoured by the paintings.*[72]

Continuum would seem to have taken this tendency as far as it could go. In entering this cylindrical work, its shape suggesting an arena, albeit on a small scale, one could say the viewer was consumed (or devoured) by the painting. The numerous claims in the press that Riley's work was aggressive or induced nausea may have primed many viewers to experience the painting as an assault well before they entered it: like the Roman Christians, they knew that the lions were waiting. Riley never again produced anything comparable; perhaps the extreme nature of the work undermined its own possibilities for manipulating the viewer's perception.[73] Nonetheless, the notion that her works in general, and *Continuum* in particular, were aggressive and violent must be seen in the context of prevailing notions of 'the violent' in contemporary culture.

The Carnival and the body

There is another way in which we may consider what might be called the performative aspect of Riley's Op paintings. One comment from the popular press in 1963 is suggestive. The *Daily Mail* questioned 'whether such a style belongs to the fine arts or to funfairs'.[74] Although intended as a derogatory joke, this comment evokes the idea of 'carnival' explored by

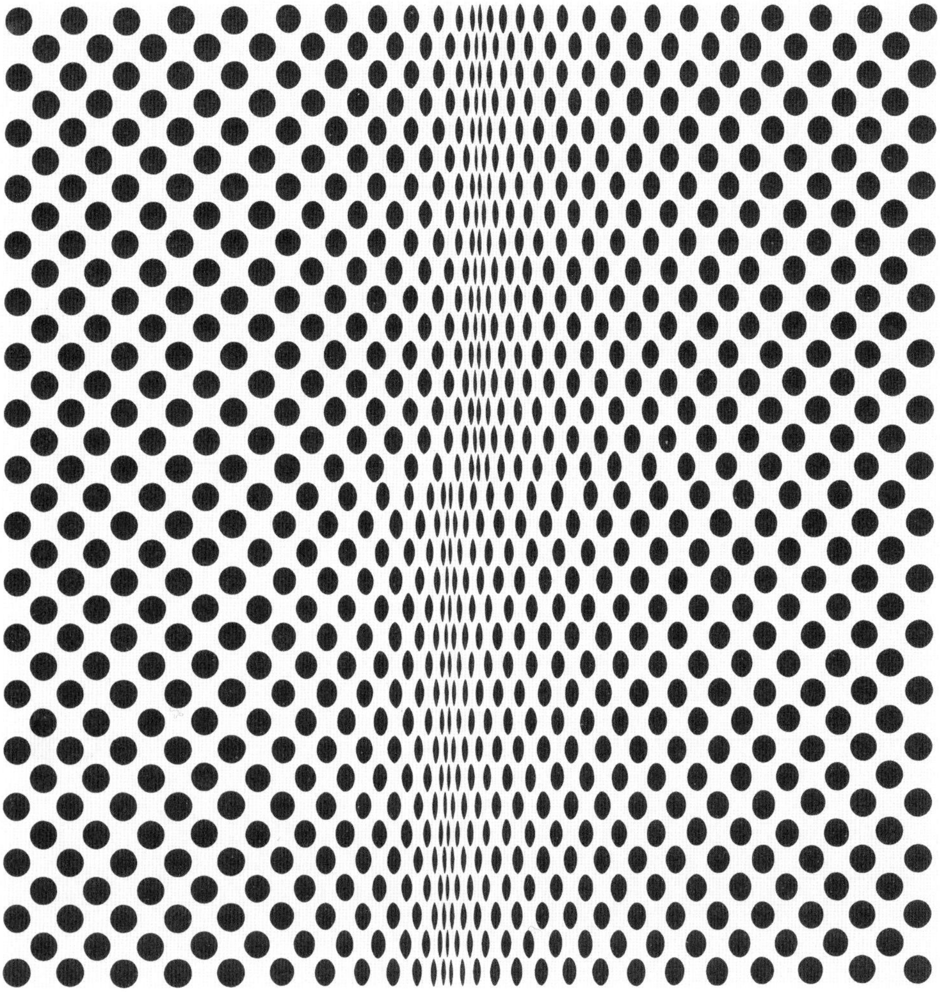

23. **Fission** 1963

Russian philosopher Mikhail Bakhtin in his work *Rabelais and his World*.[75] Bakhtin celebrated the Carnival, as it existed in pre-Renaissance times, as a site where the body was celebrated, and where laughter (a very physical act but one which expresses inner feeling or excitement: a 'psychological situation') was always ambivalent, because the spectators saw an exaggerated version of themselves mirrored in the performers. Such humour depended on the 'sense of recognition'[76] experienced by the carnival participant. A viewer of *Continuum* or of a Happening was like one of Bakhtin's carnival-goers, for whom 'there is no life outside the carnival. The people in it are both actors and spectators simultaneously'.[77] Bakhtin saw Carnival as a celebration of the body, even in its 'lower' aspects (which might include the 'seasickness' the *Mail* also associated with Riley's work).

'Carnival' was ambivalent: on the one hand it was against seriousness and encouraged the actor/spectator to laugh at him or herself. On the other hand, it also had a sinister side, as expressed by the violence of the wife-beating Punch of the English fairground, the English descendant of the Italian Carnival character Pulcinella. The *Daily Mail* sought to trivialize Riley's work but, as we have seen, for Bakhtin carnival laughter is always ambivalent and furthermore 'the body ... is part of this ambivalence. It is not closed in and private but open to the world'.[78] These words evoke the spirit of the Sixties 'Happening', where artists abandoned the privacy of the studio in order to achieve a more direct, physical contact with the world beyond it. Of course, laughter itself would not have been regarded as an appropriate response to modernist art by its practitioners or supporters: it has long been used to attack it by its detractors.[79] Such laughter may be interpreted as a failure or refusal to understand the work being ridiculed. In relation to Riley's work, however, another interpretation of this laughter may be made: not that it was an 'appropriate' response to this work but that, in its physicality, it is related (however distantly) to responses that *were* considered appropriate by some contemporary critics. It is the physicality of the spectator's response to Riley's work advocated by Ehrenzweig and later commented upon by Crow that gave this work the relationship to Happenings that Riley herself suggested. In Carnival, the beggar becomes king and the king a beggar but such role reversals only serve to accentuate the 'natural' order of things.[80] Similarly, in emphasizing the 'lowest' aspects of bodily existence, Carnival reminds us that the body is capable of more 'elevated' experiences. The sensations of nausea that some people experienced when looking at Op art also evoke Kristeva's concept of the abject: all those reminders of physical mortality – vomit, faeces, tears, mucus – which may be expelled from the body but from which the individual can never escape. Much cultural production that may be labelled 'carnivalesque' – from the revels of mediaeval carnival itself through the scatological humour of eighteenth-century political cartoons to the performances of Leigh Bowery in the 1980s and 1990s, which involved defaecation, vomiting and urination – has very evident connections with this concept of the 'abject'. In Bakhtin's Carnival, laughter at these 'lower' bodily functions provided the means to overcome fear, and specifically fear of death. When fear ends 'joyous recreation will begin ... the monster, death, becomes pregnant'.[81] The obverse of the body's 'lower' functions is the 'higher' function of procreation.

In the case of Bridget Riley's art, which of course is not itself in this Carnivalesque tradition, we may nonetheless observe parallels in the ways in which her art was interpreted by the critics. On the one hand, we have elements such as the *Daily Mail* with its claims of 'seasickness' and its relegation of Riley's art to the 'funfair' and, on the other, the claims of Ehrenzweig that her work allows the body itself to be experienced more vividly.[82] This suggests a 'higher' level of physical experience, where the body may be regarded as the site of a pleasure that borders on the spiritual.[83] It also suggests why the bodily experience of art may have been a problem for the modernist critic: it may be impossible to separate 'higher' and 'lower' bodily functions. Any suggestion of the former always risks creating associations with the latter. Creating art that emphasized bodily experience must then have been a high-risk strategy for modernists.

The *Mail*'s comment also brings to mind the fairground attraction of distorting mirrors: this is perhaps the most purely visual artefact that one associates with funfairs, where the spectator is effectively encouraged to laugh at his or her own body. That body is deliberately distorted so that 'the spectator experiences at one and the same time something known and something unknown'.[84] Looking at the distorted reflection is disorientating and disturbing; looking at the intense Op painting within the walls of *Continuum* was also said to disorientate and disturb the viewer. We may imagine parallels between the image in the funfair mirror, extended laterally and moving unpredictably with every smallest movement of the body, and the lateral extension of the image in *Continuum*, defying the eye's attempts to focus.

An 'ambivalent' response, such as described by *The Times*' critic caught between 'prison bars ...[and] a vast geometric landscape' seems appropriate to works that defy a fixed focus. In a work such as *Continuum*, it would seem that a range of possible foci presented themselves to the eye in relentless succession. The apparent simplicity of a work that consists only of black and white is confounded by the multiplicity of foci.

> *Carnival logic (the logic of ambivalence) is not restricted to the logic of binary oppositions which set limits, but is equivalent of the power of continuum (positive* and *negative).*[85]

Earlier, I made comparisons between the idea of the arena and Riley's *Continuum*. By walking into the work, the spectator participated in it: 'Carnival, in its ambivalence, focuses attention on the people as the arena for participation'.[86] On entering *Continuum* the spectator occupied 'the arena for participation' and, as *The Times* made clear, could experience this in both positive and negative ways, almost simultaneously.

While there is a theatrical element in Happenings, in the sense of their being performances, the element of participation by the 'audience' actually undermines the relationship to 'theatre'. In classical and modern theatre, the audience is usually separated from the actors and their actions. The part of the theatre building that is reserved for the actors is usually clearly demarcated and separated from the audience. Bakhtin argued that:

> *carnival does not know footlights, in the sense that it does not acknowledge any distinction between actors and spectators. Footlights would destroy a carnival as the absence of footlights would destroy a theatrical performance.*[87]

Happenings, therefore, can be seen as having an ambivalent relationship with theatre, appropriating some of its characteristics – performance and engagement with the spectator – while at the same time rejecting the physical separation of 'actor' and 'spectator'. This ambivalence can be sensed in the title of Cage's Happening *Theater Piece Number 1*, where the notion of 'theatre' is emphasized but then, as it were, retreated from: 'Number 1' suggesting both musical compositions and abstract painting, both of which could be accepted by modernists of Fried's persuasion as modernist high art, whereas theatre could not.

It is useful to think of the Happenings of the 1960s as appropriating something of the spirit of Carnival and re-producing this for a period when many artists wanted to attract an audience who would participate in their work. Like Carnival, Happenings allowed participation to circumvent representation. In likening her own work to Happenings, therefore, Riley was, perhaps unknowingly, locating it within a much older tradition of attempted subversion of the established order. This brings us back to Crow's view of her work as subverting some contemporary modernist theorizing.

Bakhtin's Carnival stood outside the social structure, neither reinforcing nor negating it but promoting values that could not find a place within it, such as the emphasis on laughter rather than seriousness, or the body rather than the mind. Carnival was a disturbance to the normal running of society, which nonetheless continued to operate around it. Happenings and Op art themselves constituted disturbances in the interpretation of modernism promoted by critics such as Fried, where 'Painting exist(s) within the indivisible present of the extremest possible perceptual intensity ... Nothing was to segment off the "now" from itself'.[88] Both the Happening and Riley's Op painting denied this sense of instantaneous ('indivisible present') – and purely intellectual – experience. They brought the spirit of the Carnival, grounded as it was in the active participation of the spectator (and with it, the notion of the artwork being experienced *through* time, rather than in spite of it), into contemporary art practice. It was as if the body itself were being insinuated into the space between 'the "now" and itself'.

'Art puts on a show'

There were a number of more positive reactions than Fried's to the theatrical aspects of contemporary art and these tended to be linked to the aggressive/destructive tendencies perceived in it. In the quotation from Bridget Riley's article, 'Perception is the medium' with which I opened this chapter, Riley said that she wanted the spectator of her work to experience 'a sense of recognition within the work ... at one and the same time something known and something unknown'. Part of what we know and yet do not know about ourselves is our own capacity for violence and to what extent our violent impulses might be channelled into something more constructive. Gustav Metzger, a proponent of 'Auto-Destructive art', argued that there was a need for 'outlets for activities that could previously be channelled to war' and that 'abject aggression might be transformed into pleasure and discharged and released through the body'.[89] This can also be a function of the theatre, where the audience derives pleasure from watching the characters engage in struggles with the major problems and questions of human life. In the films and plays of the 1960s, the struggles in which the characters engaged could be more physically violent than ever before, supporting the notion that the viewing of aggressive and violent acts could be 'transformed into pleasure'.[90] We have seen how Hess considered that 'Op ... can be used at will to produce a predictable (and once habituated, probably enjoyable) feeling'.[91] In other words, familiarization with initially-distressing Op art would render it enjoyable. The *Daily Mail*'s apparently contradictory assertion that Riley's work caused feelings of 'seasickness' but that it was suitable for 'funfairs' carried the same implication that physical distress could be transformed into pleasure.

While, for Fried, theatre lay in a no-man's land 'between the [modernist] arts', this negative view was by no means universal among modernist critics. Harold Rosenberg commented that 'Today's art is not merely shown; it puts on a show and solicits audience participation'.[92] He noted that this had 'caused some people to conclude that painting and sculpture have lost their bearing and are about to vanish into show biz',[93] however, he believed this was an unfounded fear: Futurism, Dada and Surrealism displayed the same 'impulse to turn from the art object to the art event' as did 'the interweavings of thrown pigment and fierce brush slashes of the Action Painters'.[94] Rosenberg described the Happening as 'the most extreme movement of painting towards the performing arts'.[95] He saw it as derived from Action Painting and therefore closely related to what many regarded as the epitome of 'high modernism'. For Rosenberg, art could not exist in the state of transcendent 'presentness' advocated by Fried. In the Happening:

> *painters and sculptors brought their personalities in to play as actors before an actual crowd. As in Action Painting the production of the art object was subordinated to the activity of the artist, now turned producer-director-actor. Action Painting showmanship had brought into being the mammoth canvases of Pollock and* [Franz] *Kline as literal 'arenas' for the duel of the artist with his emerging image. The viewer had been drawn into the action on the canvas as a collaborator in establishing its significance. In the Happening the image making of the artist was carried over directly into the public event.*[96]

In contrast with this dynamic view of the plastic arts in the 1960s, British theatre of the early 1950s had been considered moribund. In 1954, British theatre critic Kenneth Tynan had pronounced 'I counsel aggression because, as a critic, I had rather be a war correspondent than a necrologist'.[97] Two years later the first production of John Osborne's *Look Back in Anger* showed that Tynan's counsel was to be heeded by a new generation of playwrights. Theatre in Britain in the 1950s and 1960s underwent considerable changes and achieved a high level of engagement with the realities of contemporary life.[98] Furthermore, in Britain there was a long record of respect for the artistic value of theatre. The notion that Shakespeare, for instance, was not 'art' was not a consideration for art critic John Russell, writing in *The Sunday Times*. Russell identified theatrical parallels with Riley's work and expressed these in purely positive terms:

> *To see these pictures in terms of optical effects, as some people have done, is like seeing the storm scene in* Lear *in terms of mean rainfall.*[99]

Russell chose a play of great emotional and physical violence (Peter Brook's contemporary RSC production of *King Lear* was influenced by Artaud's theories) for comparison with Riley's paintings. Russell saw 'drama' in Riley's work – drama in the highest sense of communicating to the spectator the very essence of the central questions of human existence. He saw such questions in terms of a struggle between opposing forces. He wrote 'hazard is everywhere':

> *and that hazard stands for the hazard in human affairs to which these pictures run parallel: the moment, that is to say, at which a powerful nature is forced almost to disintegration point by pressures outward or inward (or both). Drama results, on the stage, when such a nature fights back, reforming and redefining itself in such a way that disintegration is averted; and the artist, like the playwright, can externalise and turn to good account experiences of failure and loss, breakdown and betrayal, which would destroy a frailer nature.*[100]

Russell analysed Riley's work in terms of 'situation', 'changes', 'movement', 'drama', 'unexpected pulls and thrusts'. He used dynamic, physical language to convey the experience of seeing a Riley painting. By referring to *Lear* specifically and by a general implied reference to Shakespearean drama in the passage quoted above, Russell made high claims for the value of Riley's work as 'art' in the widest sense. He created a parallel between her work and a concept of 'great' drama, rather than comparing her to contemporaries whose work might not be clearly seen as having the lasting quality and value of *Lear*. Russell was clearly interested in connections between theatre and painting but did not appear to connect either of them with Happenings.

In 1965 he wrote about developments at Stratford East's Theatre Royal. Russell wanted to see 'the infiltration of living British art into a world from which to all appearances it has too long been outlawed'. One of the key managers at the Theatre Royal, Vera Lindsay (Russell's wife) was said to want

> *to attract our best artists into the theatre and to invite them in, not as valets to the producer or the dramatist, but as prime*

movers and undisputed masters of a new kind of theatrical entertainment ... to artists in their late twenties and early thirties, it offers an escape from the solitude of the studio and a more positive – even an aggressive – function in society as a whole.[101]

Again, a connection is made between notions of theatre and of aggression, with a validation of the latter as positive in relation to 'society as a whole'. Russell also referred to the assumed need of artists to 'escape from the solitude of the studio', an aim of those artists who initiated Happenings. His words suggest the 'very explicit demand for participation' characteristic of 1960s art practice.[102] Lindsay's venture had by then extended to commissioning Bernard Cohen to paint a safety curtain and Bridget Riley to design a logo based on one of her own (untitled) paintings.[103] In contrast with the sort of views expressed by Fried, it is clear that Russell saw the theatre as part of a wider British culture from which painting had hitherto been 'outlawed', and that engagement with it would elevate the status of the painters and give them the opportunity of reaching a wider public. This attitude may explain his desire to find theatrical parallels for Riley's work. Riley herself seems to have welcomed the opportunity to explore the dramatic possibilities of her work, developing light projections for a special performance of T.S. Eliot's *Sweeney Agonistes* (1932) in June 1965.[104] Eliot's combination of modernist poetry with theatre in *Sweeney* represented an attempt to create a modernist parallel with the poetry of Shakespeare's plays and it affirms the validity of theatre within modernism. In becoming involved with this, Riley was affirming the place of her work in a broad modernist context.

Riley was to say of her own work, in 1965: 'I want the disturbance or "event" to arise naturally ... I also want it to have a quality of inevitability'.[105] For art critic David Sylvester, as for John Russell, 'theatricality' was not a negative association for painting. Sylvester anticipated Riley's remark in an earlier review, where he described parallels between Riley's painting and the experience of watching good acting. Referring to two unnamed paintings in Riley's 'unusually good' first show at Gallery One[106] in 1962, he wrote:

Both paintings, then, present a regular design that is in some way disturbed. The disturbing element is not only imaginative in conception but has the sort of rightness in its placing that a good actor has in his timing – it seems at once unexpected and inevitable. This proposing and disposing of order seems no mere game with optical effects, seems to symbolise, dramatically, an interplay between feelings of composure and anxiety.[107]

This notion of 'interplay between feelings of composure and anxiety' seems more restrained than Russell's 'moment ... at which a powerful nature is forced almost to disintegration point by pressures outward or inward (or both)'.[108] Both comments suggest the notion of dynamic inner conflict, however, a preoccupation that recurred in the writings of critics, artists and other commentators in this period. With the Happening, artists sought to dramatize art itself, often violently, and to do so in any place they chose. The Happening took action painting off the canvas and on to the street. Bridget Riley's work pulled the Happening back towards the canvas but, while the paint creating this 'Happening' was placed on the surface of the canvas, the visual impression created could not be so securely located. When confronting one of Riley's paintings, the 'spectator' could not avoid a sense of participation in the work caused by the physicality of the experience. He or she became an actor in a script determined by the artist and his or her own nervous and visual systems, unable to opt out of the 'event' so created (at least, for as long as the confrontation between spectator and painting lasted). Riley's paintings might be described as 'Happenings on canvas' but for a spectator in the 1960s the 'events' they expressed seem to have been experienced as Happenings within the body itself – perhaps the most intimate form of 'audience participation' produced in a period where such participation was so greatly valued.

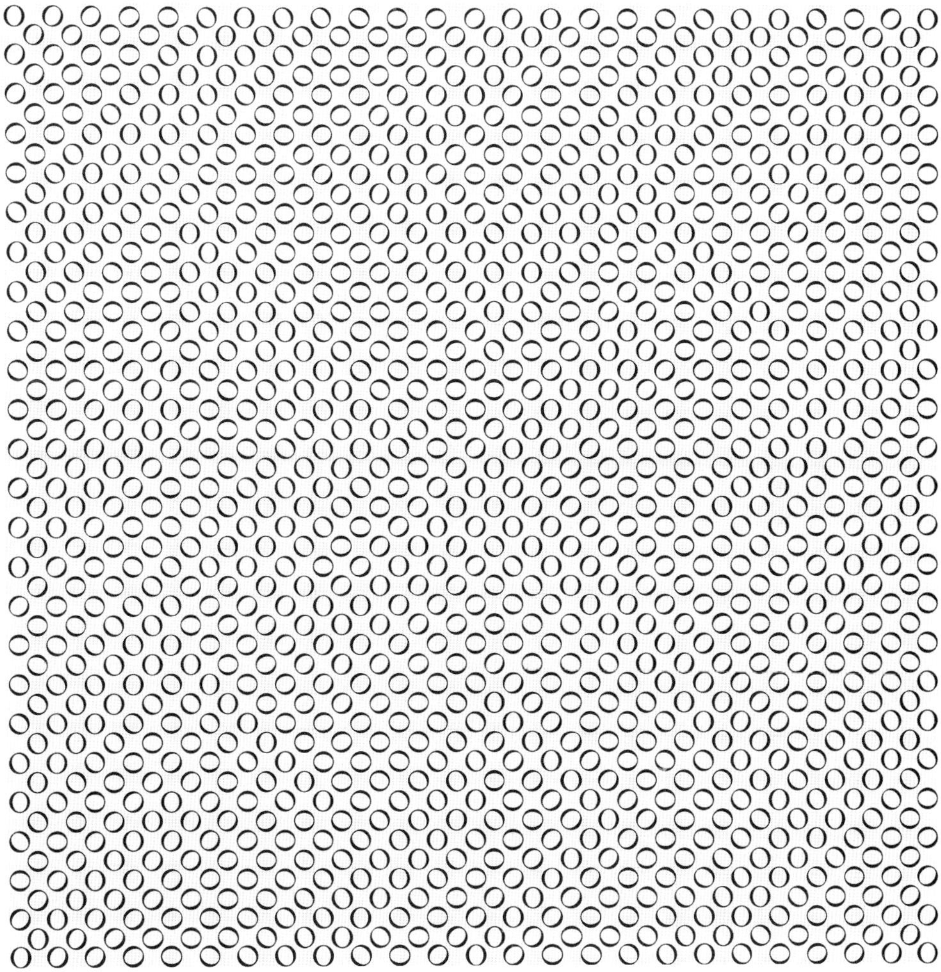

24. **Disturbance** 1964

Chapter 6 'Every Epoch Dreams the One that Follows It'

Op and the Commodification of the Future

Although there were frequent descriptions in the press of uncomfortable physical effects caused by viewing Op paintings, images copied or derived from them were widely used for the decoration of mass-produced goods: fashionable commodities for the adornment of body or home. This seems paradoxical, especially as, at the time, such commercialization of fine art was a new phenomenon, albeit presaging a future where every public art exhibition would have its T-shirts and souvenirs:

> *Fashion and graphic designers extracted the eye-fooling devices and adapted them to fit every sort of ephemeral product ... in no other case had a fine art innovation been so quickly appropriated as a marker of novelty in mass-produced merchandise.*[1]

This deluge of merchandise accompanied MoMA's 'The Responsive Eye' show in 1965, and the contemporary press was quick to seize upon this unprecedented occurrence. In May that year, a month after 'The Responsive Eye' had closed, the *Financial Times*' art critic Mario Amaya commented on the wide variety of consumer goods in 'Op' designs still being sold in New York: 'everything from evening gowns and wall paper to Holy Bibles were being designed in Op and the craze is still in full swing'.[2] Amaya implied that for fashions to last as long as a couple of months in New York was itself something of a phenomenon. By June 1965, Op fashions had also reached Britain, where the *Daily Mail* informed its readers that 'the fashion trade' was 'tottering on the brink of what looks like being a real "Op" art beano'.[3] In 1969, looking back on the summer of 1965, Christopher Booker wrote:

> *The 'Op Art Look' was the craze of the summer, having spread in barely a year from avant-garde paintings on the walls of Mayfair art galleries to hats, handbags, furniture, wallpaper and even make-up.*[4]

The Op 'craze' attracted international attention and controversy. As I shall explore in this chapter, both fashion itself and the commodities that gave it form were denigrated in modernist orthodoxy as expressions of mass culture, which was seen as trivial and transient: the antithesis of modernism. At the same time, I argue that the underlying reasons for the adoption of Op-derived patterns in mass-produced goods were connected with concerns about the future of society that were far from trivial. This was not apparent in 1965, however, and in July of that year Lil Picard expressed her reservations in a piece which suggests that the popularity of 'Op' fashions had not abated since Amaya's report in May.

> *It is obvious that the optical fashion is maybe very good for fashion, but does not help Art. Op lends itself better than other styles in Art to be exploited commercially. New York's window displays, magazine-covers, fashion shows feature Op-Designs, dots, triangles, squares, stripes are everywhere, on tableware, wallpapers, rugs, evening gowns, sweaters, paper baskets, ties.*[5]

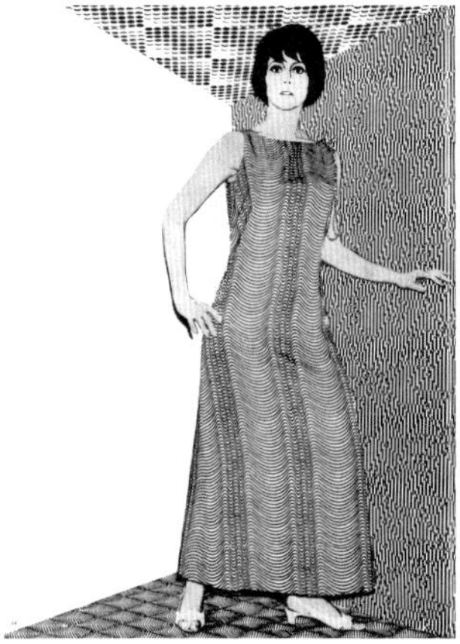

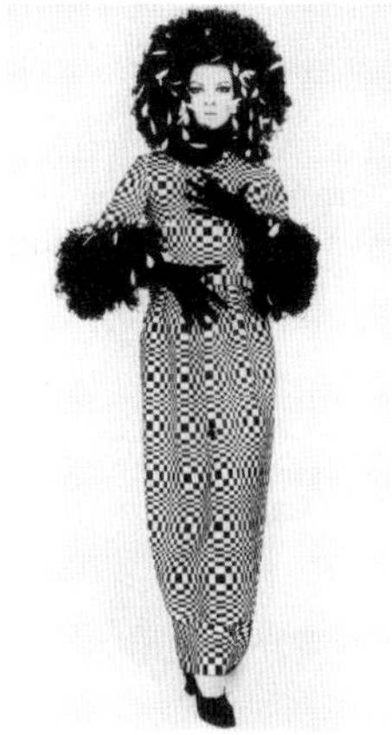

The use of Op-derived patterns in fashion was international.

25. Cover illustration, *Vogue Australia*, October 1965

26. Evening ensemble, Capucci winter collection, Paris 1965

Picard did not explain how Op invited commercial exploitation but the 'dots, triangles, squares, stripes' were easy to copy and the repetitive use of such devices in much Op was suitable for the mass-production of goods such as fabric and wallpaper. The use of black and white, rather than colour, in Riley's work – the most widely known examples of Op art – reduced the cost of such processes. All newspaper and much magazine photography was in monochrome so black-and-white items were well-suited to publicity in these media. Even the lack of specially printed fabrics did not necessarily prevent the enterprising manufacturer or home sewer from producing 'Op' dresses: 'Until more fabrics come through – and they are on the way – most manufacturers are confined to using solid chunks of colour cut into geometric shapes. But the influence is there all right'.[6]

Picard's claim that it was 'obvious' that Op-inspired designs were 'very good' for fashion was hindsight. She saw a multitude of commodities around her, all apparently selling well, even though the press reception of Op art had been marked with much comment on its rebarbative qualities.[7] Such comments, associating it with nausea and seasickness, suggest that Op art would not be an obvious design source for items intimately associated with both the domestic interior and the body: wallpapers, clothing and tableware. The prevalence of Op-inspired consumer goods cannot be easily dismissed as 'obvious' and repays investigation. As we shall see, the popularity of Op-derived images must be seen in the context of the associations which were made between Op art, technocracy and counter-cultures – the possible futures that were variously hoped for and dreaded by different elements of Western societies – and with the international prominence of Bridget Riley herself.

The spell of the commodity

The widespread appropriation of her paintings by designers of consumer goods was strongly resisted by Bridget Riley as trivializing her work. As the commodities exploiting Op-like images proliferated, concern also grew among those art critics who supported Op art.

> *The methods how* [sic] *this style is promoted and publicised have a resemblance to Seventh Avenue campaigns (the garment industry) and to Hollywood (Movie Industry). Press agents are hired, publicity girls step in, the whole slick, sickening industry is at work to start a trend and kill the artists. The gang of promoters who, as they say, have been the killers of Marilyn Monroe, are at work, this time in the visual arts.*[8] [Capitalization original.]

In this highly dramatic passage, Picard described sinister forces at work in the New York art world, apparently plotting to destroy Op's status as art. She suggests that deliberate efforts to popularize Op as a design source involved equally deliberate attempts 'to kill the artists': to destroy them *as* artists. Picard feminized both the killers and the victims in this passage: publicity 'girls' had stepped in to deal with the artists as they allegedly had with Monroe. Op as art and Op as design could not co-exist: the artists responsible for Op were being denied their status as artists by those creating the trend for consumer goods. In equating these artists with Marilyn Monroe, Picard suggested that, like the film star, they had acquired a glamorous stardom for which a high payment must be exacted. She saw both as helpless victims of a 'sickening machine,' from which they were unable to protect themselves and which, having set them up, would go on to destroy them. Monroe was easily depicted as a 'victim', as she was by film critic Alexander Walker:

> *On none are the grandeur and servitude of stardom visited more brutally than on the sex symbols ... The very way in which sex symbols are publicised brings out the latent sadism of a film studio more cruelly than the promotion of any other rank or quality of artist.*[9]

There are parallels here with Walter Benjamin's concept that each person or object possesses a unique perceptual 'aura', which is not present in photographic representations. Benjamin argued that the film actor's aura is replaced by 'the cult of the movie star, fostered by the money of the film industry [which] preserves not the unique aura of the person but "the spell of the personality", the phoney spell of a commodity' – in other words, tradable goods.[10] The unique (and unsaleable) individuality of the actor is replaced by the commercial viability of the commodity, the 'star'. The star is as much Hollywood's product as films. Likewise, photographs of art objects lacked the aura of the original and hence weakened the 'cult value' or 'magic' properties that Benjamin presumed art to have had in the past. Instead 'in photography, exhibition value begins to displace cult value'[11] and, as John Berger later put it, 'the uniqueness of the original now lies in it being the original of a reproduction'.[12]

The sheer quantity of reproductions of Op images – as prints and reproductions in books or magazines, and on domestic and clothing items – presented a particular threat to the 'aura' of such works. To replace this threatened aura, the methods of Hollywood were employed, one infers from Picard, to create Benjamin's 'phoney spell of a commodity'. As with Hollywood, where the stars and the films are both products – products intimately interlinked, where image and reality are difficult to tell apart – so in New York in 1965, Picard believed that the artists were being commodified – turned into products – along with their art. Both Picard and Walker, in different contexts, saw this process as 'cruel', even 'sadistic' – to the point of murder in Picard's case. Riley described her own 'feelings of violation and disillusionment', in *Art News* that autumn, although she was also aware that there was a serious and supportive audience for her work.[13]

There is an inherent contradiction here, as with the sex symbol, in that the mechanism set up to promote the popularity of the actress/artist as uniquely favoured, can only do so by attacking and eroding that very uniqueness. The image of what is supposedly unique, or at least rare, whether the charms of the actress or the products of artistic genius, becomes ubiquitous and available not only everywhere, but at low cost. Hence the accusations of servitude and cruelty in Hollywood and Picard's of murder; for without the aura of unique genius, the modernist painter's position *as* an artist might have been threatened, at the least. The 'conspiracy' theories concerning Monroe's death were extended here into a general view of fame and its consequences in any field. Stardom was depicted as a passive, manipulable and defenceless state, reflecting notions of the feminine, particularly those promoted by Hollywood. The commodification of Op was accompanied by an intense interest in its leading exponent, Bridget Riley, who was treated as the star of the movement by reporters who were more used to writing about female film stars than female artists. Yet Picard alluded only briefly to Riley herself: 'the optical star, the girl of the month' – suggesting *Playboy* magazine's 'Playmate of the month' and hardly enhancing the status of 'artist' that Picard seemed anxious to protect. She concentrated on reporting the views of William Seitz and the work of male artists such as Poons, Anuskiewicz, Vasarely and Albers. Her description of such established male artists as passive victims on a par with perceptions of Monroe is difficult to explain unless Op itself was 'feminizing' the men who created much of it. As we shall see, there are connections between mass culture and femininity that are relevant to the commodification of Op art. Just as critics such as Hess regarded the viewer of an Op work as a passive spectator, whose psychological and physiological reactions were determined solely by the work itself, so one might infer from Picard that the artist was in the same position, helpless to resist the power of his own creation. Once reduced to this state, the artist was apparently no match for 'press agents and publicity girls'.

Later in the same article, Picard implied that the 'sickening machine' had penetrated New York's downtown galleries where 'imitations of Optical art' were apparently already dead, being 'as lifeless and artificial as a Woolworth's gadget'. In this context one must ask what constituted 'life' for an Op painting; was it the ability to turn the viewer/painter into its helpless victim?[14] Picard did not indicate how else the viewer might distinguish between a 'real' Op painting and an 'imitation'. A concern with authenticity is central to this passage: only the 'real' Op painting can have life – a life that may be equated with Benjamin's concept of the aura.

Benjamin's analysis does not recognize another aspect of the commercialization of the art market, but can be extended to include it: the process *Burlington Magazine*'s critic Jerrold Lanes described as 'bandwagonism'.[15]

For Picard, the authenticity, the aura, of Op was doubly threatened, once by the 'mechanical' reproduction of Op paintings on dress fabrics and the like, and again by inferior artists who created paintings for purely commercial purposes. In both cases, Op's identity as art was overshadowed by an identity as a commodity. Riley was conscious that this 'alienated a section of the art-world' so that people 'could no longer see what was actually on the wall'.[16]

Fashion and abjection

Picard's article reinforces the view that Op art itself had become highly commercialized, independently of consumer goods 'spin offs'. As Jerrold Lanes put it: ' the publicity has been revolting, even for New York'.[17] The language used to criticize the promotion of Op – 'sickening', 'revolting' – seems calculated to out-do the criticisms of Op itself as physically distressing. The use of such language further sensationalized Op art; the intention was presumably not to sicken readers enough to stop them reading. Condemnation of the publicity – to which these complaints actually contributed – was intended to attract readers. The media could be said to have gorged on Op, either unashamedly or in the guise of responsible disapprobation of the gorging of others. This was as much part of the commodification of Op as the production of Op-patterned dresses. This was an art to induce vomiting; at the same time, it was an art with which to adorn the female body.

There is an apparent contradiction here between the physically repellent and the physically attractive. In both cases, Op was presented as related very specifically to the body, rather than to the mind. An intellectual or aesthetic approach to this art was apparently precluded by both physical revulsion *and* erotic attraction. The critical controversy bound the two together: either the art itself was nausea-inducing or, even if it were not, its use to adorn the female body and domestic interior was.[18] It was as though something in Op needed to be expelled from it; its capacity to adorn the body had to be rejected, vomited forth, in order to purify Op and return it to the pristine state of true art. Nonetheless, Picard's comments above show that Op *was* regarded as suitable adornment for the body and for the domestic interior (with all its female connotations) – she presented Op as being an *obvious* choice as a source for fashion textiles, as though a certain eroticism were inherent within it.

Julia Kristeva's theorizing of the 'abject' in the development of the infant is useful here: 'the abject (including tears, saliva, faeces, urine, vomit, mucus) marks bodily sites which will later become erotogenic zones (mouth, eyes, anus, nose, genitals)'.[19] The abject is neither part-of-the-body nor not-of-the-body; it can never be done away with permanently but neither can it be accepted as part of the body. For Kristeva, the abject and the erotic go hand in hand. So it was with Op: dresses intended to enhance the wearer's attractiveness were accompanied by claims that either creating such dresses was 'sickening' or that the art itself would make one sick. For some time after the MoMA show, there were continued attempts to rid Op of negative bodily associations, but also to append these to it.[20]

Mass culture and femininity

The critics who most strongly supported Op art's status as high art were naturally those most concerned about its commercialization. *New York Times* art reviewer, John Canaday, who had a high regard for Riley's work, wrote only two weeks after the MoMA opening of his horror at the commercialism surrounding Op in general and her work in particular. He noted that Riley's show at the Feigen Gallery (contemporary with the MoMA show) was sold out before it opened, many of the paintings having been bought unseen by collectors determined to have 'a Riley'. Canaday compared a woman pleading with Riley's dealer to

> *a woman pleading with her hairdresser, and from much the same point of view. If you can't go to a really smart cocktail party without the latest hairdo, neither can you give one without a Riley on the wall.*[21]

As a woman artist, Riley may have aroused concerns that relate to the 'feminine' aspects of Op discussed above. Andreas Huyssen has explored the relationship between mass culture and modernism, suggesting that mass culture itself has been perceived as 'feminine' (seductive but lacking genuine creativity) in comparison with 'masculine' (autonomous, creative) modernism. Like masculine and feminine, modernism and mass culture are bound together but:

> *the nightmare of being devoured by mass culture through co-option, commodification, and the 'wrong' kind of success is the constant fear of the modernist artist, who tries to stake out his* [sic] *territory by fortifying the boundaries between genuine art and inauthentic mass culture ... the problem is not the desire to differentiate between forms of high art and depraved forms of mass culture and its co-options. The problem is rather the persistent gendering as feminine of that which is devalued.*[22]

Canaday's likening of the would-be Riley purchaser to a woman pleading with her hairdresser equates notions of fashionability and the feminine: here was a woman seeking to extend her own self-adornment to her apartment, thus implicitly feminizing those who bought the paintings for the 'wrong' motives. To use a painting for domestic adornment was to bring it out of the realm of masculine, modernist high culture and into that of feminine mass culture. If all mass culture is feminine, fashion is particularly so regarded:

> *fashion and clothing are therefore accorded a similar profile to that enjoyed by women, that the cultural valuation given to women and feminine values is transferred, as if by metaphor, onto fashion and clothing. That is, they are either worshipped unreasonably or dismissed as secondary. Barthes refers to this phenomenon by saying that fashion 'reproduces, on the level of clothing, the mythic situation of Women* [sic] *in Western civilisation, at once sublime and childlike'.*[23]

While clearly admiring Riley as an artist, Canaday deplored the 'personality cult' around her, which he claimed distorted the public perception of her art. Perhaps the unspoken fear here was that the artist's 'mythic situation' as a woman of itself created, or at least strengthened, connections between her work and fashion. The idea of 'Woman' as a minor artist whose creation is her own, artificially adorned, body goes back at least as far as the 1860s, in the writings of Baudelaire.[24] When critics such as Canaday complained particularly of the exploitation of Riley's work for the purposes of fashion (rather than that of male artists, which was similarly exploited[25]), one suspects that it was this association that was being resisted in the arguments defending her painting as high art. I shall look more closely at the implications of Riley's position as a woman artist in the final chapter.

Art and the language of commerce

Like Riley herself, Canaday strongly objected to the use of her paintings as bases for fabric designs and the like.

> *Manufacturers of products of all kinds have been trying to give their products the Bridget Riley look, and have harassed the gallery with unwelcome offers. The most ironic proposition to date has come from the manufacturer of a headache remedy.*[26]

According to Canaday, a consequence of the heavy promotion of Op art was the neglect, by public and critics, of other kinds of art, which he claimed had become unsaleable.[27] While some of his contemporaries saw Op as part of a 'cultural renaissance' this was in fact:

> *only a high-powered adaptation of the techniques that we* [sic] *use in the sale of everything from politicians to soap ... techniques which involve not only opportunistic salesmen but the critics eager for an audience and the museums that need a big gate to survive.*[28]

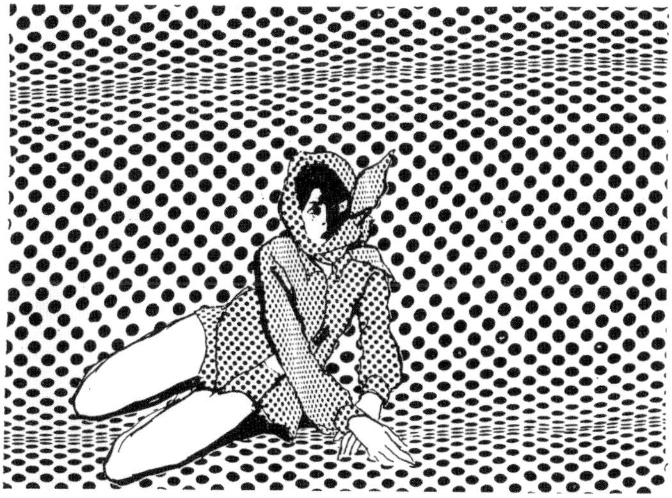

27.
Advertisement illustration, *New York Times Magazine,* as reprinted in Reyner Banham, 'Ad or Art?' *New Society,* 7 April 1966

Commercial sales methods were infiltrating areas previously considered more 'elevated' in the cultural hierarchy. If even the political process, central to a modern democracy's conception of its cultural identity, could be reduced to the level of commercial exchange, then art could hardly escape. Art was now most conspicuously patronized not by wealthy individuals but by the museums, which relied, at least partially and crucially, on that collective 'patron' of the arts, the general public, which could only be communicated to *en masse*. Commercial language had evolved for this purpose: in a culture where the same language was used to convey a sales message for soap and an electoral message from a politician, how could art avoid being affected by this language? The intensely visual nature of most mass media ensured that the language of commerce was not restricted to the written or spoken word. Images were used extensively as a commercial language and new ones were constantly required. The offer of the commodity is an offer of future satisfactions – what better images to use, therefore, than images that connoted the future? In addition, at a time when colour reproduction was still relatively expensive, paintings restricted to black and white were particularly suited to appropriation.

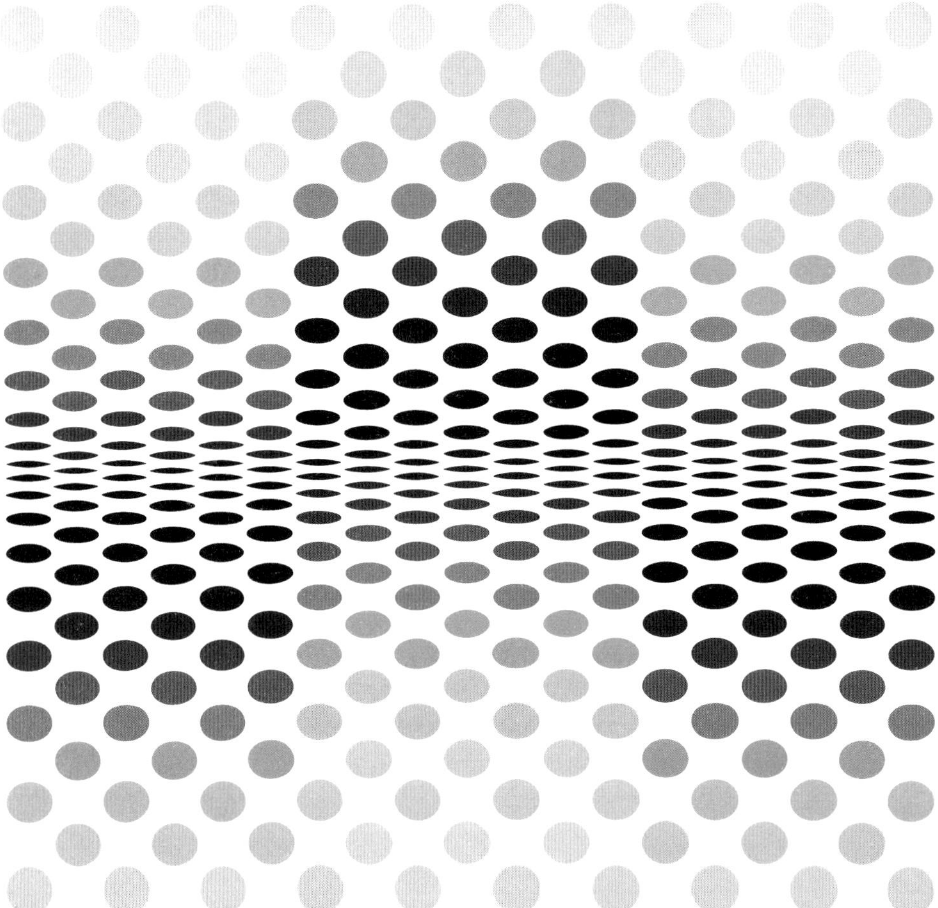

28. **Where** 1964

Against this, the many comments on the rebarbative qualities of Op would tend to militate against commercial appropriation. What might be read as an inherent mechanism of self-preservation of Op art *as* art, however, failed to protect it from commercial depredations.

Op and the spectacular society

The period in which Op art attracted the most public interest and controversy was around 1963–66. This was the period in which, in Europe, the young Guy Debord and the Situationists, a Marxist-influenced group of political and cultural theorists, were formulating the view of contemporary life that Debord was to express in *The Society of the Spectacle* (1967).[29]

> *The spectacle is the moment when the commodity has attained the 'total occupation' of social life. Not only is the relation to the commodity visible but it is all one sees: the world one sees is its world.*[30]

As Debord was arguing that contemporary society was 'the society of the spectacle', this suggests that the commodity had already attained the 'total occupation of social life' and there was no longer room for anything else except the commodity. Hence, an art which was not commodified would not be seen at all because the commodity was 'all one sees'. For Debord and the Situationists, the world of the commodity was one in which 'natural' desires were transformed into habits of consumption of commodities. Consumption had become a substitute for other relationships between people and their environment. Despite the fact that the Situationists believed that art could undermine this false relation,[31] their thesis suggests that this was impossible. The only way in which a member of the 'Society of the Spectacle' could relate to art, one could infer, was as a commodity.

Hence, for a form of art to be known to and enjoyed by a significant proportion of the population, Debord's thesis implied that such art had to be commodified. It could not be understood in any other way. 'Translation' into a commodity entailed converting it into the language of consumption, the common language of contemporary Western culture. Once commodified, art could be promoted in competition for public attention with all other commodities. It could be 'traded' as newspaper columns as well as sold in its original form or mass-reproduced as prints and on clothes and wallpaper. Although not everyone could own an Op art painting, commerce by-passed this difficulty not merely by publishing multiple reproduction prints but also by recycling the reproductions through endless permutations. The customer who had no more room on the wall for prints may have preferred a dress, a curtain or a vase. Why settle for the small size of a print when the walls themselves could be converted into one large Op image, with the appropriate wallpaper?[32] Hence the commercialization of Op art created an 'ideal' commodity – one with apparently endless permutations of form, all different yet all the same. As in the marketing technique of branding, one name could be applied to a wide variety of goods.

The attempts of artists and critics to deny and overturn the commodification of Op art can be seen as a struggle to wrest Op out of the Spectacle, to set it apart from the commercial world of the commodity and give it the role that Debord argued art should perform. Debord wanted a new society, based on creation rather than consumption, which would spring from a broadly Marxist revolution[33] and replace the commercialized world of the Spectacle of commodities, but he did not underestimate the power of the Spectacle to absorb almost any phenomenon. He admitted that every form of protest could be 'recuperated' to form part of the Spectacle; in the case of Op art, the protests of artists and critics against the commodification of art became themselves material for the newspaper columns sold as entertainment to the consuming populations. Contemporary press coverage in both the fine art magazines and the arts pages of upmarket newspapers[34] indicates that art in general was becoming 'recuperated' by the commercial Spectacle. Commodities were the essence of the Spectacle: art converted into a commodity could be incorporated into the Spectacle whereas the ideal of the 'unique' art object resisted this process. To become part of the Spectacle, art had to be converted into tradable commodities: the 1960s witnessed:

> *developments in the arts* [that] *were appropriated for purely commercial ends, the unparalleled reduction of art to objects to be 'consumed' by the well-to-do (a Henry Moore statuette, an Art Nouveau ashtray, a Campbell's soup can, all equally art 'objects'), the increasing pseudo-tolerance and unshockableness that derived from the unspoken conviction that nothing could any longer seriously disrupt the pattern of business growth, technological imperialism and the professionalization of the intelligent young.*[35]

The furore over Op arose from widespread concerns about the 'commercialization' of art and other areas of cultural life. For example, in March 1963 Katherine Whitehorn wrote a column of advice for would be art-buyers, directing her comments at people 'finding themselves not so hard up as usual and wanting to buy a picture'.[36] She particularly commented on the concern of artists not to be seen as 'decorators': 'Art is not there, they sternly feel, to be easy on the eye; and many people, aware of this, feel that to buy pictures just because they like the look of them must be cheating'. Whitehorn proceeded to give advice about buying 'affordable' pictures on the Embankment and at Hampstead Heath.

Clearly, Whitehorn was presenting art as a commodity, with the reader being reassured that this was a very commendable way to spend spare cash. The couple who were 'not so hard up as usual' had bought all the necessary utilitarian consumer goods for the home and so could move on to purely 'decorative' items. Paintings here assumed a place as furnishings, alongside decorative upholstery, wallpaper, carpets and ornaments. The physically disturbing qualities claimed for Op might have seemed likely to reduce its chances of being treated in this way; instead, Op not only took its place among the decorative items in the home, it became part of them and then extended this decorative function on to the bodies (clothing) of men and, more frequently, women. I suggest we can explain this phenomenon by considering Op's associations with contemporary notions of modernity and concerns about the future of society.

The pursuit of a projected future

Dreaming of the future

Riley's work can be related to important concerns of its time: the increasing penetration of technology into everyday life, the apparent imminence of the 'space age', the perceived emergence of new roles for women and the appearance of a 'drug culture'. These concerns were long term: they were engendered by hopes and anxieties about the future of Western societies. Politicians were stressing science/technology as a central part of their political programmes, both in Britain and the USA. The film industry was producing science fiction films rather more concerned with possible futures for mankind than the 'monsters from outer space' yarns that had characterized the genre in previous decades.[37] Films of H.G. Wells' *The Time Machine* (USA) and John Wyndham's *The Midwich Cuckoos* (UK) both appeared in 1960 and by 1964 Science Fiction films, including Kubrick's bleakly comic *Dr Strangelove*, were being made in a number of countries.[38] 'Futuristic' gadgetry was extensively used in the commercially successful James Bond films, starting with *Dr No* in 1960.[39] Meanwhile, in real life Britain, gadgets that would have seemed futuristic only a few years before were proliferating: the future was already happening, in the kitchen and sitting room.

That concerns with this projected future should find expression in the choice of decorative consumer goods to adorn the body and the home arises from the nature of consumer society itself. This process has deep historical roots.[40] Religious and social changes in the seventeenth and eighteenth centuries opened the way for modern consumer societies by encouraging the use of the imagination for hedonistic purposes. This modern hedonism contrasts strongly with traditional hedonism, in which pleasure was anticipated largely on the basis of what one remembered from previous pleasurable experiences:

> *'Modernity' means contingency. It points to a social order which has turned from the worship of ancestors and past authorities to the pursuit of a projected future – of goods, pleasures, freedoms, forms of control over nature, or infinities of information.*[41]

Colin Campbell has explored how, in the traditionally hedonist society, new objects and experiences tend to be treated with suspicion; by contrast, modern hedonists use imagination to explore possible sources of new pleasure. The pleasures of the unknown may be imagined to exceed old, familiar pleasures: 'daydreaming' and fantasy encourage the individual to believe that new pleasures will be better than old ones. In consumer societies, there is a plethora of goods on which such daydreams can focus; when the desired object is obtained, however, it is unlikely to 'live up to' the daydream so a degree of dissatisfaction is inevitable. This encourages the individual to direct his or her desire towards a new object and the process repeats. The pursuit of a projected future is one that cannot end. This phenomenon has been used to explain why there should be a fashion process or system, which emerged in Western cultures in the fourteenth century.[42] Daydreaming as we understand it may have evolved when this fashion process was well underway:

> *that distinctive cultural complex that was associated with the consumer revolution in eighteenth century England, and which embraced the rise of the novel, romantic love and modern fashion, is related to the widespread adoption of the covert habit of daydreaming. The central insight required is the realisation that individuals do not so much seek satisfaction from products as pleasure from the self-illusory experiences which they construct from their associated meanings.*[43]

Hence, consumers seek novel goods because they anticipate that these will supply novel experiences. This constant desire for new products is thus not, basically, materialistic but actually reflects a search to fulfil a sense of longing for something that is indefinable but sensed to be necessary and attainable. The fact that no actual purchase ever proves capable of satisfying this longing leads to the constant demand for new products and, therefore, is the root of the fashion process. This raises the question of what purchasers of Op-decorated goods were really longing for; what need were they trying to satisfy with these goods? This view of the fashion process as rooted in spiritual desire is completely opposed to Walter Benjamin's conception of fashion as that which 'prostitutes the body to the inorganic world'.[44] This is fashion as an exemplification of 'sin' in which 'active sensual desire is surrendered to objects and perverted into the passive desire for new sensations'.[45] Nonetheless, Benjamin believed that in every age people fantasize an image of the future that fulfils the desires of the present: 'every epoch dreams the one that follows it'.[46]

This suggests an approach to the phenomenon of Op fashions. If the acquisition of fashionable goods, particularly those which adorn the body and create the domestic environment in which the individual lives, is seen as part of a process of trying to fulfil a longing for a desired future state, then Op-derived patterns, with their connotations of a future society which was perceived as approaching but not yet attained, would seem particularly well-suited to the purpose. In this connection, it is interesting to compare this more positive view of daydreaming, or fantasy, with that of writer Christopher Booker. Booker divided fantasies into those concerned with 'vitality' (youth, power, sex, excitement, freedom) and those concerned with 'order' (security, quality, sophistication, authority, trust). These two kinds of fantasy were intrinsically opposed: vitality fantasies depended on the idea of destruction of order and those qualities associated with it. He claimed that in the 1950s and 1960s, in various aspects of popular culture such as advertising, films (e.g. James Bond) and music (The Beatles), the 'vitality fantasy' predominated.

> *Whatever form of vitality fantasy we choose to consider, ... the essence of the sensations on which it feeds is that they are, in some way, violations of order or the image of order ... It may be a violation of the aesthetic order: providing visual thrills derived from unusually angled photographs, speeded up or slow motion film, the visual tricks and unnatural juxtapositions of Surrealism, the optical illusions of Op art ...*[47]

Here, Op art is linked with the notion of the 'vitality' fantasy. While Booker's view of this appears to be largely negative, a more positive reading may, of course, be easily constructed, with destruction itself taking on a positive role if connected with ideas of destroying the evils, weaknesses or discomforts of earlier periods. I now turn to three areas relating to Op's credentials as a 'futuristic' art form and the ways in which they related to its use by designers.

Op, the space age and fashion

I have argued that Op's relationship to notions of science and the technocracy went deeper than the hotly disputed matter of whether the paintings had a basis in optical science or a 'scientific' mode of production. Claims that Bridget Riley's work was based on optical research were so widespread that, as we have seen, in October 1965 she published a detailed refutation in the American magazine *Art News*. There were, however, more subtle connections perceived between Op art and a technologically dominated society. John Canaday's views, for instance, exemplified the ways in which Op could be presented as a product of a science-based, 'space-age' society. Lil Picard also connected Op with the creations of contemporary technology.

> *The works are cool, esthetically pleasing, immaculate and visually brilliant and dazzling as Times Square by night or as fascinating as the perfectly designed business buildings on Park Avenue, of glass and steel, where also optically colorful happenings occur with reflexions of light in the metal, when one passes by car and watches the visual effects of refractions on flat surfaces of buildings.*[48]

Times Square, of course, was rendered dazzling by illuminated advertising hoardings, symbols of the commodity in a particularly 'Spectacular' form. Benjamin wrote that 'the advertisement is the cunning with which the dream imposed itself upon industry'[49] and there is a certain dream-like quality in Picard's description of the scene. Op here was presented not so much a commodity in itself as a reflection of the all-pervasive presence of commodities in American society. Her imagery was specifically urban, by implication relating Op to the city in a way reminiscent of earlier modernist painting, such as Mondrian's New York pictures, such as *Broadway Boogie-Woogie* (1942/43), Léger's imagery of machines and commerce and Robert Delaunay's Cubist celebrations of the Eiffel Tower as a symbol of the modern city. In the same month, Britain's *Connoisseur* magazine noted the uncomfortable physical sensations produced in some spectators by some Op art, and said of the MoMA show that:

> *the emphasis was placed undeniably on the daring young moderns who, in preparation very likely for space voyages, cause*

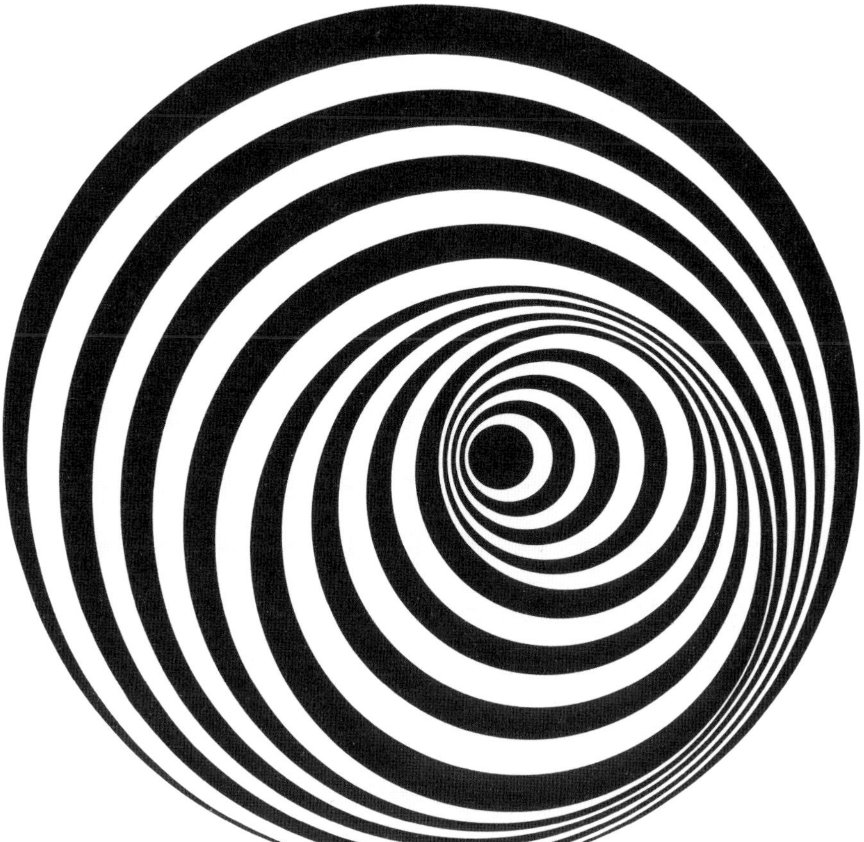

29. **Uneasy Centre** 1963

our poor heads to turn with their frantic gyrations and distortions. (According to this advance test, very few of us will qualify for the capsule to Mars or Venus ...).[50]

Such references particularly related Op to the notion of a coming space age, whose accoutrements characterized contemporary life. Like others, *Connoisseur* connected Op with physical discomfort but recast this as a reference to the rigorous training of would-be astronauts. Through the disciplined subjection of the body to regimes that would induce nausea in weaker mortals, the bodies of the astronauts could be tempered and prepared for the ordeal of space travel, an ordeal that would confine them physically even as it liberated them from the ties of Earth. Op would give everyone a taste of the physical 'punishment' *and* the elation, the sense of 'living in the future' of space travel. Notions of extreme physical discomfort were connected at this time with both space travel and Op art.

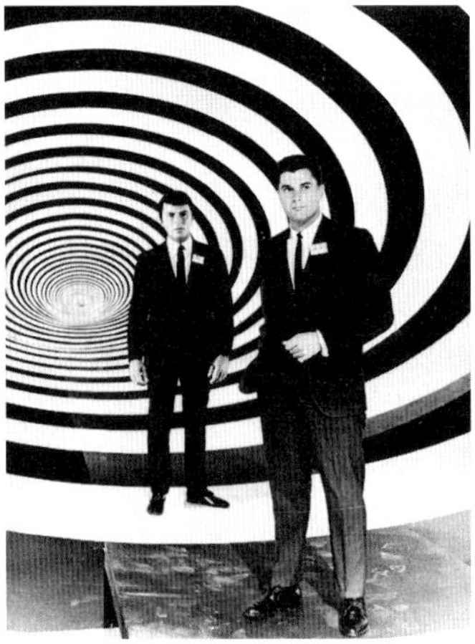

30.
'The Time Tunnel', series shown on BBC Television, 1968

The television series 'The Time Tunnel' (1968) concerned the most futuristic form of travel of all – time travel. In the set design, the entrance to the eponymous tunnel featured pulsating concentric ovals. The protagonists of the television series had to enter the time tunnel [Fig. 30] in order to reach other time periods, past and future. The tunnel thus disrupted the structure of space-time and this disruption was symbolized by the pulsating image representing its entrance. To enter the time tunnel was to enter an unknown and physically threatening place.

Fashion designers were as fascinated by a vision of the 'space age' future as the art critics. If Op art were associated with notions of the future, we might expect to find its influence in contemporary clothing. In the 1960s young Parisian designers were producing:

revolutionary clothing using technologically advanced fabrics and strident geometrical designs that simultaneously suggested the retro-chic of the twenties and the futuristic connotations of space age discovery.[51]

Trousers and tunics created a 'unisex' look reflecting women's appropriation of previously 'masculine' areas of activity beyond the home. In 1964, Courrèges' Spring Collection was dubbed the 'Space Age' collection by an enthusiastic press and he later named his mass-market ready-to-wear line 'Couture Future'. Cardin named one of his outfits from his 1966 collection 'Cosmos'. Designers such as Courrèges and Cardin designed straight-legged trouser suits with streamlined jackets whose structured silhouettes were made possible by relatively thick and rigid materials such as gabardine. Plastics, used in Courrèges' designs, created what design historian Penny Sparke has called 'a robot-like image' and 'his spaceman look'.[52] Such clothes were physically restrictive so there was a tension between their streamlined appearance and their actuality, where movement might in fact be hampered. As Sparke noted, these clothes evoked the new heroic figure of the astronaut, a figure at once cumbersome, in his massive, rigid space suit, and weightless, floating effortlessly beyond the pull of Earth's gravity.

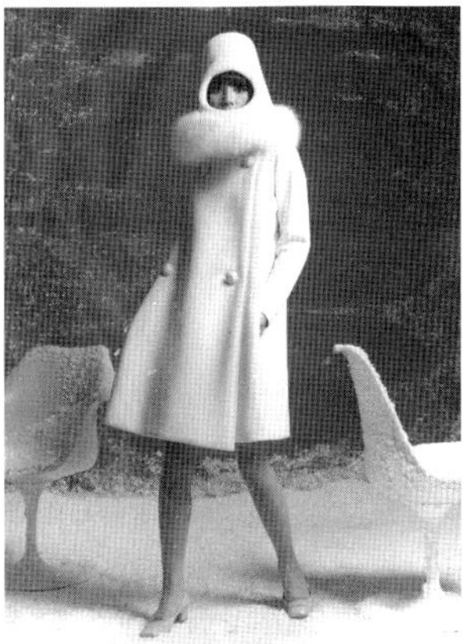

31.
Cardin 'space age' coat and hat, 1966

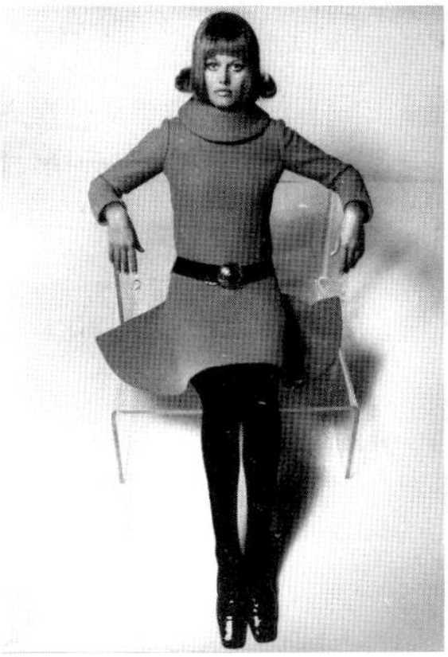

32.
Cardin dress, 1969

The clothes of Courrèges and Cardin could evoke the rigidity of the space suit but not the notion of weightlessness and physical freedom, despite the 'liberated' connotations of short skirts and trousers. These clothes tended to project a severe image of the future of women's fashion, with their simple, fairly rigid shapes and fabrics. In comparison with the often full-skirted and overtly 'feminine' 1950s styles, the so-called unisex look was a 'masculinized' style producing a very different silhouette for the female body. In contrast, the highly patterned Op-based fabric designs that began to appear in substantial numbers in 1965 and 1966[53] offered an alternative way for women to dress in a manner that reflected the space age without resorting to a 'space suit'. They allowed women to wear highly patterned fabrics – with the feminine connotations of such pronounced decorative effects – and to retain the ease of movement of more fluid fabrics, while still asserting their own right to a stake in the future [Figs. 25, 26, 35]. At the same time, manufacturers and retailers were apparently ready to attach the 'Op' tag to any spotted or striped fabric, as if milking a successful brand.

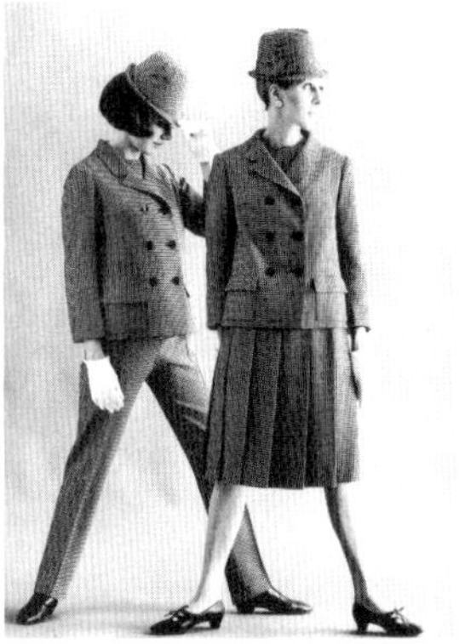

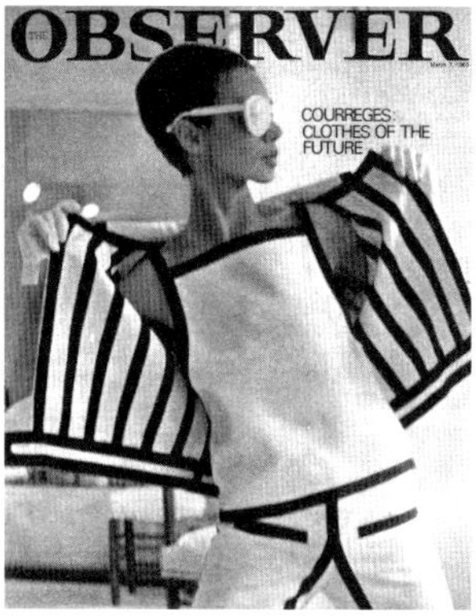

33.
Trousersuit and skirt suit by Hardy Amies, Autumn/Winter 1964 Hats adapted from men's styles

34.
Courrèges, 'futuristic' women's clothing, cover, *The Observer* magazine, 1965

In New York there was extensive press comment on the Op-inspired clothes worn by women attending the opening night of 'The Responsive Eye' show. *Time* magazine's reviewer found the art at the show upstaged by the apparel of these visitors. The language used is revealing and the passage is worth quoting at some length.

> *Gisela Oster gave* [her Op artist husband Gerald] *some dazzling competition with a turquoise and white striped long dress but Sculptor Marilyn Karp outstriped* [sic] *her by running her black and white stripes from dress to stockings to shoes. Painter Jane Wilson was completely optical in a sleek hooded sheath of white organdy, delightfully dizzy in disks of black and grey. Magazine Editor Pat Coffin wrapped herself in a giant silk stole of peristaltic black dots on a white field that was designed by Painter Bridget Riley ... Teacher-Painter Ruth Anne Fredenthal sported a polychrome print that showed Designer Emilio Pucci to be quite an Operator after all.*
>
> *Op outfitted ladies showed a tendency to linger near the pictures that best harmonized with their clothes. Collector*

Barbara Jakobson flitted among the black and white opticals, seeming to appear and disappear in a skin-tight jumpsuit with ostrich feather cuffs under a 'cage' of black chiffon, latticed with black velvet. Another black and white effect, frequently mistaken for a painting when it was standing still, was the calfskin coat by Furrier Jacques Kaplan, stenciled by Op painter Richard Anuskiewicz in a dotty pattern that focused disturbingly on Mrs Lee Lombard's pretty kidneys.[54]

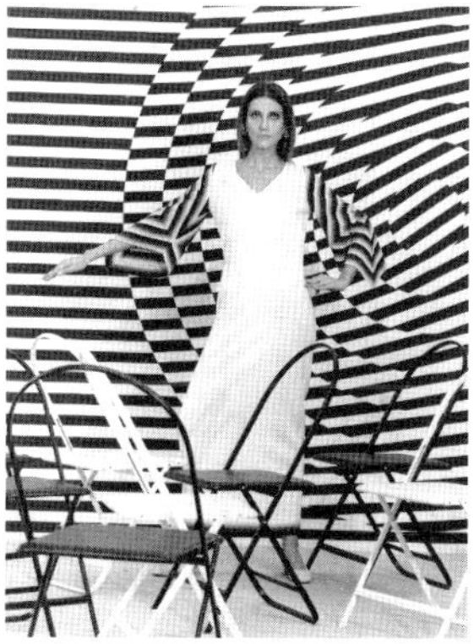

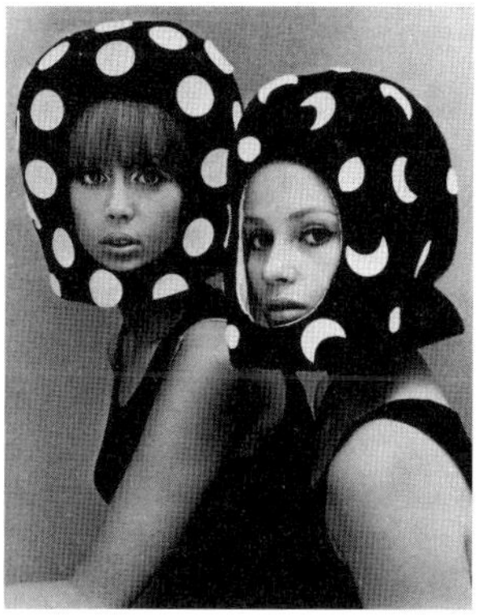

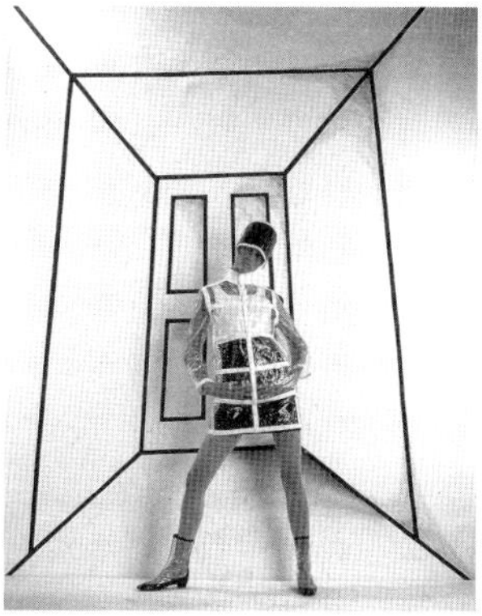

35. Op-sleeved dress by Italian couturier, 1966

36. Patti Boyd and Celia Hammond in felt helmets by Edward Mann, 1965

37. Young Jaeger PVC mini dress, 1966

Here, the reader was left to infer the appearance of the paintings from that of the clothes. There was no mention of the claims that Op induced unpleasant effects. The implications were the usual ones for fashion reportage: the clothes enhanced the attractiveness of the wearers (even the internal organs, rather than being associated with notions of abjection, were rendered 'pretty'). Gisela Oster's clothes were not seen as enhancing her husband's prestige so much as competing with it. The Baudelairean notion of woman as an artist whose canvas is her own body emerges here, but now this minor feminine art of self-adornment was presented as eclipsing the (masculine) 'high art' on the gallery walls. On the other hand, the artist Anuskiewicz had apparently used the body of a woman, Lee Lombard, as an alternative canvas; she cannot compete with his paintings because she has become one of them. Nonetheless, it is the 'painting' on her clothing which *Time* described, not the canvases on the gallery walls.[55] In the *Guardian* 13 March 1965, Hella Pick described Bridget Riley's anger with

a New York dress designer who bought one of her paintings last year [that is, before the MoMA show] *and* [who] *a few days ago attempted with a fanfare to present her with a dress copied from the painting. She stalked out without the dress.*

This may be a reference to the American designer Morton Myles who produced dress fabrics copied from several Op artists' work, including Riley's painting *Where* [Fig. 28] and other works by Julian Stanczak, Vasarely and Anuszkiewicz.[56] In 1965, there was no general copyright protection for artists in the USA. The exploitation of art in this way was so unusual (perhaps unprecedented) that clauses forbidding it were not a usual feature of the sale contracts for paintings. Riley's opposition to this situation became so well known that when a Bill was introduced to Congress to grant copyright to artists it became known as 'Bridget's Bill'.[57] Nonetheless, not everyone whom one would have expected to support Riley in this respect did so. Recalling the MoMA opening in an interview with Andrew Graham-Dixon in 1992, Riley said:

> *It was astonishing, about half the people there were wearing clothes based on my paintings and I tried to avoid having to talk to the people who were most completely covered in 'me'. There was one member of the MoMA council who was so furious that he said 'So, you don't like it? We'll have you on the back of every matchbox in Japan!'*

Graham-Dixon replied

> *that seems to suggest there was a kind of vengefulness involved in it anyway, that it was a form of not taking you seriously, it was almost like a protest against your art?*[58]

This presents the curious situation where MoMA, a key institution of American modernism, apparently encouraged the commercial exploitation of a type of art it was itself promoting. Both the artist and the person she quotes conflate the work of art with its creator: publicity for one (good or bad) is publicity for the other. This again carries suggestions of the Hollywood star system that so concerned Picard, where film/role/'star' are marketed together as a package whose parts cannot be separated. At any rate, Riley's allegation, together with *Time*'s allusion to Anuskiewicz's supposed dress-designing effort, suggests that there was considerable ambivalence, even at the heart of the New York art establishment, about the use of Op paintings as a basis for the design of consumer goods.

Op-position to technocracy

The widespread use of Op art imagery in textiles and consumer goods in the mid 1960s can be seen as part of the desire to reach out towards the space age and embrace the perceived advantages of the technological era. Misgivings about the new 'technocracy' gave rise to 'the counter-culture' and the 'Hippy movement', with their associated use of hallucinogenic drugs, as discussed in Chapter 2. Because of its perceived connections with psychotropic drugs, Op-based imagery could also be associated with counter-cultural movements that opposed the hegemony of science. Associations between Op and the perceived youthful rebellion of the 'drug culture' may have enhanced the credentials of Op-inspired consumer goods as chic, modern and 'cool'.[59] The counter-culture was, in its way, just as futuristic in its orientation as the technocracy. Where the latter promised the excitement and pleasures of the coming space age, the former advocated a future society where subjective experience would be valued. Op art, associated with strong psycho-physical reactions, was an attractive art form for those whose philosophy emphasized the importance of individual subjective experience. From early in the twentieth century, abstract art had been associated (by artists such as Kandinsky and Mondrian) with various notions of spirituality, so Op's status as abstract art also fitted it for a role as an art of a counter-culture in this respect.

We have, then, the situation where one kind of art could be seen as both expressing the new technologically dominated era and heralding its future progress on the one hand, and on the other rebelling against this apparently irresistible progress by evoking one of the most publicly visible and contentious tools of a nascent 'counter-culture', the use of psychotropic drugs. The Op-inspired dresses, carpets, wallpapers and ceramics of the mid-sixties suggest a vision of the future where 'space age' and 'counter-culture' co-exist even as they subvert each other.

Women and notions of the future

In the 1960s, the women's movement was gaining momentum, encouraging debate on possible roles for women.[60] Social categories that had previously been considered predominantly, perhaps even essentially, male – the artist and the scientist – were being penetrated by women to an unprecedented degree while, simultaneously, post-war consumerist ideology tended to emphasize women's domestic role.[61] For art, associations with fashionable consumer goods might invite corresponding associations with notions of ephemeral materialism *and* with the still-subordinate category of the feminine. For Op imagery to be used on a woman's dress doubly challenged the status of Op as art: it associated the art with notions of the ephemeral and the commercial, which were inseparable from the idea of 'fashion', *and* with the notion of feminine triviality and domesticity incompatible with the serious, public (masculine) realm of high art. The distress of artists such as Riley and Jeffrey Steele at finding their paintings reproduced on dresses and window displays can be seen as a reaction to this double downgrading of their work. By 1966, Riley had achieved public recognition of her status as an artist comparable with that enjoyed by Rachel Whiteread or Damien Hirst in the 1990s. Whereas previously women had been perceived as having a minor role in art production, in Op a woman artist had a prominent public profile. This suggests another possible aspect to the wearing of Op dresses: women who wore these clothes were displaying on their bodies a form of art whose associations included the idea of woman as artist.

With the Op dress and Op wallpaper, both art and science might have been brought symbolically within the domestic sphere. A small number of women were moving into the public realms of art and science practice, suggesting a future in which women would play a more prominent public role. At the same time, a far larger number of women were able to display their own claim to this future by wearing and using personal and domestic items adorned with traces of the art that simultaneously evoked the previously masculine-dominated domains of *both* art and science. In 1965, it was argued that Op was subverted by commercial exploitation; from another perspective, it can be argued that the more potentially subversive aspects of Op found expression on the bodies and in the homes of women who sought to stake a claim to the future in their daily lives.

Chapter **7**

The Hermaphrodite and the Gorilla

The Gendering of (Riley's) Op

> *Set to imagine the woman who could conceive and carry out these paintings, we might well picture to ourselves a barrel-bodied paragon of determination, a tenacious and fifty-ish she-gorilla given to judo and the solution in secret of championship-level chess problems.*[1]
>
> John Russell, 1965

> *The indefatigable Bridget Riley was represented by another set of her ingenuous black and white eye-irritants of which* Crest *is a perfect example. It's now all too clear that she can go on changing the pattern of her heaving and twitching geometry until she's a very old lady, but probably her only chance of developing as a painter is to drop her 'cruel' formula, which obviously gives her some sort of neurotic pleasure, and take a longer look at the black and white work of Vasarely. Otherwise, she'll have to be written off as an eccentric.*[2]
>
> Robert Melville, June 1964

Reviews of Riley's work in the early 1960s seldom suggest that her being an artist was exceptional for a woman. Her work was not characterized as being inevitably 'feminine' on the one hand, nor was it considered unexpectedly 'masculine' on the other. Yet as can be seen from the comments quoted above, gendered allusions were certainly present, although very different from those applied to Georgia O'Keeffe's work a generation earlier, which critics had said could only be created by a woman.[3] Few comments on Riley made such heavy weather of this issue as these quotations might suggest, and many reviews discussed her work in the same terms that would be used for work by a man. Nonetheless, the above quotations, from two critics associated with the 'serious' press,[4] suggest that despite any appearances to the contrary, Riley's sex was an issue. Hence we must ask what it meant, in the early 1960s, to be a professionally successful artist who was also a woman, and in particular, a woman creating Op paintings. In these quotations, both Melville and Russell were concerned with Riley's persona as an artist, rather than with her work. Here, the latter seems relevant only in so far as it enabled a picture of the artist – middle-aged she-gorilla or near-hopeless neurotic – to be drawn. One must ask if such texts would ever have been written about a man, however antipathetic the critic. Russell's words are taken from a passage that is, in fact, supportive of Riley's work. Russell's implication is that we could picture a young (and feminine) woman producing some types of paintings, but not *these* paintings. The paintings, so often represented as 'aggressive' and 'ruthless', did not, Russell implied, *appear* to be the work of a woman whom he suggested was small and delicate: 'Physically ... [she] looks as if one could pick her up with the nearest pair of tongs', as he went on to say in this article.

Melville's comments, by contrast, immediately convey an image of neither mental nor physical robustness. He presented Riley as eccentric: a neurotic woman who could only improve her art (and by implication preserve her own sanity) by studying and emulating a man artist. Vasarely's Op art was not 'cruel' but hers was – although the quote marks here suggest that this cruelty was the assessment of others, an overstatement of the effect of works that Melville could dismiss as 'eye-irritants'. The description of Riley's paintings as 'her heaving and twitching geometry' seems calculated to suggest the neurosis and instability – even hysteria – of the artist. She was not painting in order to sell her paintings in a competitive art market, nor to engage in an active visual dialogue with her contemporaries and predecessors, as expected of a modernist artist, but only (and 'obviously') for her own 'neurotic pleasure'. Melville, considering where Riley's artistic practice would lead her, portrayed 'a very old lady', neurotic, eccentric, still painting pictures identical to those of her youth. There was only one escape from this fate – she needed to learn from a man who was working in the same field but doing it so much better. Riley was here given the choice of apprenticing herself to the man or being 'written off as an eccentric'. Melville did not equate the 'cruelty' of Riley's paintings with aggression (as other critics had done and as was implied in the Russell text) but with neurosis. Both these terms are gendered: aggression being 'masculine' and directed outwards, and neuroticism 'feminine' and directed inwards. Melville chose an image that suggests frailty rather than power: a neurotic old woman in the making. Even though Melville did not openly belittle Riley's work purely on the grounds that its creator was a woman, he did this more mordantly by association and by unfavourable comparison with a man, whose work was presented as an ideal from which the aspiring woman could learn. While he implied that he was not 'writing off' Riley quite yet (she could still redeem herself by sitting at the feet of the master), the passage suggests that such elimination was not far away.

Griselda Pollock has argued that 'art is often a debate in disguised form about gender'.[5] Riley herself engaged in this debate in 1973 when she wrote:

> *It has long been established that both male and female psychological patterns are present in all of us ... the richer the personality, the more harmoniously present is the duality. The artist in particular draws upon it quite naturally while working; the artist could almost, in fact, be said to be a hermaphrodite at such times.*[6]

For Riley, the hermaphrodite represented the creative resolution of what she called male and female 'polarities': she went on to argue that in biology this created a new life, while in art it resulted in artistic production. Riley's description of the artist as an hermaphrodite suggests that the gender debate is inappropriate to consideration of an artist's work. In Pollock's 'debate about gender': 'woman is the sex, the sign of gender, perpetually the particular and sexualized Other to the universal sign Man, who appears to transcend his sex to represent Humanity'.[7] Riley's argument was that all artists transcend their sex while Pollock argues that it is only those who are male who can do so and this is inscribed in language: there are categories 'artist' and 'woman artist' but no category 'man artist'.[8]

Russell seemed concerned that his readers would not accept Riley as a 'feminine' woman *and* as the creator of her own work. She was only 34 at this time – he implied that at 'fifty-ish' she would be less feminine than a younger woman, who would still capable of the most essentially feminine form of creativity: producing babies. On the other hand, although Riley had stressed[9] that she did not use complex mathematics to create her paintings, Russell suggested this with his reference to the mathematical game of chess.[10] Chess is rational, cerebral yet highly competitive, and in this respect also resembles avant-garde art practice.[11] As we saw in Chapter 1, Jonathan Miller once described Riley's work as painting 'by dint of ruthless mathematical calculation', a procedure that seems rather more applicable to chess.[12] Associations between women and chess may still appear inappropriate: the British Chess Federation still has a 'British champion' and a 'British ladies' champion', suggesting that the sexes are not competing on equal terms even yet. References to chess and mathematics both signalled the unsuitability of women for Op art, or of Op art for women. This now looks like a way of 'masculinizing' Op and undercutting any 'feminine' associations it could have acquired.

Russell created an image of Riley as tough (a she-gorilla[13] – the conjunction suggests that a gorilla, like an artist, is 'normally' male), well past her youth, masculinized and even ugly, with colourful rhetoric of such obvious exaggeration that the reader is already prepared to learn that this image was quite the reverse of the truth. Indeed, Russell went on to demolish his possibly alarming construction by emphasizing Riley's claims to the conventional signs of femininity. The notion that she was small enough to pick up with a 'pair of [sugar?] tongs' suggests a certain vulnerability, even physical fragility, that counteracts the suggestion that she might be 'given to judo'. Russell also took pains to deny any signs of masculinity (those 'championship-level chess problems') in Riley's intellectual persona:

> *her mathematics are minimal, she was four years behind most of her class when she got to Cheltenham Ladies College at the end of the war, and her spelling has Shakespearian vagaries.*

Russell's strategy here was evidently to reassure his readers that, rather than possessing a chess champion's intellectual equipment, she was 'behind' at school and had problems with spelling. By implication, the reader was probably brighter and stronger than Riley. This raises questions of what it was about Riley's art that created associations of physical and intellectual threat.

Particular notions of what constitutes the 'feminine', and the implications of this femininity for a woman artist, were at stake here. Griselda Pollock has argued that all art produced by women has long been equated 'with femininity and femininity with bad art'[14] and that this convention has acted to preserve a hierarchy in which men artists and their work are always privileged. For a woman artist to have 'masculine' characteristics might therefore seem desirable but Russell's comments above make it clear that for Riley to possess masculine characteristics would be very undesirable. In the 1960s there was still a gulf between the notion of 'the artist' and that of 'the woman artist' which Russell did not wish, or was not able, to cross. If the artist is defined as masculine, and it is not possible for a woman to have masculine characteristics, then no confusion can arise between the 'artist' and the 'woman artist' and however good the work of the latter may be, the gulf remains. The work of the woman artist may be praised and admired but no awkward question arises as to whether it is 'as good' as that of her male contemporaries: questions of comparison can be suppressed. I would argue that this is a plausible explanation for Russell's eagerness to emphasize the femininity of his subject.

Writing on Jackson Pollock, Jeremy Lewison has suggested that in the 1940s and 1950s, it was 'unfruitful for such critics as Clement Greenberg to promote the work of women artists'.[15] He argues that US abstraction was positioned by critics as a specifically masculine art, in contrast to the 'suave sophistication of the School of Paris', which was characterized as effeminate. Women artists did not 'fit' into this narrative. By 1965, Russell was not constrained by such 'unfruitful[ness]'. He could and did enthusiastically promote Riley's work. Yet, as we have seen, his words suggest unease about Riley's status as an artist who was also a woman, specifically in relation to her Op art work. I have not discovered anything to suggest that men Op artists were regarded as offering a physical *threat* to their audience, although critics and media pundits made frequent comments on the disturbing – even aggressive – nature of much Op painting, not just that by Riley.[16] There was an emphasis on Riley's physical appearance in both the art press and the popular press that suggests a certain anxiety to which Russell's colourful rhetoric gave more direct expression. Plainly, neither Riley's paintings nor her person could offer any real *physical* threat to the individual spectator. If a painting proved too disconcerting to view, the spectator was always free to turn away. What issues, then, did Riley's work raise from which it was not so easy to turn away? To attempt an answer to this question, I will briefly return to some material presented in earlier chapters, but this time in relation to Riley's identity as a *woman* artist in the contexts of modernism and, more specifically, Op art.

The gender of modernism

Claims that Op art was in some way scientific and that this was not a normal characteristic of art can be set against the idea, put forward by Andreas Huyssen, that modernist art's 'experimental nature makes it analogous to science, and like science it produces and carries knowledge'.[17] At various times, artists have claimed that their work had a 'scientific' basis: in modernist art, Seurat's attempts to base his work on scientific colour theory is a well known example. Modernist art has a 'powerful masculinist mystique which is explicit in [the writings of] modernists such as Marinetti ... Wyndham Lewis' and others.[18] Modernism has been positioned as an essentially masculine phenomenon by successive practitioners of, and commentators upon, modernist art. This positioning has been supported by the creation of images of a polarized culture in which the 'masculinity' of modernist high culture confronts its opposite, mass culture, always gendered as feminine.[19]

Huyssen's argument is supported by cultural historian Peter Wollen, who argues that twentieth-century modernism had two originary myths, one of which was suppressed in favour of the other. The suppressed modernism was that of Matisse, whose work favoured the orientalist and decorative over the rational, European, functionalist basis of Picasso's Cubism: the latter was adopted by critics and later artists as the model of modernist art, the dominant paradigm. Wollen argues that this followed a debate over the nature of capitalism: was it primarily driven by production (with its connotations of labour, discipline, thrift and self-denial) or by consumption (which had connotations of self-indulgence and luxury, in turn connoting sensuality, eroticism, idleness)? For much of the twentieth century, production was associated with specifically male labour, and consumption with the female shopper, so that:

> *we find the contrast between a production and a consumption model of capitalism* [is] *mapped on to the gender distinction between masculine and feminine. Each reflects a different theory of the economic dynamic underlying modernism.*[20]

Matisse's version of modernism became aligned with the consumption/feminine theory of capitalism, while Picasso's modernism was aligned with the production/masculine theory. Wollen suggests that this was the view of capitalism that triumphed, and with it the paradigm of a modernism based on Picasso's art. Here, femininity is associated with a rejected view of both modernism and capitalism. Women had a subordinate role in production-oriented capitalism, which was reflected in their role in modernist art. The muse or model, like the consumer, may be necessary but is never equal to the artist or producer. The female artist, like the female producer in the wider economy, is seen as an anomaly. The relation of woman to art and of woman to commodity are relations of passivity. In capitalism, the passive image of the female consumer camouflages her essential role in driving the circulation of goods and money. Indeed:

> *since the early years of the twentieth century, the woman has been situated by a capitalist economy as the prototype of the modern consumer. ... Irigaray's*[21] *theory of the woman as commodity and the historical analysis of the woman's positioning as consumer – as subject rather than object of the commodity form – are only apparently contradictory.*[22]

Women are 'sold' images of themselves as they would like to be[23] and must then become consumers to possess the desirable items. They are buying an enhanced version of themselves. This is similar to the view that consumerism is rooted in a desire for a better life, as consumers seek new and fulfilling experiences from the products they buy.[24] The consumer does not buy mere objects but access to a life that is perceived as better or more exciting than her present life: a more exciting version of herself.[25] Woman is the ultimate consumer, continually re-buying new versions of herself. Woman, then, is central to a consumer society: indeed, she is the perfect symbol for it. Mass culture is only possible in such a society, where mass production both enables mass consumption and is itself dependent upon it. Hence it is possible to construct chains of connections between woman and mass culture. At the same time, if production's dependence on consumption is to be played down, even denied, in capitalist discourse, mass culture (and women) will be denigrated.

This is a crucial point when we come to look at the position of women active in modernist art in the mid-twentieth century. With the rejection both of the 'Matisse' model of modernism and of the consumption-driven model of capitalism, women were doubly relegated to a subordinate position in twentieth-century culture. In *Sexual Politics* (1970) the feminist writer Kate Millett characterized the period 1830–1930 as years of 'sexual revolution' and the subsequent thirty years as 'the counter-revolution'.[26] The period in which Wollen argues that the production-Cubist paradigm and the consumption-decorative paradigm were pitted against each other by economists and art factions (that is, roughly the first thirty years of the twentieth century) immediately precedes Millett's period of 'counter-(sexual)-revolution', 1930 to 1960. It would appear that, by the 1930s, the battle between these two paradigms had been won by the production/Cubist cultural paradigm. Any woman working as an artist in this period (or working in any area of production) could be seen as operating in territory that had been identified as masculine. To be a modernist artist was to work in a territory that was doubly masculinized: it was masculine not only in the sense of art's being a form of production (as opposed to consumption) but also in modernism's own now-established association with masculinity, from the 'rationality' of Picasso's Cubism to the 'virility' of Pollock's Abstract Expressionism (as opposed to the perceived femininity of Matisse's 'decorative' work).

Riley began work as an artist towards the end of Millett's 'counter-revolution', a period pithily described by novelist Angela Carter: 'It was tough in the fifties. Girls wore white gloves'.[27] By 1965, the white gloves were off: the mini-skirt – in which women could 'run ... jump ... leap, ... retain their precious freedom'[28] – had arrived, introduced by Mary Quant, who was awarded an OBE that year in recognition of her business success. The 'counter-counter revolution' could be said to have begun, and Riley was very visibly positioned in this process – certainly one of those issues that could not easily be ignored in the early years of the 1960s.

The gender of Op art

The masculinist paradigm for modernist art production faces a problem when confronted with work produced by a woman. Can the work be 'masculine' enough to qualify as avant-garde art? When the question 'Is it art?' is raised, an associated question follows: 'If it is not art, what is it?'[29] A possible answer, and one implied by the *Daily Mail*, is that the work in question is part of mass culture – like the funfair.[30] As we have seen, to relegate the work to the category of mass culture is to 'feminize' it. Riley was very sensitive to the threat to both her reputation as an artist, and to that of her work, posed by plagiarism by dress designers and other manufacturers in 1965; she commented on her feelings long after: 'I fought it in every way I could ... it was the kind of fame that would have appalled any artist'.[31] Many of the items manufactured had direct feminine connotations (women's clothing) while others had broadly recognized feminine associations (interior design and the decorative object). While most such goods were not directly based on Riley's work, it was not necessary that they should be for associations to be made between her Op paintings and the 'feminine and inferior'[32] world of mass production and mass culture that exploited Op-like imagery. A number of Op artists suffered plagiarism in the USA, while still others actively collaborated with manufacturers. Riley's high profile at 'The Responsive Eye' meant that her name was associated most immediately with Op art by the public in both the United States and Britain. As Andrew Graham Dixon later put it in a radio conversation with Riley, 'You were a household name: there was Twiggy, there was Mary Quant, there was Bridget Riley'.[33] Such a degree of public recognition indicates a certain 'notoriety', for which one must in part suspect the booming trade in 'Op' consumer goods. Hence Riley, Op art and overtly feminized aspects of mass culture could be envisaged as three points of a triangle, each directly connected with the other two. Riley had good cause to believe that her work could be devalued by the presence of elements of mass culture in this nexus of association.

Riley's attempts to 'stake out her territory'[34] included an attempt to sue those she accused of plagiarism in the United States. This proved impossible, as artists' works were not protected by US copyright law at that time. She wrote an article for *Art News* expressing her 'feelings of violation and disillusionment' at seeing her work 'vulgarized in the rag-trade'. She described what she had been through as a 'sociological phenomenon with alarming implications' characterized by 'an explosion of commercialism, bandwagoning and hysterical sensationalism'.[35]

The language Riley used in this article is itself full of allusion to the 'feminine' image of mass culture. The 'rag-trade' (the very name signalling both commerce and the transience and triviality of its products, full of feminine association) was singled out as the major source of the 'vulgarization' her work had suffered. The three witches cursing her work were 'commercialism' (inevitably the handmaiden of mass culture), 'bandwagoning' (plagiarism, imitation) and 'hysterical sensationalism'. As discussed in Chapter 5, the imitative and reproductive have long been seen as feminine by modernist critics.[36] From the late nineteenth century onwards, various authors associated the notion of the feminine with the idea of the crowd: 'male fears of an engulfing femininity are ... projected onto the metropolitan masses'.[37] The term 'bandwagoning' neatly combines both the image of the crowd and the notion of the 'imitative and reproductive'. The bandwagon is thus the crowd at its most feminine – a horde of groupies storming the gates of modernism. Finally, the feminine connotations of 'hysterical' need hardly be laboured, while 'sensationalism' indicates a form of communication targeted at the (feminine) emotions rather than at (masculine) rationality. Publishers have regarded women as a market for sensationalist literature at least since the eighteenth century.[38] Given the treatment Riley received from the press, she may have felt she had become the subject of sensationalist literature herself.

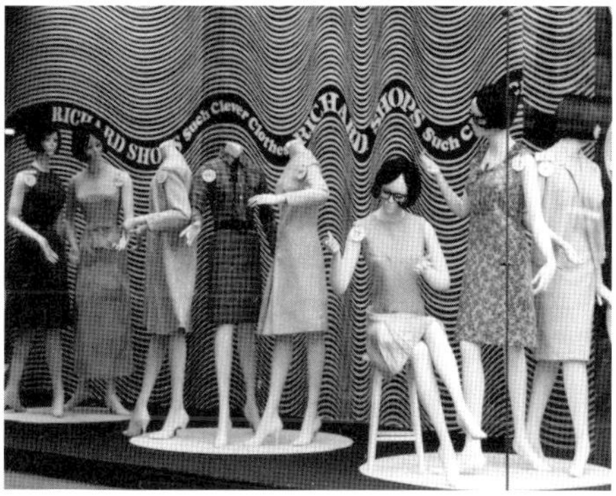

38.
Window display,
Richard Shops, London,
1966

Perhaps reacting against the lionization of Riley following her success at 'The Responsive Eye', the popular press became more aggressive in the year following the much-reported triumphs in New York. Wherever possible, Riley defended her work against commercial exploitation, as occurred when Richard Shops (a chain of boutiques) used images similar to her work as window dressing [Fig. 38] and Jonathan Miller incorporated an image suggesting one of her paintings into a book jacket, but this was not necessarily viewed sympathetically by the press. The *Daily Mail* claimed that Riley 'could be described as the high priestess of the Optical Art movement' whose 'wrathful passion' had been 'inflamed' by commercial plagiarizing of her work. She was quoted as having said that she was 'physically overcome' by it and had 'walked out of the showrooms of American designer Robert Aldritch after he offered her the first of a range of dresses based on one of her paintings that he had bought'.[39] Riley was 'involved with a London store' said to have used copies of her paintings in a window display and she was quoted as 'going to get in touch with my lawyers' over the accusations that Jonathan Miller had plagiarized a painting for a book jacket design. Riley was depicted as emotional to an unreasonable degree, apparently displaying the irrationality one might expect from a cult 'high priestess', a term that suggests a capricious and unstable beauty from a Hollywood Roman or Egyptian epic. The wording of the article is loaded with associations of mass culture. The source of the claim that Riley had made accusations against Miller was (according to the *Mail*) Riley's art dealer, Robert Fraser. Although described as 'fairly overcome' (a phrase that might suggest a distressed Victorian gentlewoman) by the sight of the offending book jacket, he was accorded cooler treatment than the artist. The person portrayed as the coolest and most reasonable figure in the dispute was Miller, who commented that 'this is the sort of hazard one faces if you do collage'. Despite the public familiarity with Riley's work that existed in 1966, Miller's creation of a book jacket which bore a clear resemblance to one of her paintings was presented as a coincidence – he was an innocent party attacked by a vengeful 'high priestess' and her acolyte, Fraser.

Riley was presented here as 'neurotic' – just as Melville had presented her in 1964. The tone of the article suggested that Riley was unreasonable – perhaps she should have been flattered by the various attempts to commercialize her work? This in turn might suggest that commercialization was appropriate for such work: why should Riley have fought the inevitable? Indeed, the *Daily Mail* claimed that what had 'inflamed [Riley's] wrathful passion ... [was] the commercial blossoming and exploitation of the Op art cult'. 'Blossoming' suggests that in being exploited by commercial interests, Op art was arriving at some kind of fulfilment of its purpose, becoming a cult of fashion and commerce with Riley as its 'high priestess'. Clearly, Riley and her work were being positioned here in ways that emphasized mass-cultural associations together with a particular image of the feminine as emotional and irrational – even neurotic, as Melville had suggested. It is as though the 'aggression' of Riley's paintings were being projected back onto the artist herself, but instead of being interpreted as strength – the individual using the law to defend her rights – this aggression is depicted as turned inward, generating neurosis and passion. Huyssen's 'male fears of an engulfing femininity' are seen here instigating a rearguard action against Riley's success at securing a central position for her work among contemporary art.

In general, those critics who wrote about Riley's person, as opposed to her art, emphasized her femininity and some of these writers made connections between her person and the more overtly feminine aspects of mass culture. This becomes especially noticeable in the publicity around 'The Responsive Eye'. Lil Picard, whose concern that Op artists should not be exploited or trivialized had not prevented her from describing Riley as 'girl of the month', reported in the same article that:

> *a long waiting list for* [Riley's] *'Opticals' is proof of the success of the new Vogue* [sic]. *Bridget Riley is the optical star, ... photographed before black and white moving lines, in a black sweater and skirt – she is a photogenic optical event.*[40]

The use of the capitalized 'Vogue' so close to the description of Riley (in fashion-model terms) is notable. Picard presented Op art itself as a fashion and Riley as a 'star', apparently casting on her Benjamin's 'phony spell of a commodity',[41] even though Picard appeared to deplore this. The description of Riley posed in front of one of (presumably) her own paintings suggests that she is modelling her painting, virtually 'wearing' it. Picard's use of the word 'Vogue' brings to mind Cecil Beaton's 1951 photo-shoot, for *Vogue* magazine, of models posed in front of Jackson Pollock's paintings [Fig. 39]. In those photographs, the painter himself is out of sight, while the 'action' of his paintings remains as a trace of his masculine creativity and a dramatic contrast to the poised passivity of Beaton's models. Although Picard was an artist herself, her piece suggests she found it easier to present Riley as a model than as an artist. Like a *Playboy* centrefold, Riley was the 'girl of the month', a phrase that itself expresses both the notion of celebrity and the transience of all fashion: the *Vogue* of the month, one might say. It also conveyed a degree of youthfulness that was inappropriate for a woman in her thirties. Riley's painting was not even identified: perhaps for Picard they were all just 'black and white moving lines', as non-particularized as the lines making up that icon of mass culture, the television screen. In this passage, even though no picture accompanied it, Riley's work and her position as a mature artist were effectively absorbed into a fashion-magazine 'spread'; painting and artist were indistinguishable.

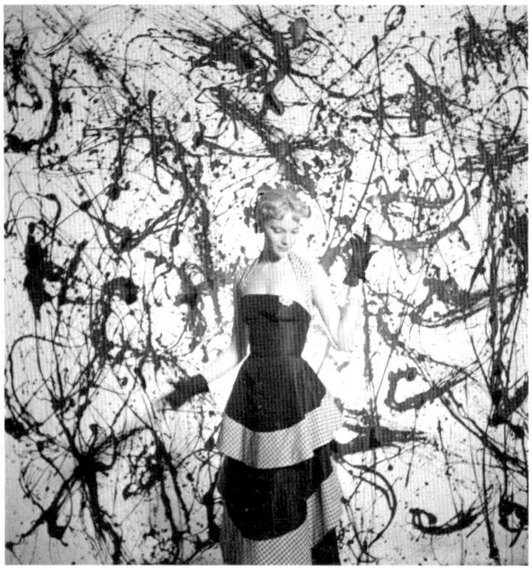

39.
Cecil Beaton: fashion model with Jackson Pollock's *Autumn Rhythm*, 1951

Another artist had been presented in this way only the previous year. In 1964 the Pop artist Marisol exhibited at New York's Stable Gallery and attracted great press attention in the USA. According to Cécile Whiting, press coverage 'included photographs that posed Marisol with her sculpture as if artist and artwork were indistinguishable from one another'.[42] Whiting describes how 'several magazines cast the artist Marisol as a fashion model'[43] [Fig. 40] and she argues that in doing this they were continuing an established practice. In 1957, the US magazine *Life* had presented a number of Abstract Expressionists:

> *posed ... seated casually, sometimes even provocatively, next to or on top of* [their] *completed paintings. ... Even if their poses did not stress their seductive feminine allure, the women's outfits matched the colours of their paintings as if artist and artwork were nothing more than decorative elements in a colour-co-ordinated interior.*[44]

These women had at least been photographed in their studios [Fig. 41]. Whiting argues, however, that Marisol's work as an artist was often presented in women's magazines as subsidiary to her role as a fashionable woman; this heavy press coverage was noticed by the art critics and journalists.

> *References in art criticism to her role in the fashion press reinforced the ascription of femininity to Marisol, an ascription that ... worked against her identity as a genuine modernist artist.*[45]

While Marisol may have been thought to have encouraged conflation of her person with her work, by using her own features on many of her sculpted female figures, the austerity of Riley's clothes would seem a sharp contrast to the pronounced optical liveliness of her works. That these works contained a lot of black seems to have been excuse enough for the press. Riley's black sweater and skirt, perhaps suggesting 'chic' of Audrey Hepburn, or the clothes of the Beat Generation, may have seemed austere compared with the clothes of her Abstract Expressionist predecessors. In connection with the black used in her paintings, and the associations with Marisol's public image that such pictures may have invited, however, these photographs left her open to Picard's description of her as a 'photogenic optical event'. To so describe a woman dressed entirely in unflamboyant black clothing is improbable in any other context.

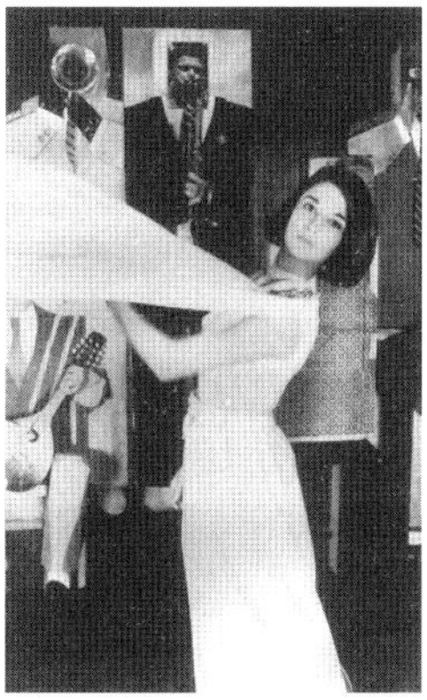

40.
Duane Michals:
Marisol Escobar,
photographed for
Harpers Bazaar,
October 1963

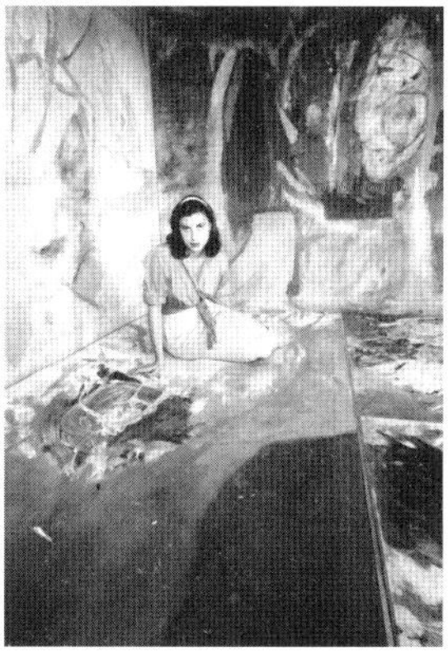

41.
Gordon Parks:
Helen Frankenthaler,
photographed for
Life, 13 May 1957

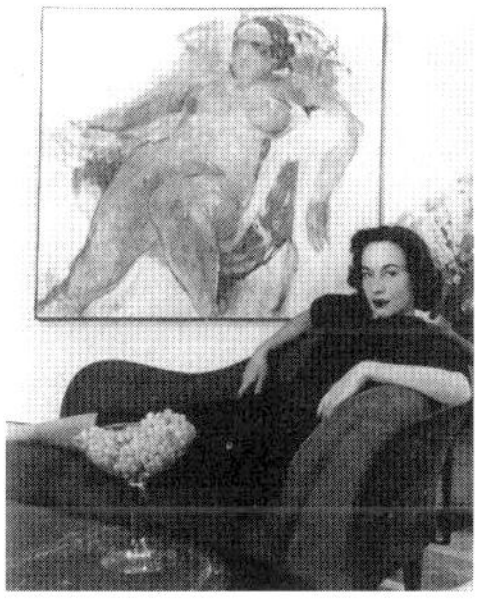

42.
Gordon Parks:
Jane Wilson,
photographed for
Life, 13 May 1957

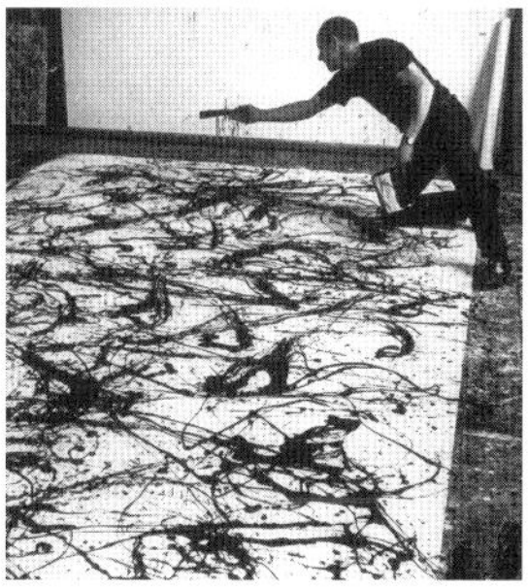

43.
Hans Namuth:
Jackson Pollock at work
1950

By 1965, in the USA at least, picturing women artists with their work – not in the act of creating it but posed against it like models – had become something of a representational convention in the media [Fig. 42]. Such a convention forms a striking contrast with the widely circulated pictures of Jackson Pollock actively at work [Fig. 43], and with the image of the artist promoted in 1965 by the film *The Agony and the Ecstasy*,[46] featuring Hollywood he-man Charlton Heston as Michelangelo. The film made a visual equation between Michelangelo's struggles to paint the Sistine Chapel ceiling and the 'warrior pope' Julius' activities on the battlefield. Virility was equated with artistic production in both this film and Hans Namuth's film of Pollock (1951, discussed in Chapter 5). This idea of the artist had apparently not changed in the intervening years. Indeed, Lewison quotes the catalogue of the Pollock retrospective of 1957–58 (about half way between the Namuth and Heston films), which celebrated Pollock's 'aggressive spirit of revolt' 'bursting masculinity' and engagement in '"violent combat" in the "arena of conflict and strife"'.[47] The arena, site of combat, necessarily connotes masculinity.

The pictures of Pollock (and of Heston as Michelangelo) emphasized his role as an active producer; art was something that he did. Women artists posed in elegant attire in front of their own works were denied this active engagement with their own work. Without accompanying text identifying them as producers, they could be taken for purchasers of the works: consumers – the role that Wollen argues had become identified with women over the course of the early twentieth century. Ample conventions existed for portraying women in this role, from the most basic advertising to Cecil Beaton's models [Figs. 39, 44].

44.
1960s' models posed with works of art. Photographs by Horst in 'Looks Men Like at Home', *Vogue*, November 1966

Left
with Tom Wesselmann's *Mouth #7*

Centre
with Vasarely's *Onix 2* and *Minta*

Right
with George Segal's *Walking Man*

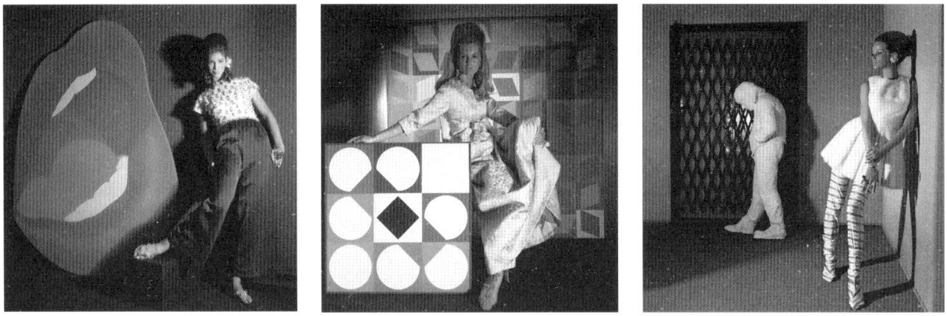

How was the active, producing woman to be represented when the accepted paradigms of production denied her existence? In addition, Riley recalls seeing 'windows full of versions of my paintings on dresses, in window displays, everywhere' on her arrival in New York for 'The Responsive Eye'.[48] 'Converting' the paintings into dresses and displaying them on mannequins equated them with consumption. In the shop window display, production (whether of the original paintings or of the dresses themselves) was hidden beneath a fantasy of consumption ('wear this dress and become someone more alluring/glamorous/exciting'). The presence of such window displays, as much as the dresses themselves, served to align Riley's paintings with the feminine principle of consumption.[49]

Whiting has argued that Marisol was marginalized by the media's creation of a 'model girl' image for her.

> *A number of critics found Marisol a suitable artist to situate in a space peripheral to 'hard core' Pop, a space necessary as the foil against which to demarcate the centre ...*
>
> *Without a feminine Pop, there could not have been a masculine Pop in opposition; without a soft periphery, there could have been no hard core.*[50]

Whiting's idea that the 'hard core' exists in relation to a 'periphery' is reminiscent of Huyssen's argument that modernism needs a mass culture to which it can stand in opposition. It also applies to the way that women Abstract Expressionists were promoted in the media in the previous decade. Posed like fashion models in smart clothes [Fig. 42], they evoked notions of (subsidiary, peripheral) consumption rather than (primary, central) production. Hence the visual representations of women Abstract Expressionists worked against written descriptions of them as producers and identified them with the 'peripheral' role of consumers. Just as Marisol could be positioned as a peripheral figure among Pop artists, so women Abstract Expressionists before her had been silently relegated to a peripheral position by photographs that ostensibly celebrated their role as artists. Photographs in which women artists appeared in model-like poses allowed an image of them as fashionable and feminine women to be 'sold' to publics both within and outside the art establishments. Their status as artists was denied even as it was apparently asserted: the (masculine) status quo was reinforced by such pictures.

By the early 1960s, however, posing the woman artist in elegant attire next to her pictures – as if she were the artist's patron (or the artist's patron's wife) rather than the artist herself – became insufficient to maintain a convincing image of femininity within which she might – just – be contained. The active, producing woman was becoming highly visible. By 1961 women made up a third of the UK workforce, more than half of these being married.[51] In the USA, Betty Friedan promoted the idea that married women should work outside the home in *The Feminine Mystique* (1963).[52] Prompted by Eleanor Roosevelt, President Kennedy set up a Commission on the Status of Women in 1961.

> *The Commission's report in 1963 marked a watershed between the 1950s mystique of femininity and the liberal and radical egalitarianism which was to follow in the 1960s. It opposed sex discrimination in government employment and demanded 'equal pay for comparable work' ... However, it dithered on whether education should prepare girls for motherhood or lift 'women's aspirations beyond stubbornly persistent assumptions about "women's roles" and "women's interests" and result in choices that have inner authenticity'.*[53]

While there was no consensus on women's social and economic roles, the assumptions of the previous decade were no longer seen as secure in the early 1960s. Preserving the masculine ideal of the modernist paradigm needed rather more effort than merely photographing women artists in passive poses. On the other hand, the image of the fashion model, the archetype of the passive woman, had moved on. Models such as Jean Shrimpton were promoted as lively, active young women who dressed for a lifestyle rather than to display their husbands' wealth through expensive clothing.[54] A new notion of young femininity was being promoted by authors such as Helen Gurley-Brown, author of *Sex and the Single Girl* (1962 – she was later editor of US *Cosmopolitan* magazine), in which the single woman was presented as achieving her identity through work rather than domesticity.[55] Nonetheless:

> *As if in response to the hyperdomesticity of consumer imagery directed toward women in the 1950s, the Single Girl emerged as the new feminine ideal of consumerism. ...* [She] *is a working girl, prepared to pay her way if necessary, competent and reliable beneath her girlishness, with her eye on the bottom line.*[56]

In this context, there was no need to picture Riley in an elegant suit seated before her pictures in order to present her in that most essentially feminine role, the consumer. Presented more dynamically, as Picard's 'photogenic optical event' she nonetheless fitted the new brief for the female consumer.[57]

So where did the US press position Riley as an artist? She had come to the USA from Britain in 1965 to promote her work at 'The Responsive Eye' and at the commercial Feigen Gallery in New York. As we have seen, she was highly successful in this respect. It is worth repeating here that the MoMA show was substantial and featured many established (male) European and American artists, yet it was Riley's work that was chosen for the cover of the catalogue and her work attracted very considerable attention in the press. To a great extent, therefore, in both the USA and Britain, the press treated Riley's work as the 'hard core' of Op art. The photographic conventions established for portraying the artist who happened to be female, however, were tied to the depiction of woman as consumer: the model being the Sixties' ideal of the young, swinging consumer, peripheral to all forms of production. Just as Marisol had been presented, not as though she were the producer of her work but, rather, as though both she and it were the product of some unseen third party – as if brought into being by the (male) gaze behind the camera lens, so the simply-dressed Riley became an 'optical event'. Like the female Abstract Expressionists who had posed before their pictures wearing the same colours as in their paintings, she wore the predominant colour in her own work; like Marisol she is attractive and relatively young. So although fresh conventions had been established for photographing the peripheral woman artist, there were none available for representing one working at the masculine core.

The Feigen Gallery, which had a strong interest in promoting Riley as an artist rather than a fashion icon, avoided a 'model girl' portrayal.

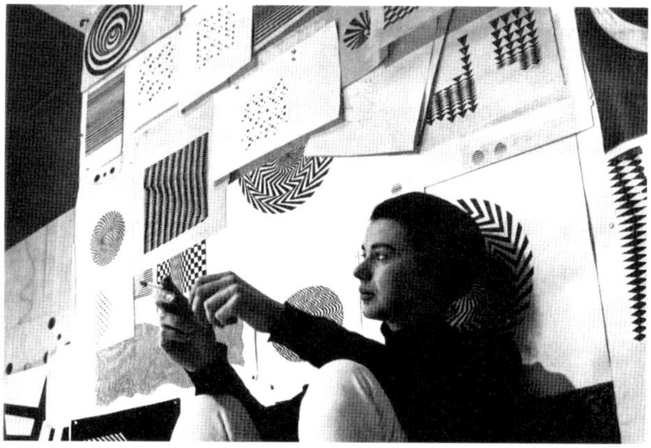

Bridget Riley - March '65 - Richard Feigen Gallery New York City

45. Advertisement for Riley's show at Richard Feigen Gallery, *Art International*, February 1965

Its advertisements for her exhibition there show Riley sitting on the floor with knees drawn up but photographed, nonetheless, from below [Fig. 45]. The display of her clothing is minimized in this shot; she holds a partly smoked cigarette and looks away from the camera, apparently directing her close attention at someone or something across the room.

This is not the self-absorption or self-advertisement of the model; the eye is drawn upwards to the mass of drawings of her work, pinned in overlapping profusion and indicating 'work in progress'. The Feigen Gallery may or may not have been concerned about the peripheralization of an artist they were backing; but, consciously or not, they chose an image that says 'here is an *artist*'. Newspapers, of course, had no such axe to grind. When, in April 1965, *The Times* applauded Riley's success in New York, they accompanied the article with a picture of her in her studio, posed in front of a single large drawing, with one hand held behind her head and looking upwards, patently at nothing at all, with a rapt expression [Fig. 46]. Here, the conventions for photographing a 'pretty young woman' were applied, notwithstanding her success as a mature artist, attested to by the accompanying text. By contrast, pictures in the *Tatler* in 1965 show Cecil Collins and Philip Sutton posed as though working in their studios [Figs. 47, 48].

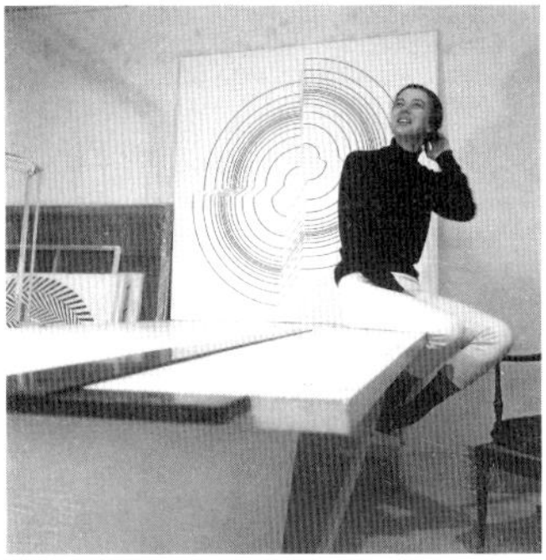

46.
Bridget Riley in her studio, photograph for 'Miss Bridget Riley and optical art', *The Times*, 19 April 1965

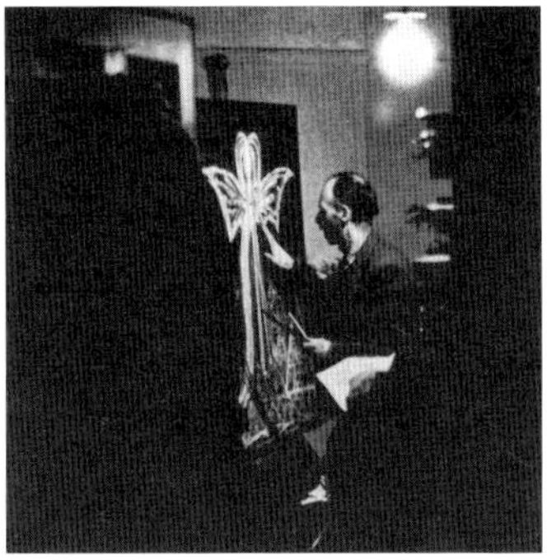

47.
Cecil Collins, apparently at work, *Tatler*, February 1965

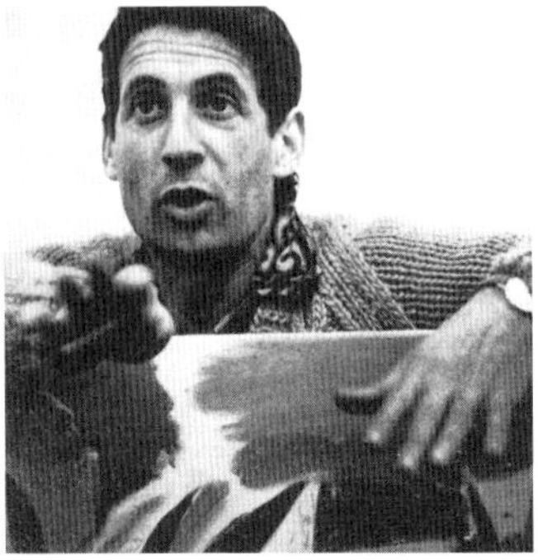

48.
Philip Sutton, apparently at work, *Tatler*, February 1965

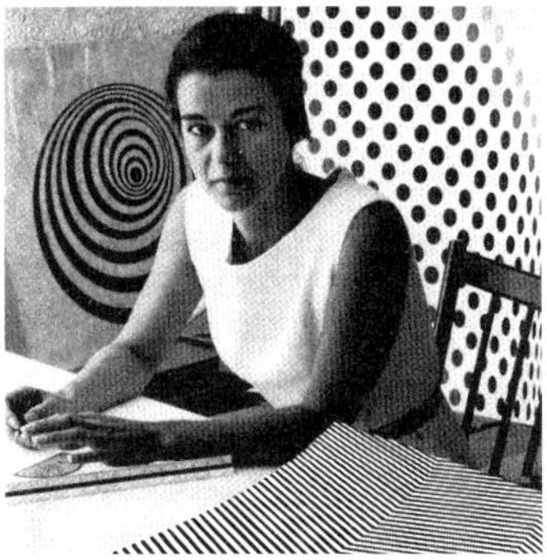

49.
Bridget Riley, apparently at work, *Vogue Australia* October 1965

Riley's treatment by the press during her US visit, and indeed at home, indicates the tensions generated between long-standing notions of the peripherality of the woman artist and the seizure of a central position by Riley herself. While Riley's dealers had an interest in portraying her as very much the artist, one section of the press plausibly had a similar interest, although for very different reasons. Some publications directed at women moved away from the 'model girl' presentation of Riley's person. A picture in *Vogue Australia*, October 1965 [Fig. 49] shows her in medium close-up, sitting at a table with her work in front of and behind her, looking directly at the camera with a serious expression. Her hands reach towards something in front of her and she seems to have glanced up in the middle of working. A shot in the US fashion industry journal *Women's Wear Daily* shows Riley in front of some of her work, gesticulating with cigarette-holding hand, apparently talking animatedly with someone off-camera (Fig. 50).[58]

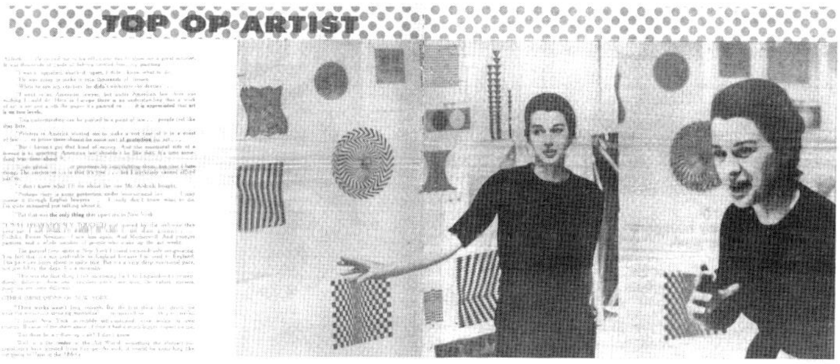

50. Bridget Riley in animated conversation, *Women's Wear Daily*, 11 May 1965

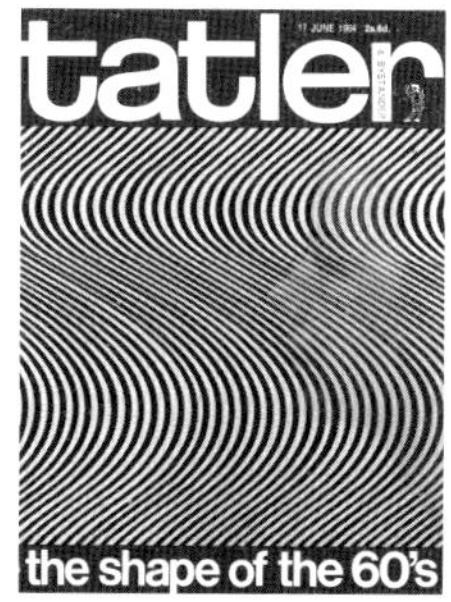

51. Cover, *Tatler* 17 June 1964

A montage on the cover of *Tatler* (1964) [Fig. 51] shows her profile, over which is superimposed a detail from one of her paintings (possibly *Current* or *Fall*) [Figs. 14 and 13].[59] Too little of Riley's face is visible for her to be mistaken here for a standard cover model. The caption beneath it, 'The shape of the sixties', conveys the impression that the image communicated something fundamental about the decade then nearing its midpoint. It is as if Riley herself had given 'shape' to the decade. This presentation of Riley *as an artist*, in publications directed at women, illustrates the point made in Chapter 6 that many women in this period sought to attain their own 'stake in the future'. Riley represented the possibility of attaining success in even the most male-dominated areas of work. While it might seem contradictory that the very publications that promoted Op clothes – and thereby seemed to trivialize Riley's art – also visually presented her most seriously as an artist, the contradiction is more apparent than real. The women who bought such clothes, I would argue, did not think of themselves as trivializing the art, but were appropriating it as part of their own claim to a place in society as active, producing individuals. That one of the most prominent creators of Op art was a woman would have made it all the more suitable for this purpose.

Within a few years the tendency to photograph female and male artists differently seems to have disappeared. By the 1970s photographs of

Riley tend to show her in her studio, as an active, producing artist. A photograph from *The Times* in 1971 (only six years after the hand-behind-the-head 'model' pose of Fig. 46) shows her surrounded by her own canvases in a studio and posed as though working,[60] while in 1998 another press shot[61] positions her between a foreground packed with brushes and paints, and work in progress behind her. In 1999 she appears apparently mixing paint,[62] with containers of paint and coloured sketches massed in front of her. Riley was no longer a young woman by this time, and so not likely to be shown as a 'model'; the sort of pose shown in Fig. 42 might, however, have been thought appropriate for a photograph of a mature woman, but it was not used. In every case, the press now chose to portray her very definitely as an artist. In 1965, it simply did not occur to photographers to depict a female artist using the conventions that were commonplace in representing her male counterparts.[63] Hence, in the press lionization of Riley we see uneasy shifts of focus. Coverage of Riley's *work* placed her at the artistic centre, while the photographic and verbal coverage of her *person*, and the frequent associations made between her work and mass culture, placed her at the periphery.

Another issue arises here, in relation to the USA. In Chapter 4, I looked at the disquiet expressed in the USA at the success of what Sidney Tillim called 'European-type Op'.[64] Tillim had argued that, in effect, European Op art should be marginalized. By implication, the high profile Riley acquired in the USA in 1965 could not have been welcome to anyone sharing Tillim's views. The prevailing representations of the woman artist – beautiful, fascinating but artistically impotent – might also have been modes of representation preferred by critics such as Tillim for European Op artists in general. In other words, any suggestion that Riley herself was marginal might be seen as implying that European Op art was also marginal. From this point of view, the promotion of a woman artist as the leading light of European Op, a promotion which involved representing her in ways already associated with the 'peripheral' woman artist, could be read as an attempt to relegate European Op itself to the periphery of art practice. We have seen above that Greenberg associated the 'School of Paris' with a 'feminine' conception of art, which he denigrated.[65] Furthermore:

> *Greenberg never turned his pen to Riley's work and through this omission he effectively excommunicated her from his fold. The consensus of her generation was that it was better to receive Greenberg's admonition than not to receive any notice at all. At*

least if he was critical, it meant an artist's efforts were carefully considered.[66]

The associations between Riley's work and elements of mass culture, which the press had variously celebrated and deplored, created 'the biggest barrier to the appreciation of Riley's work'.[67] This may have deterred Greenberg from addressing Riley's work but, given his long championship of American art, it may also be possible that he wished to avoid acknowledging the work of a European artist who, for some months in 1965, dominated the New York art scene. Rather than engage with the issues raised by the success of Riley's art, Greenberg may have hoped that if he ignored them they would noisily drown in a sea of (feminine) commercialism, leaving Abstract Expressionism and its heirs on the intellectual (masculine) high ground. If Op art were seen in some quarters as a European successor to the School of Paris, and one likely to steal the centre-stage position from Abstract Expressionism and its (US) heirs, its 'femininity' could hardly be better guaranteed than if associated primarily with a woman artist. In such a climate, why search for new ways to depict and discuss a successful European woman artist?

Woman artist as new woman

It is possible to take a more positive view of the way Riley's identity as a woman artist was promoted in the press. Whiting has argued that for the women's press, promotion of Marisol as a fashionable woman 'who happened to be an artist'[68] was a way of promoting a concept of femininity that was not tied to domesticity. Nonetheless, too much emphasis on her profession might also have made Marisol appear unfeminine. It is a truism that photographs are open to multiple interpretations. When women in the 1950s saw articles in *Life* about women Abstract Expressionists, did they see only images of fashionable middle-class women, or, as Whiting suggests, might the bright colours of their clothing, co-ordinated with the colours of their paintings, have had 'bohemian' connotations opposed to domesticity? In the case of the Marisol coverage, a concept of femininity was promoted that was still very much tied to notions of consumption: not the 'rational' consumption of household necessities, but rather the consumption of fashionable luxuries for personal adornment. As a woman who also very visibly worked – ostensibly, the reason for featuring her in magazines was her celebrity as an artist – Marisol could be said to represent an ideal specimen of Gurley Brown's 'Single Girl': self-supporting and having a great time as the centre of media attention and well-publicized 'success'.

In Bridget Riley, British women had their own example of a woman who had successfully contested a male preserve – the art world – and won visible rewards within it. Unlike Twiggy and Mary Quant, for instance, her success seemed to be independent of men (Twiggy was photographed and managed by men, Quant was married to her business partner). Whilst it may have been, to some extent, the influence of Riley's work in the area of mass culture that brought her to the attention of many women in Britain, she *was* recognized as an artist, not as someone directly identified with the feminine sphere of dress design and fashion promotion. Furthermore, Riley's reception in the USA at the time of 'The Responsive Eye' was extensively reported in the British media. As discussed in Chapter 4, Riley's work appears to have received rather more attention in Britain after that show than before it. One British reporter suggested that few people in the USA or Britain had heard of her before the show and indicated the extensive media coverage she had received in New York.[69]

Riley represented an ideal of the successful woman: young, attractive and yet not peripheral to the men normally found at the centre of discourses on art (or other professions). In this context, photographs of Riley posed with her pictures, which may have read as 'glamour' shots that marginalized her status as an artist to some viewers, could have served as reassurance to some women viewers that it was possible for a woman to achieve such success without being 'desexed'. The difficulty of presenting a woman as both feminine *and* successful in a male profession, in 1965, is shown so tellingly in John Russell's comments quoted at the beginning of this chapter. The visual vocabulary of the 'model girl' shot, deployed on an active, producing woman might be seen as the visual riposte to Russell's rhetorical image of a 'fifty-ish she-gorilla'.

Russell's comments, especially his reference to judo, can be interpreted as alluding to the 'aggression' that some critics associated with Op art.[70] The frequent media allusions to the supposed aggression of Riley's work could not be explained by any 'butch' physicality of the artist herself. Millett's contention that a counter (sexual) revolution had been in progress from about 1930 to about 1960 and that the 1960s saw a renewal of sexual revolution, suggests that one reason for the emphasis on this aspect of Riley's work was a concern with the threat of feminism. Christopher Booker commented:

> *To the dream images of pop, the Beatle portraits of Peter Blake, the stark dream-shapes of 'Hard Edged Abstractionism', the year* [1964] *added a new craze – for the restless, startling patterns of Op art,*

painted by Miss Bridget Riley, a product of that one-time citadel of upper middle class feminism, Cheltenham Ladies College.[71]

Booker seems to have hesitated to say that Riley was a feminist. If Cheltenham Ladies College was a 'one-time citadel of upper middle class feminism' was it still so when Riley attended it? It would seem that Riley was being identified here as 'upper middle class' and so in some way not representative of 'ordinary' women. Feminism itself, in this passage, was being labelled as the pastime of a class-based elite, something confined to places, such as a private girls' school, divorced from normal life. Booker's account of Op art was as pessimistic as the rest of his book. In this passage Op is a 'craze' promoted by a woman who comes from a world of protected privilege and might be a feminist, to boot. References to the art schools attended by Riley[72] would have been more relevant to her career as an artist than her secondary schooling, but Booker cited her school for its 'feminist' and 'class' associations, or both. The qualifying 'one-time' gives the impression that Cheltenham Ladies College could no longer be described in these terms (although as a private school it could hardly be said to have transformed itself into a classless comprehensive). Presumably it is the 'feminism' that Booker saw as having passed: the elite school and its feminist ethos were by now passé. As a 'craze', perhaps Op itself would soon – the author hoped – become similarly passé. Here Booker actively made connections between Op art, privilege and feminism. Yet if Op art were a craze – implying a very widespread and intense interest – it is difficult to see how it could be a sign of privilege.

The purpose of mentioning a school attended by Riley in the 1940s was clearly to associate her above all with 'upper middle class feminism' and to imply that this was something that had had its day. By the time Booker wrote this, however, feminism was far being a concern of a small and privileged section of the female population. By 1964 Kate Millett's thirty-year counter-revolution was over. Many women, from all levels of society, who may not have thought of themselves as feminists, had expectations very different from their mothers' generation. Trade unions were pressing for equal opportunities for women; at the TUC conference in 1965 a woman delegate raised the question of birth control. By the time *The Neophiliacs* was published in 1969, years of debate and pressure from women's groups in the UK had culminated in the Ford sewing machinists' strike for equal pay in 1968. It is plausible that masculine anxiety about 'how far' women would go underlies Booker's scorn for Cheltenham Ladies College and, by extension, Riley.

Russell's solution to the question of Riley's identity as a woman and as an Op art painter was to use a rhetorical, humorous approach. It was a relatively benign way of confronting the notion that Op paintings could not be created by a 'normal' (feminine) woman and to demonstrate the overt femininity (as he saw it) of a painter whose work he supported critically. Whereas, for Booker, Riley was by implication an 'upper middle class feminist' responsible for an unhealthy craze, for Russell, she was an artist whose sex was a problem to be addressed in negotiating her work. Both men expressed unease about Riley's public image. While Booker was afraid that she would be taken seriously, for Russell the opposite was the case: if Riley could really be perceived as some sort of aberrant freak, her work could also be dismissed. He may have chosen humour as a strategy because he wished to avoid becoming entangled in any debate over the status of women artists and their work. The lack of direct reference in the media generally to Riley's position as a woman artist may reflect a widespread reluctance to engage with this issue, rather than being a sign that critics and other writers no longer saw any distinction between men and women artists. In other words, it may be an early example of what we now call 'political correctness', rather than a reflection of genuine assumptions of equality.

Given the views Booker expressed throughout his book, where he attacked virtually every new cultural and social development of the period, Riley's success was probably reason enough for his concern. This very success, however, might be thought to be enough to allay Russell's anxiety, but this was not so. While most reviews in the British press did not attack Riley as a woman artist per se, Melville's review, quoted at the start of this chapter, expressed attitudes that Russell may have encountered elsewhere than in print. Little more than a year after that review, and in the wake of 'The Responsive Eye', however, Melville's views had softened.

He now discerned 'an illusion of movement, produced by a subtle handling of subdued colours' [73] and as if answering his own criticism of the previous year, he offered that this replaced 'the cruel twitch with a rhythmic undulation'. Melville continued: 'The effect is rather like the steady pounding of one's heart or the sensation of floating on the tide' [Figs. 52, 53].[74] This description suggests a sensuous, even feminine, eroticism, 'ingratiating and enveloping'. Instead of Vasarely's Op art, Riley's work was now compared to the work of Rothko and Olitski. Following 'The Responsive Eye' it would seem that, whereas Greenberg had seen Abstract Expressionism as a 'masculine' art, Melville could see 'feminine' principles at work within it – or at least within the 'homogenous surfaces' of Olitski

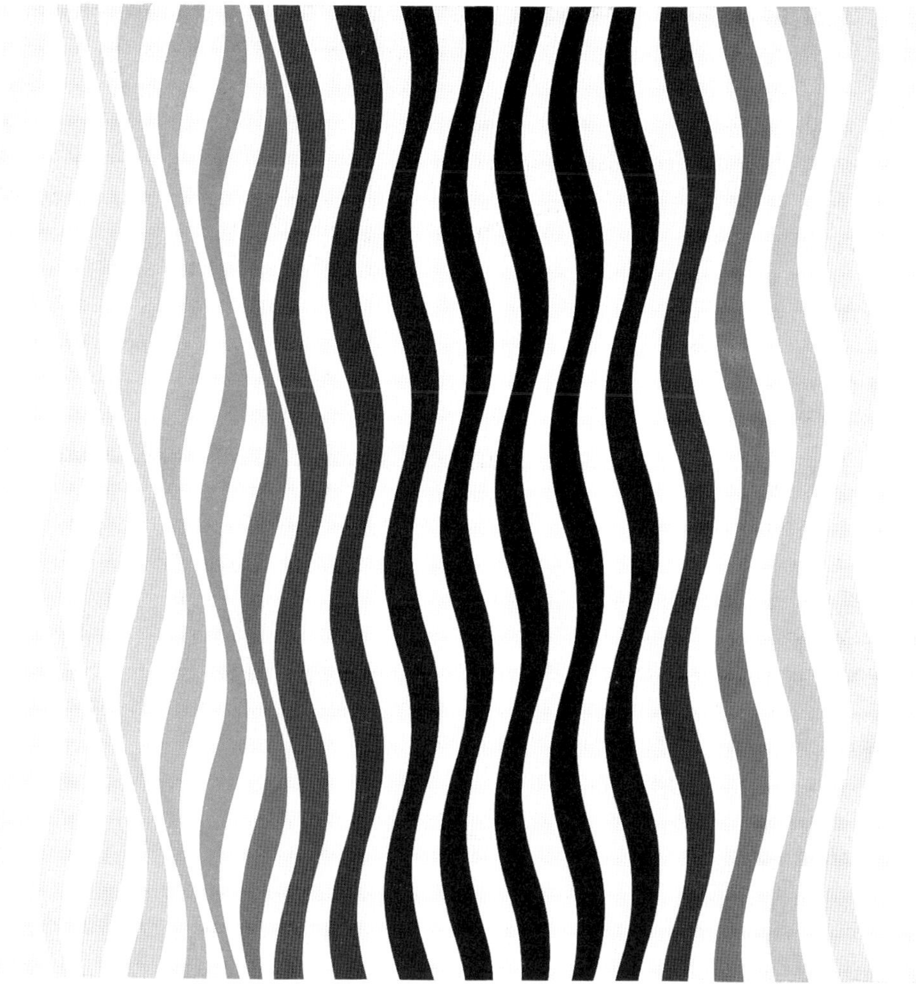

52. **Arrest 1** 1965

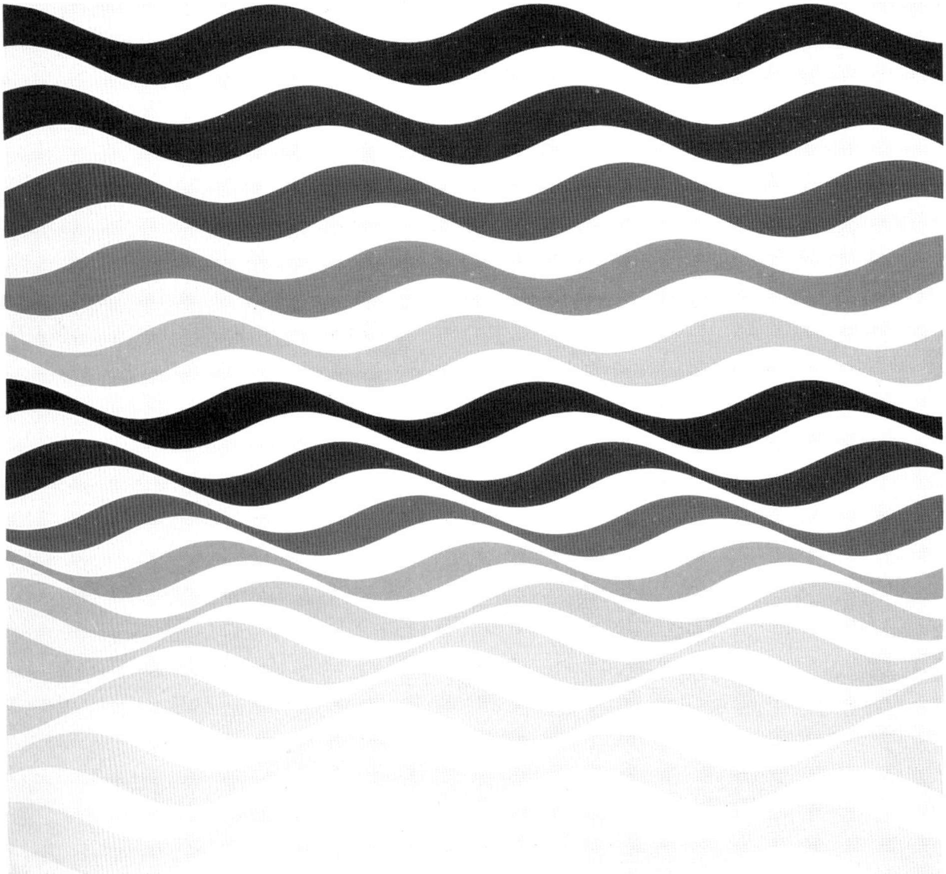

53. **Arrest 3** 1965

and Rothko, which he described as 'regressive images of Nirvana'. Melville closed his review with the thought that:

> *If the 'abstract sublime' school is now going to reinforce its effects with the illusion of rhythmic movement, I can foresee the time when paintings will restore adults to the peace of the rocking cradle.*[75]

This seems an ambiguous note on which to end, suggesting the sensuality and mindlessness of a sleeping infant, or perhaps Matisse's view of his own art as being as relaxing as an armchair. It represents an enormous psychological leap from the 'eye irritants' of the previous year and the 'cold ferocity' Melville claimed to have seen in Riley's earlier work. The feminized eroticism he now found in Riley's art (and that of Rothko and Olitski) could lead, via a sort of inverted maternalism, to the passivity of infancy. Here, feminine passivity was transferred from artist to spectator. So even while Melville apparently enjoyed Riley's latest work, and seems to have moved beyond the simple promotion of masculinist ideals in art production, he revealed anxiety about where this feminine art might lead: complete passivity might be pleasurable but perhaps debilitating. It is as though in this passage, Riley becomes Delilah, unmanning the hapless art lover, the aggressive attack of her earlier work merely softening him up for the final fatal seduction.

Breaking the barriers

Any investigation of Bridget Riley's treatment by the press – both the popular press and the more serious publications – cannot be conducted with the disregard to her status as a woman artist that Riley herself might have preferred.[76] As with other aspects of her work, no unambiguous interpretation emerges. It cannot be said that she was overlooked or dismissed; clearly she had tremendous critical support, while attacks on her work do not as a rule labour her position as a woman artist. Melville's comments on her 'neuroticism', and the *Daily Mail*'s similar implicit attack, are exceptions. Yet it would surely be wrong to infer from this that there was no anxiety about a woman artist achieving a degree of prominence previously reserved for men artists. In this chapter I have sought to show how that anxiety was expressed, 'between the lines' of written commentaries and embodied in the visual language of photographs of Riley and other women artists of the 1950s and 1960s. Russell's words quoted at the start of this chapter demonstrate the difficulties faced by critics wishing to support Riley and her work, yet clearly not at ease with the fact that such work should be produced by a woman. Where Riley, in 1973, presented the notion of 'the artist as hermaphrodite' as a seamless fusion of male and female natures within the creative being of the artist (of either sex), Russell's depiction of the woman artist as 'she-gorilla' was another take on the notion of hermaphroditism. Here, however, the hermaphrodite is not an ideal being but a grotesque monster who lurks in Riley's shadow, threatening to destroy, if not her, at least her credibility as she tries to maintain an almost impossible role: that of the woman artist. Yet Riley did indeed carry off this role in a way that gained much critical support for her work. The extreme attacks of the popular press, such as that by the *Daily Mail*[77] and of some more serious critics – even the fact that Greenberg never wrote about her work – may suggest that she broke down barriers that were previously considered unbreachable – those between the 'woman artist' and the 'artist'.

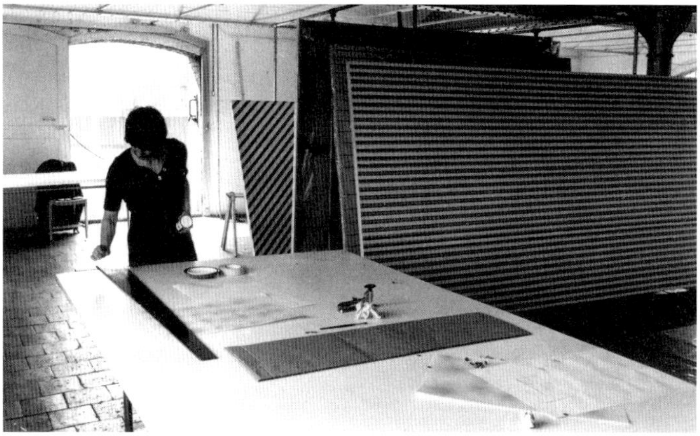

54.
Bridget Riley in her studio, *The Times*, 1971

Postscript

The 1980s saw a revival of interest in Op art among younger artists. The work of Ross Blaekner, Philip Taaffe and Peter Schuyff shows the influences of Riley and Vasarely. Michael Archer has connected this with fears of AIDS:

> *Ross Blaekner suggested in 1987 that 'people in their early twenties are thinking about death more now'. The use of Op by these artists was a way of dealing with this. Coming as it had at the very end of the modernist trajectory, Op stood as the most played out, most empty, non-referential, non-art of the entire century.*[1]

For Archer, Op art (and specifically Riley's work, as he mentions her as a prime influence on these younger artists) was an art of negation and death. Such a view recalls Bataille's views on the destructive basis of art and, more specifically, the views of some of Riley's contemporaries that her work was 'aggressive'. The Sokol cartoon [Fig. 22] shows a man being devoured by one of Riley's paintings: under the humour, death is implied. The connotations of aggression and destruction attributed to Riley's work, and even the associations made with nausea or seasickness, suggest the possibility of death, and connotations of drug use are also open to this interpretation.

In sharp contrast, however, Riley's work was also received by her contemporaries as the expression of the life of their time. Rather than being played out and empty, one could argue that for both its admirers and detractors, Riley's work was full of sensation (at a literal, physical level) and replete with connotations of dreams of, and fears for, the future. It involved the body in the act of experiencing art in a way that earlier art (such as Pollock's work), may have attempted but had not achieved so forcibly. The work of the Abstract Expressionist action painters had associations of dynamism and movement but Riley's work communicated dynamism and movement to the viewer at the level of his/her own physical experience. I have argued that assertions that Riley's work induced feelings akin to 'swimming or perhaps sky-diving'[2], or that might be experienced by astronauts in training, or members of the counter-culture on an LSD trip, were connected with desires and fears for the future of Western societies. People who focused on desires for improving the world were more concerned with life than with death. Those for whom fears outweighed hopes, however, could view space voyages, sky-diving and LSD trips as undertakings filled with the risk of imminent death.

Archer describes Op as 'non-referential' – indeed as being the most non-referential art of the twentieth century. This may be interpreted as a reformulation of Jasia Reichardt's claim, quoted in the introduction, that 'Op paintings do not lend themselves to intellectual exploration'.[3] A lack of 'references' suggests a lack of material on which to gain intellectual purchase. Alternatively, as I have argued, Riley's work can be seen to be filled with apparently contradictory associations of the space age and its antithesis, the counter-culture. Furthermore, the central point of reference for Riley's work is the body itself, a point from which no viewer can escape. Her admirers and detractors may have disagreed on whether the sensations induced in the body of the spectator were pleasant or unpleasant, but nobody suggested that no sensations were induced. This was an art that affirmed the centrality of the body to all perception, even that experience most *apparently* restricted to the mind: that of aesthetic pleasure. In calling Op 'non-art', Archer reminds us of the *Daily Mail*'s questioning of 'whether such a style belongs to the fine arts or to fun fairs': the *Daily Mail*'s correspondent implied that Op is 'non-art'. Many of the critics quoted in this book either promoted such interpretations or were concerned that such interpretations might prevail. In its rich hoard of associations with early modernism (Seurat, Monet), however, and with art of the post-war period (Jackson Pollock, Yves Klein, performance artists, Lucio Fontana and Michelangelo Pistoletto), Riley's work has in fact made a major contribution to the art created 'at the very end of the modernist trajectory'. Rather than indicating the 'death' of modernism, a dead-end to its trajectory, Riley's work may now be seen as part of a re-assessment of what modern art was or could be, which gave rise to many different movements in art as the 1960s progressed. In its concern with the body it was a source of renewed energy, an attempt to revitalize a modernism that had become associated most strongly with Abstract Expressionism ('the poor, tired tag end of a great tradition'[4]) and latterly with Pop art, which might also have reached the end of its possibilities for development.

In the 1960s Riley's art could connote a life in which body and mind were increasingly regarded as interdependent. If her early work has had a special appeal to the 'AIDS generation' then this may be because of its connotations of death, destruction and aggression. Alternatively, perhaps that appeal arises from her work's ability to elicit a celebration of the life of the embodied mind, which may be especially valued when human longevity appears less assured than in the 1960s. Riley's work embodied not only the vision of the artist, but also that of the spectator. Riley herself said in 1965 that: 'Knowledge of a painter's intentions may be of interest, but in the last analysis stance alone will never make a work of art'.[5] In saying this, she recognized above all the importance of the spectator's own individual reaction to a work. 'Ultimately, the degree of visual sensibility is the vital agent in transforming a concept into the indefinable experience which is presented by a work of art.'[6] Is this the artist's 'visual sensibility' or that of the spectator? The very nature of Riley's work seems to insist that both may be inferred (if not consciously implied) here. Visual sensibility does not exist partitioned off from the intellect and from the rest of one's experience of life, but is informed by the whole being and lived experience of both artist and spectator. Hence the multiple associations that Riley's work evoked in the writings of critics and other commentators in the early 1960s.

New associations will be made for works of art as time passes. These may well be very different from those the artist might wish. Riley herself feared the associations of commercialism engendered by aspects of her work's reception in New York in 1965: 'I remember thinking that it would take twenty years before anybody could look at my paintings again.'[7] Nonetheless, Riley has kept in her own archive a photographic record of this commercialization (see Fig. 38), as if preserving a reminder of both the power of the spectator to take their own 'stance' in relation to her work *and* her own ultimate success in overcoming such threats to the credibility and reputation of herself and her work.[8] As I have shown, Riley was not happy with other aspects of the reception of her work, such as the associations made with science and psychotropic drug use. It is now possible to re-read the views expressed at the time and appreciate that connections made then may not have been as shallow as the contemporary press made them appear. Art historian Ron Hunt has said of Blaekner and Taafe that:

> *They, and others, reworked Op in the early '80s. In their view, Op with its concomitant design and lifestyle, was emblematic of a failed Utopia, which twenty years later, could be appropriated and deflected in order to reveal something else.*[9]

In the reception given to Op in the 1960s, Hunt recognizes its connections with notions of the 'future', although he connects Op with only one Utopian vision (and does not say what sort of Utopia). Neither the hippy dream counter-culture, which never took form beyond the dissociated activities of a small section of society, nor the technocracy, which may be thought to have triumphed in some respects, delivered problem-free and unanimously contented societies. Op may now be said to emblematize these 'failed Utopia[s]'. As both counter-culture and technocracy represented dystopias for certain sections of the population, however, even their failure cannot be regarded unequivocally. More positively, Riley's work may represent, for a less idealistic age, the dreams, hopes and fears of people who, forty years ago, flocked to see her work or purchase items adorned with Op-derived patterns.

It is part of the fascination of this work that the vision it embodied for one spectator might be quite opposed to that embodied for another. 'Embodied' is a key word here, whatever the interpretations or associations made by the individual spectator, as attested to by the emphasis on the physical made by so many commentators, from the most serious to the most frivolous. While at one time Riley may have feared that the latter group would succeed in determining how her work would be perceived, her subsequent career has not suffered from these unwelcome attentions. For the art historian, even the most trivializing detraction may yield a wealth of insights into the multiple meanings a work of art may have had for contemporary viewers.[10] Utopia, as usual, has been postponed, but perhaps in the pulsating optical resonance of a Riley Op painting, there are optical echoes of the diverse outlines, shifting in and out of focus, of utopian visions of the early 1960s. The utopias dreamt of at that time seem to have been more than political or philosophical ideals, but very much worlds in which the importance of the body as a site of experience was recognized. The reality of experience lived in the body was central to the hippy commune and its ideal of free love, as well as to space age exploration testing astronauts to physical extremes. Such diverse utopias reverberate in the embodied visions of Bridget Riley's work.

Notes

Introduction
pp.9-19

1. Herbert Read, *To Hell With Culture*, London 1963, p.28.
2.T.J. Clark, *Image of the People: Gustave Courbet and the 1848 Revolution*, London 1973, 1982, p.10.
3. Ibid. p.12.
4. Anon. 'Op art: pictures that attack the eye', *Time*, 23 October 1964, pp.42–44. For simplicity, I have used the term Op art throughout this book, regardless of the date of the work discussed.
5. Lil Picard, 'Op–report', *Kunstwerk*, July 1965, p.8.
6. For example, Marco Livingstone, 'Pluralism since 1960', in David Britt, *Modern Art: Impressionism to Post-Modernism*, London 1989, pp.359–405.
7. 'Op' art suggests a particular form of the general concept of 'art', whereas 'Op Art' might be looked on as a style or fashion separate from true 'art' (like Art Nouveau, for example), while 'op' art might also seem trivializing, given that terms such as 'Impressionism', 'Abstract Expressionism' are usually capitalized.
8. Jasia Reichardt (1966) 'Op art' in Nikos Stangos, *Concepts of Modern Art*, London 1981, p.243.
9. Ibid. p.243.
10. Norbert Lynton, 'Recent painting and sculpture', *The Story of Modern Art*, London 1989, p.301.
11. Bridget Riley, conversation with the author, 1995.
12. Michael Fried, 'Art and objecthood', *Artforum*, vol.5, no.10, Summer 1967, pp.12–23.
13. Roger Fry, 'An essay in aesthetics' (1909) in Charles Harrison and Paul Wood, *Art in Theory 1900–2000: An Anthology of Changing Ideas*, Oxford 2003, p.80.
14. Maurice Merleau-Ponty (1960), 'Eye and Mind' in Galen A. Johnson, Michael B. Smith (eds.), *The Merleau-Ponty Aesthetics Reader*, Illinois 1993, p.124.

Chapter 1
Venus and Mars: The Marriage of Art and Science
pp.21-61

1. Bridget Riley, 'Perception is the medium', p.33, *Art News*, October 1965, pp.32, 33, 66.
2. Cyril Barrett, *An Introduction to Optical Art*, London 1971, p.36. GRAV's manifesto was entitled *Enough of Mystification* 1961.
3. Much early work on the subject of optical illusion and visual perception had been done in the 1940s by the US psychologist Adelbert Ames (*The Ames Demonstrations in Perception*, Princeton 1952). His bibliography listed over 50 books which had made use of Ames' 'demonstrations' and according to W.H. Ittelson, (1968) the number of works citing Ames' work grew rapidly after 1952. His 'demonstrations' were often better known than their creator, appearing unaccredited in textbooks and encyclopaedias.
4. Radio lecture 'Modernist painting' (1961), reproduced in Francis Frascina and Jonathan Harris (eds), *Art in Modern Culture*, London 1992, pp.308–314, esp. p.312.
5. In conversation with Maurice de Sausmarez' (1967) in Robert Kudielka (ed.), *The Mind's Eye: Bridget Riley Collected Writings 1965–1999*, London 1999, p.61.
6. Greenberg's first important contribution was 'Avant-garde and kitsch' published in 1939 but he had his greatest influence in the 1950s and 1960s.
7. For example, Fry's (1909) 'Essay in aesthetics' and Greenberg's (1961) 'Modernist painting'. Fry (1866–1934) and his protégé Clive Bell (1881–1964) produced a formalist critical framework further developed by Greenberg (1909–94). See Charles Harrison and Paul Wood (eds), *Art in Theory 1900–2000*, Oxford 2003.
8. See Alan Wallach (1992) 'The museum of modern art: The past's future' in Francis Frascina and Jonathan Harris, 1992, op.cit., pp.282–91.
9. See for example, Norbert Lynton, *The Story of Modern Art London*, 1989, p.301, on Riley 'In 1960 she began to adapt diagrams through which scientists were studying perceptual processes in order to paint powerful black and white paintings'. Lynton here makes the sort of statement that generated lively controversy in the 1960s but he expresses it as established fact.
10. Herbert Read, 'Civilization and the sense of quality' in Herbert Read, *To Hell With Culture*, 1963, p.175.
11. The Federation of British Industry *Civil Research Policy* June 1963 quoted in Tom Wilkie, *British Science and Politics Since 1945*, Cambridge 1991, Mass. and Oxford. The Federation did not suppose that the new ministry was the way to achieve this aim.
12. Tom Wilkie, 1991, Op cit., p.19.
13. Riley's article in *Art News* (see note 1) made no mention of technology; she defended her work against associations with 'optics' 'mathematics' and 'science'.
14. C.P. Snow, 'The Two Cultures' (The Rede lecture, Cambridge, 1959), quoted in Wilkie, 1991, op.cit., p.69. Snow argued that the humanities and sciences had become totally separated, with those involved in each failing to understand one another.
15. Thomas B. Hess, 'You can hang it in the hall', *Art News*, Vol. 64 No 2, pp.41–43, 49–50, see p.50.
16. Wilkie, 1991, op.cit. p.19.
17. John Profumo, a Conservative minister, had had an affair with Christine Keeler, who was simultaneously involved with a Russian diplomat, presenting the risk of security breaches.
18. Harold Wilson, speech at the Labour Party Conference, 1 October 1963, quoted in Wilkie, 1991, op.cit., p.39. Here, the 'scientific revolution' was presented as a social panacea. According to Wilkie, the pro-nationalizers interpreted this as an argument for an extension of public ownership in relation to scientific research while the anti-nationalizers interpreted it as a move away from the whole question of nationalization. Hence both sides rallied to the new policy.
19. Vernon Bogdanor (1970), 'The Labour Party in opposition 1951–1964', Vernon Bogdanor and Robert Skidelsky (eds), *The Age of Affluence 1951 to 1964*, Basingstoke 1970, p.104.
20. Church of England baptisms declined sharply after the war (Grace Davie, 1994, *Religion in Britain since 1945*). Arthur Marwick claims that 'At the beginning of the fifties under 10% of the population were regular churchgoers', *British Society since 1945*, London 1996, p.97.
21. Anon., 'Gallery Guide', *The Observer*, 27 May 1962, p.27.
22. John Canaday (1965a), 'The Responsive Eye: Three cheers and high hopes', *The New York Times*, 28 February 1965.
23. Harold Rosenberg, *The Anxious Object*, Chicago, 1964/1966, p.270.
24. Barbara Rose, 'Beyond vertigo: Optical art at the Modern', *Artforum*, April 1965, p.32.
25. H.J. Seldis, 'With Op art the eyes have it', *Los Angeles Times*, 3 October 1965.
26. Bernard Levin, *The Pendulum Years: Britain and the Sixties*, London 1970, p.178.
27. See Wilkie, 1991, op.cit., p.22. Wilkie argues that British governments have consistently had interest in science only for its military applications; funding for research of civilian importance has always been haphazard.
28. It is significant that women artists and scientists were becoming increasingly visible at this time; I examine the possible implications of this in chapter 7. As a well known artist working within Op itself, Riley is an obvious example, but women were establishing themselves as a successful and highly visible minority in other forms of art and in scientific disciplines.

29. Anon., *Daily Mail*, 10 September 1963.
30. Andrew Forge, 'Presentation', *New Statesman*, 24 April 1964, p.655. Forge was himself a painter.
31. See David Thomson and Geoffrey Warner, *England in the Twentieth Century*, 1965.
32. The idea that knowledge is dangerous is expressed in the Judaeo-Christian creation myth and arises repeatedly in relation to post-Enlightenment cultural production. Its frequency increases as the impact of science intensifies: e.g. Mary Shelley's *Frankenstein* (1818), H.G. Wells' *Island of Dr Moreau* (1896), Fritz Lang's *Metropolis* (1925–27) and numerous science fiction books and films thereafter.
33. Anon., 'Some critics are already throwing their weight behind op in dubious battle with pop', 'Op art: pictures that attack the eye', *Time*, 23 Oct 1964. *Kunstwerk*'s critic Lil Picard commented on the term, *Kunstwerk* 'Op-Report', July 1965, p.8.
34. The term 'technocracy' had been coined by US engineer W.H. Smyth (1855–1940) but was popularized by James Burnham's *Managerial Revolution* (pub. 1942). The term implied what Smyth called 'rule by technicians'.
35. Not everyone regarded Op as a 'new' art form. See the discussion on Martin Gardner later in this chapter. It was widely recognized that Vasarely had been working on Op-type paintings since at least the early 1950s.
36. The theories of Schrödinger and Einstein lead to the view that the position of the observer affects what is observed, so that phenomena are in some way products of observation, not independent of it.
37. C.G. Jung, 'Psychological Commentary' (1954) quoted in Jose A. Argüelles, *Charles Henry and the Formation of a Psychophysical Aesthetic*, Chicago and London 1972, p.18.
38. This heading is taken from the book of that title by Paul Wood, Francis Frascina, Jonathan Harris and Charles Harrison.
39. See Alan Wallach, 1992, op.cit.
40. Jonathan Miller, 'à la Mod', *New Statesman*, 29 May 1964, p.853.
41. Miller was here referring to the highly fashion-conscious youth subculture that flourished in London and south-east England in the early 1960s.
42. 'Purple hearts' were an amphetamine drug popular with Mods and other young people. The use of this term suggests the physically stimulating (even over-stimulating) effect of the pictures.
43. Harold Rosenberg, 1966, op.cit., p.269.
44. 'Cool' was also used to describe some aspects of cultural production by communications theorist Marshall McLuhan.
45. Views from Adolf Loos' 'Ornament and crime' (1908) to Greenberg's insistence on the primacy of 'flatness' and 'self-criticism', which rejected the 'ornamental' as merely frivolous, held considerable influence. See C. Greenberg (1992, originally published 1961), 'Modernist painting' reproduced in Fancis Frascina and Jonathan Harris (eds), 1992, op.cit., London: Phaidon, pp.308–314.
46. Jonathan Miller, 1964, op.cit., p.853.
47. The 'space race' was now in progress and speculation about what would be found on the moon included the possibility of a surface deeply covered with fine sand or 'dust'.
48. In Lewis Carroll's *The Hunting of the Snark* (1876), the Boojum is the imaginary (although dangerous) alter-ego of the imaginary Snark.
49. Robert Melville, 'Miscellany', *Architectural Review*, August 1962, pp.132–4.
50. Andrew Forge, 1964, op.cit., p.655.
51. Barry Curtis has pointed out that Marshall McLuhan, who introduced the terms 'hot' and 'cool' to cultural debate, may have considered Op to be 'hot', because it could be argued that it produces a response without the viewer's voluntary engagement, whereas 'cool media are high in participation or completion by the audience' (Marshall McLuhan, *Understanding Media*, London, 1964, reprinted 2002, p.25). Alternatively, 'participation or completion' for Op paintings could be seen as a process that did depend on the viewer's engagement: his or her willingness to submit to the experience, rendering the art 'cool'.
52. Robert Hewison, *Culture and Consensus: England, Art and Politics Since 1940*, 1995, p.129.
53. Thomas B. Hess, 1965, op.cit., p.43.
54. Ibid., p.50.
55. In contrast, it is interesting to note an opposing view: 'Modernism is craftsmanship, even in its wildest moments' T.J. Clark, *Farewell to an Idea*, New Haven & London 1999, p.328.
56. Thomas B. Hess, 1965, op.cit., p.50.
57. Ibid., p.50.
58. For example, Alan Wallach argues that in the 1930s MoMA developed a 'complex modernist aesthetic construct based on Bauhaus architecture and design, Fauvism ... Cubism ... and Surrealism' (1992, op.cit, p.284), which was expressed in the architecture of the MoMA building ('... this technologised space' (p.286) '[a] signifier of corporate modernity' (p.286)). Domesticity also connotes the feminine, a subject discussed in Chapters 6 and 7.
59. Thomas B. Hess, 1965, op.cit., p.50.
60. See Chapter 2 for a discussion of Barr's chart. See Griselda Pollock, 'Modernity and the spaces of femininity' (1992) and Alan Wallach, 1992, op.cit., both in Francis Frascina and Jonathan Harris, 1992, op.cit.
61. T.J. Clark, 1999, op.cit. p.10.

62. 'The immediate aims of the Modernists were, and remain, personal before anything else, and the truth and success of their works remain personal before anything else.' Clement Greenberg 'Modernist painting' in Francis Frascina and Jonathan Harris (eds), 1992, op.cit., pp.308–314, see p.312.
63. The USSR's Society of Young Artists, OBMOKhU, exhibited what they called 'laboratory work' in Moscow in 1921. B. Fer, 'The language of construction' in Briony Fer, David Batchelor, Paul Wood, *Realism, Rationalism, Surrealism: Art Between the Wars*, London 1993.
64. Nigel Gosling, 'The shapes of the Sixties', *The Observer*, 10 February 1963, p.21. Gosling was to change his position with regard to Riley's art by the end of the decade, e.g. 'Seduced by Riley', *Observer*, 27 July 1969.
65. Robert Melville, 'Surrealists and others', *Architectural Review*, February 1964, vol.135, no. 804, pp.137–40.
66. *Blaze 1* was executed entirely in black and white paint.
67. Robert Melville, 1964a, op.cit.
68. Anne Massey, *The Independent Group: Modernism and Mass Culture 1945–59*, Manchester 1995, pp.43–45.
69. As already noted, Op would later be related to Constructivism by a number of commentators.
70. Anne Massey, 1995, op.cit., pp.42–45.
71. Herbert Read, 'The psychology of reaction' in Herbert Read, 1963, op.cit., p.140.
72. Anne Massey, 1995, op.cit., p.45.
73. Herbert Read, 'The great debate' in H. Read, 1963, op.cit., pp.177–83. Greenberg was also antagonistic to increasing materialism.
74. Margaret Garlake, *New Art New World*, 1998, p.108.
75. For example, furniture designer Ernest Race, who used ideas derived from images created by molecular biologists. See Anne Massey, 1995, op.cit., p.11.
76. William Feaver in Mary Banham and Bevis Hillier (eds), *A Tonic to the Nation: the Festival of Britain 1951*, 1976, p.51.
77. See Mary Banham and Bevis Hillier (eds), 1976, op.cit., p.61. Reilly's assertion of British prowess in crystallography is not unreasonable; only a few years later the rare high quality of Rosalind Franklin's X-ray crystallographic photographs of DNA would be invaluable to Watson and Crick in their discovery of the structure of DNA.
78. Quoted by Reilly. See Mary Banham and Bevis Hillier (eds), 1976, op.cit., p.61. Anne Massey has argued that the Festival Style was based on a combination of British and Scandinavian influences as well as crystal structures and images from molecular biology. Anne Massey, 1995, op.cit., pp.7–11.
79. See Chapters 3 and 4 for a discussion of national identity issues in relation to Op and the question of its supposed scientific content.
80. Harold Rosenberg, 1964/66, op.cit., p.51.
81. Anon., 'Op art: Pictures that attack the eye', *Time*, 23 October 1964, p.42. This article was attributed to John Borgzinner by Thomas B. Hess, in his article 'You can hang it in the hall'.
82. Ibid., p.42.
83. Ibid., p.43.
84. Ibid., p.43.
85. Ibid., p.45.
86. Note, however, that this article appeared over a year after Oster and Nishijima's *Scientific American* article on scientific applications of moiré patterns, which is discussed below.
87. Lil Picard, 'Op-report', *Kunstwerk*, July 1965, p.8.
88. Op was associated with the notion of fashion in the sense that it generated considerable public interest. In addition, it was widely drawn upon by designers of mass-produced domestic goods and women's clothing (see Chapter 7).
89. Carlo McCormick, 'pOPTOMETRY', *Art Forum*, vol. 25, November 1985, p.88.
90. Ibid., p.88.
91. See, for example, Lil Picard, 1965, op.cit., p.8. The magazine is also cited by T. B. Hess, 1965, op.cit.
92. Gerald Oster and Y. Nishijima, 'Moiré patterns', *Scientific American*, May 1963, pp.54–63.
93. Anon., 'Op art: Pictures that attack the eye', *Time*, 23 October 1964, pp.42–44, see p.45.
94. Martin Gardner, 'Mathematical games: 'On the relation between mathematics and the ordered patterns of Op art', *Scientific American*, July 1965, pp.100–103.
95. William Seitz, Catalogue for 'The Responsive Eye', MoMA, New York 1965.
96. In the widest possible sense of the term – 'The Responsive Eye' included much that was not regarded strictly as Op by contemporary critics (see Thomas B. Hess, 1965, op.cit.).
97. Art historian Alan Wallach (1992, op.cit., p.286) has argued that MoMA's influence on contemporary art was waning by the 1960s and that 'The Responsive Eye' exhibition (which he wrongly dates to 1967) was 'a last pathetic gesture' in its attempts to maintain that influence.
98. Thomas B. Hess, 1965, op.cit., p.41. It is not clear if he meant in the USA or worldwide, or how well substantiated this claim was, but in any case his claim suggests a very high level of interest in this kind of art. Op was not a minority interest in 1965.

Chapter 2
Painting the Doors of Perception
pp.63-92

1. Laura Cumming, 'Riley, ace of stripes', *Observer Review*, 15 November 1998.
2. Alfred Hickling, 'The life of Riley', *Guardian*, 17 November 1998.
3. For example, in the UK the Dangerous Drugs Act 1964 increased controls on the supply of cannabis and amphetamines; LSD was made illegal in 1966.
4. Presumably a reference to marijuana. *Fall* was painted in 1963 [Fig. 13].
5. Quoted in Michael Bracewell, 'A plea for painting', *Guardian Weekend* (supplement), 15 March 1997, p.18.
6. Quoted in ibid.
7. R. L. Gregory, *Visual Perception*, London 1973, cites a number of publications in this period, e.g. J.J. Gibson *Perception of the Visual World* (1950); R.L Fantz 'The origin of form perception', *Scientific American* 240 (1961); D. N. Hubel and T. N. Wiesel (1962) 'Receptive fields, binocular interaction and functional architecture in the cat's visual cortex', *Journal of Physiology* 160; C. S. Penrose and R. Penrose (1958) 'Impossible objects: a special type of illusion', *British Journal of Psychology* 49, and so on. E.H. Gombrich, *The Image and the Eye*, London 1982, cites a number of publications in this period concerning the perception of apparent movement in static images.
8. As promoted in Aldous Huxley, *The Doors of Perception*, London 1954, republished 1994.
9. Christopher Booker, *The Neophiliacs: A Study of the Revolution in English Life in the Fifties and Sixties*, London 1969, pp.298–9. Booker was not only one of the founders of *Private Eye* in 1962, he also wrote sketches for television's satirical review *That Was the Week that Was*.
10. See Briony Fer (1995), 'Poussière /peinture: Bataille on painting' in Carolyn Bailey Gill, *Bataille: Writing the Sacred*, 1995, p.157.
11. Picard, an artist in a number of media, including performance, was known as 'grandmother of the hippies' and 'muse of the American avant-garde'. www.uiowa.edu/~ournews/2000/january/0110picard.html
12. Banham (a one-time student of Nikolaus Pevsner) had once worked in the aircraft industry. As a founder member of the Independent Group, Banham displayed an early interest in mechanization and new technology in relation to cultural developments.
13. Reyner Banham, *Los Angeles: The Architecture of Four Ecologies*, London 1973, p.23. For Banham, 'the language of design, architecture and urbanism in Los Angeles is the language of movement ... So, like earlier generations of English intellectuals who taught themselves Italian in order to read Dante in the original, I learned to drive in order to read Los Angeles in the original'.
14. There had been earlier modernist interest in technology and the body, as shown in Vertov's film *Man with a Movie Camera*, 1928, or the ideas of Le Corbusier and others in the 1920s.
15. John Canaday, 'The Responsive Eye: Three cheers and High Hopes', *The New York Times*, 28 February 1965.
16. Elizabeth Stevens, 'Bridget Riley' (a short review of Riley's show at New York's Feigen gallery), *Art News*, vol. 4, no. 62, April 1965, p.14.
17. Norbert Lynton, 'London letter', *Art International*, October 1963.
18. Harold Rosenberg, *The Anxious Object*, Chicago 1964-1966, Phoenix edn 1982, p.269.
19. See Charles Harrison and Paul Wood, 'Modernity and modernism reconsidered' in Paul Wood, Francis Frascina, Jonathan Harris, Charles Harrison, *Modernism in Dispute: Art Since the Forties*, New Haven and London 1993, p.195.
20. Briony Fer, 1995, op.cit.
21. Antonio Melechi, 'Drugs of liberation: from psychiatry to psychedelia' in Antonio Melechi (ed.), *Psychedelia Britannica: Hallucinogenic Drugs in Britain, London*, p.23.
22. Ibid., p.26.
23. See Theodore Roszak, *The Making of a Counter Culture: Reflections on the Technocratic Society and its Youthful Opposition*, London 1970.
24. David Alan Mellor, 'The Sixties in Britain' in David Alan Mellor and Laurent Gervereau (eds), *The Sixties*, London 1997, p.274. Among those attending was Pete Townsend, later to form The Who, known for destroying their instruments on stage.
25. Quoted in Andrew Wilson 'Moving times – new words – dead clocks: Sigma, London counter-culture' in David Alan Mellor and Laurent Gervereau (eds), 1997, op.cit., p.255.
26. William Seitz, Catalogue to 'The Responsive Eye', 1965, p.31, (*Current*, Fig. 14).
27. Oster was a polymer chemist interested in perception, as well as an artist and contributor to *Scientific American* (see Chapter 1). The use of psychotropic drugs for research or personal use was not illegal at the time.
28. William Seitz, 1965, op.cit., p.31.
29. Quoted in Michael Bracewell, 1997, op.cit. There are similarities of construction between *Fall* (1963) and *Current* (1964).
30. Briony Fer, 1995, op.cit. p.159, discussing Bataille's views as given in *The Accursed Share* (1949) and other writings.

31. This can be related to the writings of Greenberg, who Rosalind Krauss recalls used the term 'hallucinated literalness' in the 1950s. She states this was in relation to Jackson Pollock's work, to 'set up just the right kind of tension between the pictorial wall's flatness and the optical illusions it none the less released'. Rosalind E. Krauss, *The Optical Unconscious*, Cambridge, Mass. and London 1993, p.246.
32. Leading to the legal bans on their use in the USA, 1965 and UK, 1966.
33. Anton Ehrenzweig, 'Introduction' Catalogue to Bridget Riley's one-person show at Gallery One, London May 1962. Ehrenzweig does not specify a particular painting.
34. Anton Ehrenzweig, *The Hidden Order of Art: A Study in the Psychology of Artistic Imagination*, London 1967, p.85.
35. Aldous Huxley, *The Doors of Perception* (1954), London, edn 1994, p.46.
36. Quotations from ibid., pp.8, 11, 32, 41, 42.
37. Ibid., p.34.
38. Clive Bell, 'The aesthetic hypothesis' (1914), in Charles Harrison and Paul Wood, *Art in Theory 1900–2000*, Oxford 2003, p.109.
39. Francis Frascina, 'Introduction' in Francis Frascina (ed.), *Pollock and After: The Critical Debate*, 1985, p.17.
40. Quoted in T.J. Clark, 'Arguments about modernism: a reply to Michael Fried' (1983), in Francis Frascina (ed.), *Pollock and After: The Critical Debate*, London 1985, p.87.
41. Ibid., p.86.
42. Charles Harrison and Paul Wood, 1993, op.cit., p.195. Harrison and Wood see this notion as occurring in modernist criticism since the writings of Roger Fry and Clive Bell, not as a view unique to Fried.
43. Ibid., p.250. A being outside space and time would necessarily be bodiless, as a body could not exist without space and time. 'Grace' is Fried's term – see T.J. Clark 'Arguments about Modernism: a reply to Michael Fried' (1983), in Francis Frascina (ed.), 1985, op.cit., p.87.
44. Aldous Huxley, 1954, op.cit., p.17.
45. Michael Fried, 'Art and Objecthood', *Artforum*, Summer 1967, vol. 5, no 10, pp.12–23, see p.22.
46. Carlo McCormick, 'pOPTOMETRY', *Artforum*, November 1985, pp.87–91, refers to 'Op and its low IQ brother psychedelia' (p.88), arguing that Op in part gave rise to so-called 'psychedelic art'.
47. Thomas B. Hess, 1965, op.cit., p.43.
48. This concern was reflected in the work of the artist Bruce Lacey, who addressed the matter of drug addiction in a sculpture exhibited in London in January 1965. Frank Whitford described this in the *Arts Review*: ('London Galleries: British painters', 23 January–6 February 1965, p.8): 'his drug addict has a system filled entirely with pills, and a machine at the end of the large intestine dispenses purple hearts (genuine) ... when a penny is put into the slot'. Francis Bacon's *Lying Figure with a Hypodermic Syringe* (1963) has been described by historian Stuart Sillars as 'both a rejection of the emerging drug culture—the psychedelic sixties—and an assertion that we are all somehow part of it.' (Stuart Sillars, 'Caro verbum factus est: British art in the 1960s' in B.J. Moore-Gilbert and John Seed (eds), *Cultural Revolution? The Challenge of the Arts in the 1960s*, London 1992, p.256.)
49. In 1967, Mick Jagger and Keith Richards were to be controversially imprisoned for possession of illegal drugs and the Beatles' song 'A Day in the Life' was banned by the BBC for supposed drug references.
50. It was made illegal in Britain the following year.
51. Ehrenzweig also used similar language in 'The pictorial space of Bridget Riley', *Art International*, February 1965.
52. Thomas B. Hess, 1965, op.cit., p.50.
53. Given that in the USA and UK in the 1960s wine was not the everyday drink that it has subsequently become, Op was being likened to a fairly pricey commodity whose consumption was limited to an economic elite. Elsewhere in his article, Hess expressed contempt for Op's popularity with the 'Public' and the 'mass mediums [*sic*]', so there may be a suggestion here that Op was an art for the *nouveau riche*, not the established 'upper class' who patronized Abstract Expressionism.
54. The word Soma itself means 'body' but the effects suggested by Huxley are psychological and quantifiably predictable: 'one cubic centimetre cures ten gloomy sentiments' (Aldous Huxley, *Brave New World*, London: Flamingo Modern Classic, edn. 1994, p.48). Soma is routinely served with coffee (p.67), which again indicates the safe predictability of its effects.
55. Theodore Roszak, 1970, op.cit., p.23.
56. Albert Hofman, LSD, *My Problem Child* (1983), quoted in Antonio Melechi, 1997, op.cit., p.64. Ellipses in Melechi.
57. Leary emphasized this by entitling his autobiography *High Priest* (pub. 1968); he belonged to a hippy commune called the Brotherhood of Eternal Love, which imitated Mexican Indian mescaline-based religious ceremonies. (See Antonio Melechi, 1997, op.cit., esp. p.100.) Roszak claimed 'Leary ... preferred to come on during his LSD camp meetings with all the solemnity of the risen Christ, complete with white cotton pajamas *[sic]*, incense and the stigmata of his legal persecutions' (Theodore Roszak, 1970, op.cit., p.166).
58. This contrasts, for example, with the early nineteenth-century Fourierist dream of a future utopia based on a 'scientifically' planned social structure.
59. Theodore Roszak, 1970, op. cit., p.186.

60. Roszak's work is related to that of another American writer, Paul Goodman, who also wrote about the disaffection of contemporary youth. Goodman founded the Gestalt school of psychoanalysis and became well known in 1960s' counter-cultural circles. The growing influence of the Gestaltists, which had begun earlier in the century, may be partially attributed to Goodman, the success of whose *Growing Up Absurd* (1960) may have attracted readers to his earlier works such as *Gestalt Therapy* (1951). As early as 1962 there was evidence in the USA of young people seeking an alternative to the existing social structure. The American organization 'Students for a Democratic Society' published its first manifesto, the 'Port Huron Statement', in 1962, expressing 'a yearning to believe that there is an alternative to the present, that something can be done to change circumstances in the school, the workplaces, the bureaucracies, the government' (B.J. Moore Gilbert and John Seed (eds), 1992, op.cit., p.52.).
61. Theodore Roszak, 1970, op.cit., p.187.
62. Anton Ehrenzweig, 'The pictorial space of Bridget Riley', *Art International*, February 1965, p.21.
63. Ibid., p.21.
64. Maurice de Sausmarez, *Bridget Riley*, London 1970, p.26, quotes this passage and tells us that Riley had read Severini.
65. Maurice Merleau-Ponty (1960), 'Eye and Mind' in G.A. Johnson and M. Smith (eds), *The Merleau-Ponty Aesthetics Reader*, 1993.
66. Ibid., p.127.
67. Ibid., p.124.
68. Guy Burn, 'The New Generation', *The Arts Review*, 44–18 April 1964, p.10. Italics original. Riley exhibits included *Tremor* (1962, Fig. 5), *Shuttle* (1964, Fig. 9), *Hidden Squares* (1961) and *Crest* (1964, Fig. 20).
69. There are also suggestions of the concept of 'eternal life': the Roman Catholic belief that Eucharistic transubstantiation is a key to this and the alchemists' belief that finding the secret of converting base metal to gold would also reveal the means to defeat death.
70. Maurice Merleau-Ponty (1945), *Phenomenology of Perception*, (trans. Colin Smith, English edn, London 1962, p.68). In this work, Merleau-Ponty argued that 'the body is neither subject nor object but an ambiguous mode of existence that affects all knowledge'.
71. Rudolf Arnheim, *Art and Visual Perception*, London 1954, p.8.
72. Ibid., p.8.
73. Rosalind E. Krauss, 1993, op.cit., p.205–6.
74. Briony Fer, 1995, op.cit., p.159.
75. Rosalind E. Krauss, 1993, op.cit., p.215–216.
76. Briony Fer, 1995, op.cit., p.159. See also B. Fer, *On Abstract Art*, New Haven and London 1997, p.63. Fer relates Bataille's concern with destruction to Freud's notion of the 'death drive'.
77. Anon., 'Something to blink at', *Time*, May 1964, p.45.
78. Briony Fer, 'Poussière/peinture' in Briony Fer, 1997, op.cit., all quotations p.79.
79. Thomas Crow, *The Rise of the Sixties*, London 1996, p.113.
80. Ibid., p.113.
81. 'The increasing divergence of opinion and valuation discernible during the sixties between orthodox Modernist criticism and a broader Modernist culture of modern art may have had its roots in a significant divergence in artistic practices during the previous decade'. Charles Harrison and Paul Wood, 1993, op.cit., p.185.
82. 'Jackson Pollock ... reopened the break that Picasso had plugged: he began to paint on the ground, to walk on his pictures, to make gravity itself an agent of his process of inscription. The role played by this horizontalization in the rupture Pollock introduced in the history of painting was immediately repressed by Clement Greenberg's modernist interpretation (according to which, Pollock's paintings contributed to an "optical mirage").' Yve-Alain Bois, 'Liquid words' in Yve-Alain Bois and Rosalind E. Krauss, *Formless: A User's Guide*, New York 1997, p.126.
83. Op art was discussed in terms that clearly show it was regarded as modernist even by its detractors, see e.g. Sidney Tillim's comments relating it to Constructivism and the Bauhaus (see Chapter 4 and Sidney Tillim, 'Optical art: pending or ending?', *Art Magazine*, January 1965, pp.16–23). Riley's supporters likewise discussed her work in modernist terms (see e.g. Anon. 'Painters who explore the mechanics of vision', *The Times*, 1 October 1963, where comparisons were made to Monet's late work). Riley herself insisted 'I do not mean my paintings to look three dimensional ... I work in two dimensions' (quoted in Anon., 'Miss Bridget Riley and Optical art', *The Times*, 19 April 1965) – a reference to the modernist insistence on respecting the flat plane of the canvas. Other claims she made for her work were typically modernist in character: see, e.g. Bridget Riley, 'Perception is the medium': 'It is absolutely untrue that my work depends on literary impulse or has any illustrative intention. The marks on the canvas are the sole and essential agents in a series of relationships which form the structure of the painting', 1965, pp.32–33.
84. Roger Fry, 'An essay in aesthetics' (1909) in Charles Harrison and Paul Wood (eds), 2003, op.cit., p.80.
85. Thomas B. Hess, 1965, op.cit., p.49.
86. Quoted in Cyril Barrett, *An Introduction to Optical Art*, London 1971, p.36.
87. Thomas B. Hess, 1965, op.cit., p.49.
88. Anton Ehrenzweig, 'Introduction' to the catalogue of Riley's one-person show at Gallery One, May 1962.
89. Thomas B. Hess, 1965, op.cit., p.43.
90. Cyril Barrett, 1971, op.cit., p.36.

91. For example, 'The plight of our culture: industrialism and class mobility', *Commentary*, 15 June 1953; 'Modernist painting' (Radio broadcast, 1961) reproduced in Francis Frascina and Jonathan Harris (eds), *Art in Modern Culture*, London 1992; 'Avant-garde and Kitsch' in Clement Greenberg, *Art and Culture Critical Essays*, Boston 1961, edited reprint.
92. Robert Hewison, *Culture and Consensus: England, Art and Politics Since 1940*, London 1997, p.88.
93. Partly promoted by the British Council, which travelled throughout the USA in 1965.
94. Leon Kraushar, collector, quoted in Cécile Whiting, *A Taste for Pop: Pop Art, Gender and Consumer Culture*, Cambridge and New York 1997, p.96.
95. Andy Warhol's studio, where he had the help of various assistants, was known as the 'Factory' whereas Op art collectives tended to describe their studios as 'laboratories', the former had more 'proletarian' associations than the latter. Warhol's choice of name seems calculated to challenge notions of art as 'aristocratic' or elite, whereas the reference to laboratories suggests a different kind of elite: the professional scientist or 'technocrat'. See my comments on the class-based distinction between science and technology, in Chapter 1.
96. Kenneth Coutts-Smith, 'London: The new scene', *Arts Review*, 17 April–1 May 1965, p.3. Italics original.
97. Cécile Whiting, 1997, op.cit., p.117. My argument here follows Whiting.
98. Ibid., pp.30–31.
99. Ibid., p.39.
100. Ibid., p.41.
101. A claim supported by Hess' assertion in *Art News* (1965, p.41) that 'some forty or fifty thousand 'Op exhibitions had been shown in the period 1963–5 prior to 'The Responsive Eye' – Hess does not say whether this is a US or international tally – only large attendances would explain such a phenomenon.
102. Robert Melville, 'Abstract illusionism', *New Statesman*, 16 October 1964d, p.588.
103. David Thompson, 'London Commentary – Concentric circles', *Studio International*, June 1966, p.268.
104. Thomas Crow, 1996, op.cit., p.113.
105. See Serge Guilbaut, *How New York Stole the Idea of Modern Art: Abstract Expressionism, Freedom and the Cold War*, Chicago, 1983, for an account of the different audiences for various types of art.
106. Maurice Merleau-Ponty, 1945, op.cit., p.68.

Chapter 3
A Modern English Art
pp.93-121

1. Charles Harrison, *English Art and Modernism 1900–1939*, London 1994, p.viii.
2. Benedict Anderson, *Imagined Communities – Reflections on the Origin and Spread of Nationalism*, London 1983/1991, p.6 (emphasis original).
3. Ibid., p.141.
4. William Vaughan, 'Pevsner's art history'. Lecture given at 'Pevsner's "The Buildings of England"' Conference, Victoria and Albert Museum, 13 July 2001.
5. Ibid.
6. Nikolaus Pevsner, *The Englishness of English Art*, London 1956, p.19.
7. Ibid., p.181.
8. The terms 'English' and 'British' were used interchangeably at this time, more frequently than today, with an implicit assumption that England was the dominant country in the UK (compare the use of Union Jacks by England supporters in the 1966 World Cup football contest with more recent use of the St George Cross; in the 1960s, to the English at least, the Union Jack was the English, as well as the British, flag). In this chapter I shall use 'Britain' to mean England, Scotland and Wales, where many of the media quoted here circulated, but the reader should be aware that at the time 'England' may well have been used either to mean all three countries or with the implication that Wales and Scotland were of little perceived relevance.
9. David Thompson, 'International recognition for British painting', *The Times*, 31 December 1963.
10. Bryan Robertson in Bryan Robertson, John Russell and Snowdon, *Private View*, London 1965, p.49.
11. The Peter Stuyvesant Foundation, established by a tobacco company, supported and promoted young British artists to enhance its founder's reputation, and that of its products, with both government and affluent young people. See Simon Faulkner, 'Art, cigarettes and visual culture in the sixties: the Peter Stuyvesant Foundation and the "New Generation" exhibitions, 1964–66', *Visual Culture in Britain*, 2000, vol. 1, no 1.
12. Edward Lucie-Smith has more recently argued that Riley's Op paintings do contain a 'landscape element' (*Art Today*, Third ed., Oxford 1989, p.304), but this is not claimed in his earlier writings.
13. Edward Lucie-Smith, 'Introduction' in the catalogue for 'One Year of British Art', Arthur Tooth & Son, London 21 January–9 February 1963, p.2.
14. By 1951 80% lived in towns/cities: Arthur Marwick, *British Society Since 1945*, London 1996, p.32.
15. Nanette Aldred (1987) 'A Canterbury tale' in David Mellor (ed.), *A Paradise Lost: The Neo-romantic Imagination in Britain 1935–1955*, London 1987, p.118.

16. David Mellor (1987) 'The body and the land' in ibid. p.34. During the war, the American-funded Pilgrim Trust charity had commissioned British artists to paint historic country houses, as a record in case they were destroyed by bombing. These properties, belonging to a tiny minority of people at the top of the (specifically) English social system, were seen as a central and irreplaceable expression of the nation's heritage and identity. The millions of homes in large towns and cities, which were more likely to form the targets of enemy attacks, were not considered by the Trust as subjects for artistic record. The project's title, 'Recording Britain', implied that this small number of up-market residences constituted Britain. The Trust employed 63 artists and produced 1,549 paintings and drawings featuring elite rural properties in 32 English counties and four Welsh ones (none in Scotland!)

17. Jacquetta Hawkes' book *A Land* (described by Mellor as a 'fantasia' and illustrated by Henry Moore), was published in 1951. She later joined the Campaign for Nuclear Disarmament (CND) and took part in at least one of the Aldermaston Marches organized by CND between 1958 and 1963 (Jeff Nuttall, *Bomb Culture*, London 1968, p.51).

18. David Mellor, 'The body and the land' in David Mellor (ed.), 1987, op.cit., p.24.

19. Robert Hewison, *Culture and Consensus*, London 1995/1997, p.24.

20. David Sylvester, *Henry Moore* (1968, exhibition catalogue); introduction reproduced in *About Modern Art*, London 1997 edition, p.192.

21. Martin J. Wiener, *English Culture and the Decline of the Industrial Spirit 1850–1980*, London 1981/1992, p.78. The 'literary reviewer' was Anthony Thwaite, writing in the *New Statesman*.

22. Anon., *The Times*, 2 April 1964; Lil Picard, 'Op report', *Kunstwerk*, July 1965, p.8.

23. Bryan Robertson, John Russell and Snowdon, 1965, op.cit., p.7.

24. Charles Harrison, 1994, op.cit., p.234.

25. David Thomson and Geoffrey Warner, *England in the Twentieth Century*, Harmondsworth 1981, p.203.

26. Arthur Marwick, 1996, op.cit., p.18.

27. Alan Sked and Chris Cook, *Post- war Britain: A Political History* (Third edn), London 1990, pp.26–28, 106.

28. David Mellor, 1987, op.cit., pp.67 and 68.

29. See Frances Donaldson, *The British Council: The First Fifty Years*, London 1984, p.238.

30. In 1969 Clement Greenberg was to claim that linearity was central to all stylistic developments of the 1960s, appearing in the 1950s in Vasarely's work in France and in that of Ellsworth Kelly, Barnett Newman, David Smith and Robert Rauschenberg in the USA. (Clement Greenberg, *Avant-garde Attitudes: The John Power Lecture in Contemporary Art*, 1969). In 1956, however, Pevsner (*The Englishness of English Art*) presented linearity as an English characteristic dating back to the Perpendicular style of architecture.

31. Clive Bell, 'The aesthetic hypothesis' in Charles Harrison and Paul Wood (eds), *Art in Theory 1900–2000*, Oxford 2003, p.108. Ultimately, one could trace this line in Western thought back to Plato, with his distrust of imitative art.

32. David Mellor, 1987, op.cit.

33. David Thompson, 1963, op.cit.

34. Ibid. Interestingly, Thompson appears to imagine the artists themselves as a 'community' within the wider (imagined) community of the nation. In this review, the 'senior generation' could be taken for the direct progenitors of the 'younger generation'. All are presented as working toward a common goal.

35. Ibid. It is not clear whether Thompson implicated Riley's black-and-white work in his statement 'It [British painting] is generally cautious about colour' or if the boldness of such a limited palette is one of the exceptions implied in 'generally'. Perhaps he regarded the precision of her work as an avoidance of 'the sensuous, material, physical aspects of art', or its direct stimulation of the nervous system as a rare British engagement with these qualities.

36. Ibid.

37. As early as 1948 Greenberg had correlated the rise of New York painters to international prominence with the rise in US industrial and commercial power and corresponding national wealth.
See Clement Greenberg, 'The decline of cubism', *Partisan Review*, 1948, vol. XV, no 3, pp.366–369.

38. G.S. Whittet, 'G.S. Whittet says', *The Studio*, no. 847, November 1963, p.179.

39. Ibid.

40. Andrew Forge, 'Presentation', *New Statesman*, 24 April 1964, p.655.

41. David Thompson, 'Introduction' to the catalogue to *The New Generation*, Whitechapel Gallery March–May 1964.

42. Alan Bowness, *Recent British Painting. The Peter Stuyvesant Collection* pub 1968 (text written in 1967 for a catalogue of the same name published that year), 1967, p.12.

43. Charles Harrison has shown (1994, op.cit., pp.285–287) how English Constructivism was shaped by the involvement of Russian artist Naum Gabo.

44. Ibid. The associations with landscape discussed above may have been seen as more important, in this respect, than associations with a 'foreign' art form.
45. Norbert Lynton, 'Bridget Riley', *Art International*, September 1962, p.47.
46. Max Kozloff, 'British painting today', *Encounter*, vol. xxii, no 1, January 1964.
47. John Russell, 'Towards grown-up greatness', *The Times*, 3 February 1963a.
48. Thompson also felt 'good taste' to be something of a liability in a painting, David Thompson, 1963, op.cit.
49. Auerbach, Blake, Hockney, Hoyland, Hughes, Irwin, Latham, Phillips, Riley, Jack Smith, Stephenson and the sculptors George Fullard and David Hall.
50. Edward Lucie-Smith, 'Introduction' in the catalogue for 'One Year of British Art', 1963, p.2.
51. John Russell, 1963a, op.cit.
52. John Russell, 'Hazard is everywhere', *Sunday Times*, 15 September 1963b. See Fig. 13.
53. John Russell, 'Downright professional', *Sunday Times*, 19 July 1964.
54. Robert Melville, 'Abstract illusionism', *New Statesman*, 16 October 1964d, p.588.
55. For an interesting discussion of the distinction between 'illusion' and 'illusionism', see Richard Shiff, 'Bridget Riley: The edge of animation' in Paul Moorhouse (ed.), *Bridget Riley* (catalogue), Tate, London 2003.
56. Norbert Lynton, 1962, op.cit.
57. Anon., 'The gestures British artists make', *The Times*, 29 July 1964.
58. Ibid.
59. John Russell, 1963a, op.cit.
60. David Thompson, 1963, op.cit.
61. Anon., 'The gestures British artists make', *The Times*, 29 July 1964.
62. Robyn Denny, 'London Letter', *Art International*, May 1964, p.53.
63. Bryan Robertson in Bryan Robertson, John Russell and Snowdon, 1965, op.cit.
64. Bryan Robertson writing about Eduardo Paolozzi in Bryan Robertson, John Russell and Snowdon, 1965, op.cit., p.79.
65. Now known as *Water Lily Pond*, National Gallery, London 1916–26.
66. Anon., 'Painters who explore the mechanics of vision', *The Times*, 1 October 1963.
67. Martin J. Wiener, 1981/1992, op.cit., p.15.
68. Ibid., p.16.
69. Ibid., p.15.
70. Bryan Robertson in Bryan Robertson, John Russell and Snowdon, 1965, op.cit., p.143.
71. Ibid., p.143.
72. Ibid., p.168.
73. Ibid., p.145.
74. Arthur Marwick, 1996, op.cit., p.41.
75. Michelle H. Bogart, *Artists, Advertising and the Borders of Art*, Chicago 1995. See esp. chapter 6.
76. Thomas B. Hess, 'You can hang it in the hall', *Art News*, 1965, vol. 64, no 2, pp.41–43, 49–50, see p.50.
77. Christopher Booker, *The Neophiliacs*, London 1969, p.153. A number of similar comments appear here.
78. Ibid., p.31, see also p.30.
79. In the index to *The Neophiliacs*, 'professionalism' is listed as '"Professionalism", cult of as symptom of fantasy', neatly summing up the book's approach to the phenomenon.
80. Peter Blake, Anthony Caro, Eduardo Paolozzi et al. letter to *The Sunday Times*, June 1963, quoted in David Mellor, *The Sixties Art Scene in London*, London 1993, p.91.
81. David Thompson, 1963, op.cit.
82. Charles Harrison, 1994, op.cit., p.240.
83. John Russell, 1963b, op.cit.
And see Figs. 13 and 18, *Fall*.
84. John Russell in Bryan Robertson, John Russell and Snowdon, 1965, op.cit., p.209.
85. John Russell, 1964, op.cit.
86. According to Marwick, average earnings rose 34% between 1955 and 1960 (while inflation was 15% over the same period) and continued to rise steeply through the 1960s (Arthur Marwick, 1996, op.cit., p.123).
87. For example, John Osborne (*Look Back in Anger*, 1956), John Braine (*Room at the Top*, 1957). When these works were published, the writers were 27 and 35 respectively: as Marwick says 'not youths', but not middle-aged either.
88. Arthur Marwick, 1996, op.cit., p.123.
89. Barry Curtis has pointed out that American poet and songwriter Shel Silverstein, who coined the term 'swinging London', attributed the city's new image to a combination of European, American and traditional British influences. The effects of perceived infiltration of foreign influences on life in the capital may themselves have contributed to concerns about loss of national identity.
90. Sainsbury was also chairman of his family's supermarket chain, an example of how those made wealthy by the developing consumer culture could exert considerable influence in other areas of national life.
91. John Sainsbury, 'Introduction' *British Painting in the Sixties*, Tate and Whitechapel Galleries, June 1963.
92. John Russell, 1964, op.cit.
93. Sidney Simon, 'From England's green and pleasant bowers', *Art News*, April 1965.
94. Hella Pick, 'New York's Responsive Eye', *Guardian*, 13 March 1965.
95. Gorer analysed the major public attitude survey in 1955, finding that in a largely urban country 'most people picture their country as rural'. Quoted in Martin J. Wiener, 1981/1992, op.cit., p.75.

96. Anon., 'Miss Bridget Riley and Optical Art', *The Times*, 19 April 1965.
97. See Michael Bracewell, 'A plea for painting', *Guardian Weekend* supplement, 15 March 1997, p.14.
98. Edward Lucie-Smith, 'Bridget Riley's Venice success', *The Times*, 29 October 1968.

Chapter 4
Un-American Activities:
The Reception of Riley's Work in America
pp.123-141

1. Jerrold Lanes, 'Current and forthcoming exhibitions: New York', *Burlington Magazine*, April 1965, vol. 92, no. 745, pp.219–20.
2. Norman Rosenthal, 'American art: a view from Europe' in Christos M. Joachimedes and Norman Rosenthal (eds), *American Art in the Twentieth Century*, London 1993, p.13.
3. Nigel Wheale, 'Modernism and its consequences: continuity or break?' in *The Postmodern Arts*, London 1995, p.16.
4. Serge Guilbaut, *How New York Stole the Idea of Modern Art: Abstract Expressionism, Freedom and the Cold War*, Chicago 1983.
5. Ibid., p.55.
6. See Alan Sked and Chris Cook, *Post-war Britain: A Political History* (Third edn), London 1990, p.51.
7. Eva Cockcroft 'Abstract Expressionism, weapon of the cold war' (1974) in Francis Frascina and Jonathan Harris (eds), *Art in Modern Culture*, London 1992.
8. Ibid., p.83: '[A]lmost every [US] secretary of state after the end of the second world war, right up to the present [1974] has been an individual trained and groomed by the various foundations and agencies owned and controlled by the Rockefellers. The development of American cold war politics was directly shaped by the Rockefellers'.
9. Particularly interesting in view of the European and Russian origins of much of the MoMA aesthetic.
10. Serge Guilbaut, 1983, op.cit.
11. US consumer credit increased by 800% between 1945 and 1955 while GNP rose 250% between 1945 and 1960. Douglas Tallack 'Culture, politics and society in mid-century America' (1993) in Christos M. Joachimedes and Norman Rosenthal (eds), op.cit., p.29.
12. One 'hot' manifestation of which was the USA's involvement in the war in Vietnam, escalating from the supply of 'military advisers' in the early 1960s to large-scale bombing and troop deployment from 1965–73.
13. Nancy Marmer, 'Los Angeles' in *Artforum*, December 1964, pp.11–12.
14. Sidney Simon, 'From England's green and pleasant bowers', *Art News*, April 1965, pp.28–31, 64.
15. Thomas B. Hess, 'You can hang it in the hall', *Art News*, 1965, vol. 64, no 2, see pp.42–43.
16. See Chapter 2.
17. Quoted in Harold Osborne, *Abstraction and Artifice in Twentieth Century Art*, Oxford 1979, p.149.
18. Thomas B. Hess, 1965, p.41.
19. Nan Rosenthal, 'New York: Gallery notes', *Art in America*, 1965, no 1, pp.114–6.
20. Elizabeth Stevens, 'Bridget Riley', *Art News*, vol. 64, no 2, April 1965, p.14.
21. Harold Rosenberg, *The Anxious Object*, Chicago 1964/1966, p.269.

22. Sidney Tillim, 'Optical art: pending or ending?', *Art Magazine*, January 1965, pp.16–23.
23. Ibid., p.18.
24. Ibid., p.21. Tillim claimed this term was used in Europe but I have not come across it in my own research.
25. Ibid., p.21.
26. Ibid, p.18.
27. Ibid., p.21.
28. P. Cézanne, 'Letters to Emile Bernard', excerpted in Charles Harrison and Paul Wood, *Art in Theory 1900–2000*, Oxford 2003, p.33.
29. Amédée Ozenfant 'Foundations of Modern Art' (1928) in Charles Harrison and Paul Wood, 2003, op.cit., pp.369–71.
30. Rosalind Krauss, 'Bridget Riley, Richard Feigen Gallery', *Artforum*, June 1966, p.51.
31. 'In conversation with Maurice de Sausmarez' (1967) in Robert Kudielka (ed.), *The Mind's Eye: Bridget Riley Collected Writings 1965–1999*, London 1999, p.62.
32. Tillim is cited by Barbara M. Weise as one of Greenberg's 'closest followers': 'Greenberg and the group: a retrospective view' in Francis Frascina and Jonathan Harris, 1992, op.cit., pp.225–63.
33. Anon., 'Painters who explore the mechanics of vision', *The Times*, 1 October 1963.
34. Anon., 'The gestures British artists make', *The Times*, 29 July 1964.
35. Rose was married to Frank Stella, who in turn was critically supported by Michael Fried, who like Tillim was another member of Greenberg's 'group'.
36. Barbara Rose, 'Beyond vertigo: Optical art at the Modern', *Artforum*, April 1965, pp.30–32, see p.32.
37. Lisa G. Corrin, 'Continuum. Bridget Riley's 60s and 70s. A view from the 90s', in L.G. Corin et al. *Bridget Riley Paintings from the 1960s and 70s*, London 1999.
38. See Alan Wallach, 'The Museum of Modern Art: The past's future' (1991) in Francis Frascina and Jonathan Harris, 1992, op.cit.
39. See chapter 7 for more on this issue.
40. John Canaday, 'The Responsive Eye: Three cheers and high hopes', *The New York Times*, 28 February 1965.
41. Anon., 'Something to blink at', *Time*, 1 May 1964, p.45.
42. Anon., 'Op art: pictures that attack the eye', *Time*, 23 October 1964, pp.42–44.
43. Anon., 'Uptown', *Time*, 5 March 1965, p.6.
44. Anon., 'Art in New York' (review page), *Time*, 26 March 1965.
45. John Canaday, 'That's right, it's wrong', *New York Times*, 14 March 1965b.
46. Lil Picard, 'Op–report', *Kunstwerk*, July 1965, p.8.
47. Hella Pick, 'New York's Responsive Eye', *Guardian*, 13 March 1965.
48. Nancy Marmer, 'Bridget Riley, Feigen-Palmer Gallery', *Artforum*, December 1965.
49. For example, the 'Situation' exhibition in London in 1960 showed the work of a number of young British artists who had been particularly impressed by the sheer scale of the American works. See Roger Coleman's introduction to the catalogue, reproduced in David Mellor, *The Sixties Art Scene in London*, 1993, pp.90–91.
50. Mario Amaya, 'When Op becomes Pop', *Financial Times*, 26 May 1965.
51. Bridget Riley, 'Practising abstraction. Talking to Michael Craig-Martin' in *Bridget Riley Dialogues on Art*, London 1995, p.69. I shall turn to a more detailed discussion of the plagiarism of Riley's work by the fashion industry in Chapter 6.
52. Jerrold Lanes, 1965, op.cit.
53. Ibid. Note the essential agreement here with Tillim, above.
54. I am grateful to Barry Curtis for pointing out this possible connection.
55. See Herbert Read, 'What is revolutionary art?' in Charles Harrison and Paul Wood, 2003, op.cit., pp.510–514.
56. Anon., 'The gestures British artists make', *The Times*, 29 July 1964.
57. David Mellor, 1993, op.cit., p.131.
58. Anne Massey, *The Independent Group*, Manchester 1995, p.106.
59. For example, *Lee I* and *Lee II* (both 1961, private collection), based on a motif derived from Lee brand jeans. David Mellor, 1993, op.cit., pp.124–6.
60. Marco Livingstone, 'The artist thinks', *Pop Art: A Continuing History*, New York 1990, pp.93–113.
61. Laurence Alloway, 'The development of British Pop' in Lucy Lippard, *Pop Art*, London 1970, pp.27–67.
62. Mario Amaya, 'When Op becomes Pop', *Financial Times*, 26 May 1965. Amaya was very familiar with the New York art scene: three years later he was with Andy Warhol the day Valerie Solanas shot him, and was also wounded.
www.warholstars.org/chron/andydies68n33.html
63. Bridget Riley, 'Perception is the medium', *Art News*, October 1965, p.32.

Chapter 5
Happenings on Canvas:
Notions of 'The Theatrical' in Relation to Riley's Op Art
pp.143-169

1. Bridget Riley, 'Perception is the medium', *Art News*, October 1965, pp.32, 33, 66, see p.33.
2. Michael Fried, 'Art and Objecthood' (1967) as quoted in Charles Harrison and Paul Wood 'Modernity and modernism reconsidered' (1993), in Paul Wood, Francis Frascina, Jonathan Harris, Charles Harrison and Paul Wood, *Modernism in Dispute: Art Since the Forties* (1993) (ellipses and italics in Harrison and Wood). By contrast, according to Susan Sontag (1966), the Italian Futurist Marinetti 'envisaged the theatre as a final synthesis of all the arts'. See 'Film and theatre' in Gerald Mast, Marshall Cohen, Leo Braudy, *Film Theory and Criticism*, New York and Oxford 1992, pp.362–74, see p.372.
3. Thomas Crow, *The Rise of the Sixties*, London 1996, p.113.
4. Andreas Huyssen, 'Mass culture as woman: Modernism's other' in *After the Great Divide: Modernism, Mass Culture and Postmodernism*, London 1986, p.51.
5. Ibid., p.53. See also my chapters 6 and 7.
6. See Michael Fried, 'An introduction to my art criticism' in *Art and Objecthood*, Chicago and London 1998, p.48.
7. Michael Fried, 'Art and objecthood', *Artforum*, Summer 1967, vol. 5, no 10, pp.12–23.
8. Michael Fried, 1998, 'An introduction', op.cit., p.42.
9. In this chapter I give my own understanding of Fried's essay, in terms of its apparent, though unintended, implications in relation to Op art. The reader is referred to 'Art and objecthood' and *Art and Objecthood* for Fried's full argument.
10. Michael Fried, 1967, op.cit., p.12.
11. Ibid., p.15.
12. Quoted in ibid. Morris wrote this passage in 1966.
13. Anton Ehrenzweig, 'The pictorial space of Bridget Riley', *Art International*, February 1965, pp.20–24; and see Chapter 2.
14. Art which 'theatricalized the body, put it endlessly on stage', Michael Fried, 1998, op.cit., p.42.
15. Michael Fried, 1967, op.cit., p.22. Italics original.
16. Ibid. Italics original.
17. Fried did not argue in 'Art and objecthood' that it was actually possible to appreciate a work of art in an 'instant', but claimed that for some (modernist) works 'at every moment the work itself is wholly manifest' (Michael Fried, 1967, op.cit., p.22) – implying that such instantaneous appreciation was theoretically possible, if not a practical proposition. He argued that this could be true of a sculpture, even though at one instant one could only have a single view of it (from among the many possible views), and would need to walk round it (in time) to see all views. Nonetheless, this argument opposes Ehrenzweig's emphasis on the need to experience one of Riley's paintings over time, to allow the physical and psychological sensations engendered to develop in one's nervous system. There is no suggestion that it would be even theoretically possible to experience such sensations 'instantaneously'.
18. Anton Ehrenzweig, 'Introduction' in the catalogue to Bridget Riley's one-person show at Gallery One, London May 1962.
19. William Seitz, 'The Responsive Eye' catalogue, MoMA, New York 1965, p.30.
20. Robert Morris and Donald Judd, whose quotes are not always individually attributed, and Tony Smith. There is a point of similarity between Fried's criticism of Minimalist art and Hess' criticism of Op art some two years earlier. Both men found it problematic that true art could be accessible to a wide public. While Thomas B. Hess ('You can hang it in the hall', *Art News*, 1965, vol. 64, no 2, pp.41–43, 49–50, see p.49) insisted that art was 'difficult, serious, remote, aristocratic', Fried took issue with Minimalist sculptor Tony Smith's 'praise of Corbusier [*sic*] as "more available" than Michelangelo ... "It's something everyone can understand." It is, I think, hardly necessary to add that the availability of modernist art is not of this kind' (Michael Fried, 1967, op.cit., p.19). An anxiety about who is experiencing this art, as well as the nature of that experience, apparently underlay both men's criticisms of the art forms of which they expressed disapproval.
21. Michael Fried, 1967, op.cit., p.22. Fried admitted the difficulty poetry and music faced, in being time-dependent and saw music as particularly hampered by the similarities between a concert and a theatrical performance.
22. Interestingly, Fried asserted that film, 'by its very nature, escapes theater entirely'. He claimed that it did this 'automatically' but was not explicit about how film 'provided ... a refuge from theater' (Michael Fried, 1967, op.cit., p.21).
23. Fried's opening paragraph in 'Art and objecthood' implies that he saw Op and Pop art as neither modernist nor 'literalist' but he did not expand on this.
24. Günter Berghaus (1995) 'Happenings in Europe' in Mariellen R. Sandford (ed.), *Happenings and Other Acts*, London 1995, pp.310–88, see p.369. Berghaus notes that Allan Kaprow arranged another event the next day. Neither performance was well received by the Festival organizers.
25. Stuart Sillars, '*Caro verbum factus est*: British art in the 1960s' in B. Moore Gilbert and John Seed (eds), *Cultural Revolution? The Challenge of the Arts in the 1960s*, London 1992, p.257. Fried placed considerable importance on 'shape' in modernist painting. See Fried, 1967, op.cit., pp.12, 15.
26. T.J. Clark, *Farewell to an Idea: Episodes from a History of Modernism*, New Haven & London 1999, p.300.
27. Thomas Crow, 1996, op.cit., p.33.
28. See note 37 below.

29. Arthur Marwick, *The Sixties: Cultural Revolution in Britain, France, Italy and the United States c.1958–c.1974*, Oxford 1998, p.191.
30. Riley used assistants to help execute her own paintings.
31. Sidra Stich, *Yves Klein*, London 1995, p.175.
32. Barbara Moore 'New York Intermedia: Happenings and Fluxus in the 1960s' in Christos M. Joachimedes and Norman Rosenthal (eds), *American Art in the Twentieth Century*, p.100/102. Dine's work was entitled *The Smiling Workman*.
33. Robert Bernasconi, 'Maurice Merleau-Ponty' in Ted Honderich (ed.), *Oxford Companion to Philosophy*, Oxford 1995, p.554.
34. Maurice Merleau-Ponty (1945), *Phenomenology of Perception*, trans. Colin Smith, English edition, London 1962, p.68. In this work, Merleau-Ponty argued that 'the body is neither subject nor object but an ambiguous mode of existence that affects all knowledge' (Robert Bernasconi, 1995, op.cit.).
35. Maurice Merleau-Ponty, 'Eye and Mind' (1960) in G.A. Johnson and M. Smith (eds), *The Merleau-Ponty Aesthetics Reader*, Illinois 1993, p.127.
36. For example, Gunter Berghaus, writing on the work of performance artist Jacques Lebel, who produced Happenings in France, England and Italy in the 1960s, claims that for Lebel 'Happenings are not designed to be contemplated by spectators but to force them into active intervention'. (Gunter Berghaus, 1995, op.cit., p.352).
37. Claims of Pollock's bodily connection to his work are various. According to Pollock's biographers, Steven Naifeh and Gregory White Smith (*Jackson Pollock: An American Saga*, London1989), Pollock suffered from 'ocular migraines' which caused him to see moving, 'swirling images' which, he later claimed, resembled his drip paintings (pp.538–39). They report that 'When a woman asked him "How do you know when you're finished [with a painting]?" Jackson replied "How do you know when you're finished making love?"' (p.541). They quote Pollock: 'On the floor I am more at ease. I feel nearer, more a part of the painting, since this way I can walk around it, work from the four sides and literally be in the painting' (p.552, italics original).
38. A degree of public familiarity with Pollock's work may be deduced from the fact that it was shown in London as part of 'Modern Art in the USA' at the Tate Gallery in 1956, when the BBC screened the Namuth film and a lecture on Pollock by Meyer Shapiro. (See Jeremy Lewison, *Interpreting Pollock*, London 1999, p.8.) Mellor tells us that British artist Gillian Ayres' 'understanding of Pollock's Action technique [was] based primarily on a viewing of the Hans Namuth film of Pollock painting (which may also have been the inspiration for Ken Russell's film of William Green [British artist, participant in the 'Situation' exhibition], *Painting an Action Painting*)'. David Mellor, *The Sixties Art Scene in London*, London 1993, p.86.
39. Quoted in Giuliano Briganti (1989), 'Cultural provocation: Italian art of the early sixties' in Emily Braun (ed.), *Italian Art in the Twentieth Century*, London 1989, p.304.
40. Michael Fried, 1967, op.cit., p.21.
41. This again recalls Bataille's interest in the 'dust and dirt' found at 'ground level' and the importance of the horizontal axis in his work, which is, as John Lechte puts it, 'the axis of sacrifice, loss, chance and eroticism' (J. Lechte, *Fifty Key Contemporary Thinkers*, London and New York, p.98).
42. It was related to Monet's work at the time: see chapter 3 and Anon., 'Painters who explore the mechanics of vision', *The Times*, 1 October 1963.
43. Anon., Untitled item in a gossip/trivia page, *Daily Mail*, 10 September 1963. By contrast, Jasia Reichardt seems hardly to have noticed any physical sensation, mentioning only an 'effect of optical instability [which] could also be said to involve the spectator' (Jasia Reichardt, 'London: Bridget Riley', *Architectural Design*, August 1963).
44. Anon., 'Painters who explore the mechanics of vision', *The Times*, 1 October 1963.
45. Anton Ehrenzweig, 1962, op.cit.
46. Maurice de Sausmarez, *Bridget Riley*, London 1970, p.29.
47. Harold Rosenberg, *The Anxious Object*, Chicago 1964/1966, Phoenix Edition (1982), p.41.
48. Ibid., p.41.
49. Quoted in Caroline Tisdall, 'Materia: the context of Arte Povera' (1989) in Emily Braun (ed.), 1989, op.cit., p.367.
50. Michael Fried, 1967, op.cit., p.16.
51. In late 1963, Fried expressed unease about 'an element of coercion' in Larry Poons' Op art work. See Michael Fried, 1998, op.cit., p.310.
52. I discuss Debord's ideas in more detail in Chapter 6.
53. Artaud quoted in John Fraser, *Violence in the Arts*, Cambridge 1974, p.118. Ellipsis in Fraser.
54. Christopher Booker, *The Neophiliacs: A Study of the Revolution in English Life in the Fifties and Sixties*, London 1969, p.235. His reaction seems to echo the reception given to modernist drama from the early years of the twentieth century, e.g. Kokoschka's *Murder Hope of Women* (first performed Vienna, 1909) or Stravinsky's dance-drama *Rite of Spring* (first performed 1913), both of which were condemned for 'barbarism' and 'primitivism' (Christopher Innes 'Modernism in drama' in Michael Levenson (ed.), *Cambridge Companion to Modernism*, Cambridge 1999, pp.140–141.) According to Booker, however, 'violence' and 'freakishness' were products specifically of 1960s' culture.
55. Such as his production of Peter Weiss' *Marat/Sade*, 1964.
56. Robert Hewison, *Culture and Consensus: England, Art and Politics Since 1940*, London 1995, p.143.

57. *Le Théatre et son Double* (1938), a collection of essays translated as *The Theatre and its Double* (1958).
58. The Royal Shakespeare Company's own 'Theatre of Cruelty' season was directed by Peter Brook in 1964. Bond's *Saved* (1965) featured a baby being stoned to death and was later described by Bernard Levin as the play in which cruelty 'reached extremes never seen before outside Grand Guignol, or possibly even inside' (Bernard Levin, *The Pendulum Years*, 1970, p.350).
59. Robert Hewison, 1995, op.cit., takes this view, p.143.
60. David Thompson, 'Introduction' *Peter Stuyvesant Foundation – The New Generation: 1964*, London 1964, p.8.
61. Anon., 'Something to blink at', *Time*, 1 May 1964, p.45.
62. Robert Melville, 'The new generation', *The Architectural Review*, 1964b, p.448.
63. Robert Melville, 'Pom-pom', *New Statesman*, 6 August 1965, p.196. I am grateful to Tag Gronberg for pointing out the possible connection with the film.
64. This phenomenon echoes the earlier history of avant-garde movements, where the destruction of the 'old order' is seen as necessary for the creation of something 'better' – in the words of the Italian Futurist Marinetti: 'art can be nought but violence, cruelty and injustice'. (Quoted in Charles Harrison, *English Art and Modernism 1900–1939*, New Haven and London 1994, p.87.)
65. A belief of the counter-cultural movements of the period, one member of which later remembered wanting 'a kind of undefined Armageddon that would somehow leave the countryside pure and unsullied but ... all the bad things kind of vaporised' (quoted in Jonathon Green, *Days in the Life: Voices from the English Underground 1961–1971*, London 1988/1998, p.130).
66. Austrian performance artists. According to RoseLee Goldberg, Nitsch saw himself as 'illustrating Aristotle's notion of catharsis through fear, terror and compassion ....[and] as an extension of action painting' RoseLee Goldberg, *Performance Art: From Futurism to the Present*, London 1979, p.163.
67. British performance artist.
68. 'sTigma' (from February 1965) was a Happening created by Nuttall and a number of other artists, including John Latham (who from 1964 destroyed books in his Skoob Tower Ceremonies). See Jonathon Green, *All Dressed Up: The Sixties and the Counterculture*, London 1999, pp.135–136.
69. Godwin owned Better Books, which stocked 'counter-cultural' literature and had a basement that various groups of artists used for Happenings and exhibitions. Godwin was also editorial director of Penguin Books. See Jonathon Green, 1999, op.cit., p.35.
70. Jeff Nuttall, *Bomb Culture*, London 1968, p.137. John Calder published counter-cultural literature and campaigned against censorship. (See J. Green, 1999 op.cit., p.131.)
71. See S. Connor, entry on Bataille in M. Payne (ed.), *Dictionary of Cultural and Critical Theory*, Oxford 1997, p.49.
72. Anton Ehrenzweig, 1965, op.cit., p.21.
73. In relation to Hess' view that art should be 'difficult' (see note 20 above) it is perhaps hard to imagine a more challenging work than *Continuum*; had it not been subsequently lost it might now be better appreciated as a most significant work of this period.
74. Anon., Item in a gossip/trivia page, *Daily Mail*, 10 September 1963.
75. Published in English in 1965. My analysis here relies largely on the account of Baktin's work given by John Lechte, 1994, op.cit., and Pam Morris, *The Bakhtin Reader: Selected Writings of Bakhtin, Medvedev and Voloshinov*, London 1994.
76. Here I use Riley's expression from the very different context of the quotation at the beginning on this chapter. B. Riley, 1965, op.cit.
77. John Lechte, 1994, op.cit., p.8.
78. Ibid., p.9.
79. See, for example, the use of humour to attack Manet's *Olympia*, as described by T.J. Clark in *The Painting of Modern Life: Paris in the Art of Manet and his Followers*, London 1985. See especially pp.92 and 97.
80. Roger Malbert, 'Exaggeration and degradation: Grotesque humour in contemporary art' in Timothy Hyman and Roger Malbert, *Carnivalesque*, London 2000, pp.74–96. Malbert follows Umberto Eco' in his account.
81. Mikhail Bakhtin 'Rabelais and his world' (extract) in Pam Morris (ed.), 1994, op.cit., p.209.
82. Anton Ehrenzweig, 1962, op.cit.
83. Ibid.
84. See Riley's words quoted at the opening of this chapter.
85. J. Lechte, op.cit., p.9., italics original.
86. Ibid., p.9.
87. Quotation from Mikhail Bakhtin *Rabelais and his World* in Gary Saul Morson and Caryl Emerson, *Mikhail Bakhtin: Creation of a Prosaics*, Stanford California 1990, p.92.
88. As Rosalind Krauss has expressed the notion of 'presentness' promoted by Fried. Rosalind E. Krauss, *The Optical Unconscious*, Cambridge Mass and London 1993, pp.213–214.
89. Gustav Metzger, 'Auto-Destructive art at the AA', 1966, p.6, quoted in David Mellor, 1993, op.cit., p.134. Metzger's December 1962 lecture at the Ealing School of Art may have inspired Pete Townsend to smash his guitars on stage.

90. This idea was explored particularly in Michael Powell's film *Peeping Tom* (1959), where the protagonist films the deaths of women as he kills them.
91. Thomas B. Hess, 1965, op.cit., p.50.
92. Harold Rosenberg, 1964/66, op.cit., p.260. This 'solicitation' was what Fried objected to, of course.
93. Ibid., p.261.
94. Ibid.
95. Ibid., p.266.
96. Ibid., p.267.
97. Quoted in Juliet Gardiner, *From the Bomb to the Beatles*, London 1999, p.119.
98. Martin Priestman 'A critical stage: drama in the 1960s' in B. J. Moore Gilbert and John Seed (eds), 1992, op.cit. For Priestman the key events initiating these changes were the first English staging of Samuel Beckett's *Waiting for Godot* (August 1955), John Osborne's *Look Back in Anger* (May 1956) and a visit to Britain by Bertolt Brecht's Berliner Ensemble (August 1956).
99. John Russell, 'Hazard is everywhere', *Sunday Times*, 15 September 1963b.
100. Ibid.
101. John Russell, 'The newest thing in London', *Art in America*, 1965, no 1, pp.139–142. See p.142.
102. Arthur Marwick, 1998, op.cit., p.191.
103. Later sold at Riley's show at the Feigen gallery in New York, March 1965.
104. David Mellor, 1993, op.cit., p.170.
105. Bridget Riley, 1965, op.cit., p.33. See opening of this chapter.
106. Gallery One was associated with the performance of Happenings, e.g. 'The Festival of Misfits', autumn 1962. M.R. Sandford (ed.), 1995, op.cit., p.342.
107. David Sylvester, 'Fences', *New Statesman*, 25 May 1962, p.770.
108. John Russell, 1963b, op.cit., and see above.

Chapter 6
'Every Epoch Dreams the One that Follows It': Op and the Commodification of the Future
pp.171-194

1. Thomas Crow, *The Rise of the Sixties*, London 1996, pp.111–112.
2. Mario Amaya, 'When Op becomes Pop', *Financial Times*, 26 May 1965, p.28 and see Chapter 4.
3. Liz Atkinson, 'Enter the fashion that dances before your eyes', *Daily Mail*, 9 June 1965.
4. Christopher Booker, *The Neophiliacs: A Study of the Revolution in English Life in the Fifties and Sixties*, London 1969, p.20.
5. Lil Picard, 'Op–Report', *Kunstwerk*, July 1965.
6. Atkinson, op.cit.
7. See for example, Anon., *Daily Mail*, 10 September 1963; Robert Melville, 'Surrealists and others', *Architectural Review*, vol., 135, no 80, 4 February 1964a; Anon., 'Art in New York', *Time*, 26 March 1965.
8. Lil Picard, 1965, op.cit.
9. Alexander Walker, *Sex in the Movies* (orig. pub. 1966), 1968, p.121.
10. Walter Benjamin, 'The work of art in the age of mechanical reproduction' (1992) in Gerald Mast, Marshall Cohen , Leo Braudy, *Film Theory and Criticism*, New York and Oxford 1992, p.673.
11. Ibid, p.670.
12. John Berger, *Ways of Seeing*, London 1972, p.21. Italics original.
13. Bridget Riley, 'Perception is the medium', *Art News*, October 1965, pp.32, 33, 66.
14. The MoMA exhibition encouraged a large number of Op exhibitions in New York, of variable quality according to contemporary reports. See e.g. Norman Rosenthal, 'New York: Gallery Notes', *Art in America*, 1965, no 1, p.114; Lil Picard, 1965, op.cit., p.8; M.L. D'Otrange Mustai, 'The foundations of "Op" art', *Connoisseur*, July 1965, p.215.
15. Jerrold Lanes, 'Current and forthcoming exhibitions: New York', *Burlington Magazine*, vol. 92, no 745, April 1965, p.219. The term was also used by Riley (1965) op.cit.
16. Bridget Riley, 1965, op.cit.
17. Jerrold Lanes, 1965, op.cit., p.219.
18. Presumably, if Op paintings *did* induce reactions such as retching, the use of Op-derived patterns on clothing would have had the same effect. In fact, I have not found any claims to this effect.
19. Elizabeth Grosz (1992), entry on Julia Kristeva in Elizabeth Wright (ed.), Feminism and *Psychoanalysis, A Critical Dictionary*, Oxford 1992, p.198.
20. David Thompson ('From Caliban to Ariel', *The Observer*, 3 July 1966)referred to Bridget Riley's 'recent ordeal' of having her work 'subjected to fashionable exploitation of the most trivialising sort' while her most recent paintings were described as 'a malevolent machine for inducing bilious attacks' later that year (Robert Melville, 'Paraphrases', *New Statesman*, 5 August 1966).

21. John Canaday, 'That's right. It's wrong', *New York Times*, 14 March 1965b.
22. Andreas Huyssen, 'Mass culture as woman: Modernism's other' in *After the Great Divide: Modernism, Mass Culture and Postmodernism*, London 1986, p.53.
23. Malcolm Barnard, *Fashion as Communication*, London 1996, p.22.
24. Charles Baudelaire (1863) translated and edited Jonathan Mayne, *The Painter of Modern Life and other Essays*, London 1964.
25. Op paintings by Jeffrey Steele were reproduced on bathing costumes; according to Anon., *Art in America*,, April 1965, p.110, Stanczak's, Anuskiewicz's and Vasarely's paintings were adapted by US fabric designer Morton Myles, who also based fabrics on Riley's work.
26. John Canaday, 1965b, op.cit. This apparently relates to the many claims that Riley's work would induce headaches, seasickness and other unpleasant physical symptoms. Headaches were presented as predominantly *female* maladies – for instance, the use of female models in advertisements for products such as Anadin.
27. Ibid.
28. Ibid. This language also suggests a gendering of mass culture, in that 'soap' would be sold primarily to women shoppers; so there may be a suggestion here that the political process was becoming 'feminized' as the same methods used to sell soap were used to promote politicians.
29. Sadie Plant, *The Most Radical Gesture: The Situationist International in a Postmodern Age*, London 1992.
30. Guy Debord, *The Society of the Spectacle* (1967) quoted in the introduction in Elizabeth Sussman, *On the Passage of a Few People Through a Rather Brief Moment in Time: The Situationist International 1957–1972*, Boston 1989, Mass. p. 8.
31. Sussman, 1989, op. cit. p.4: 'In the late 1950s and early 1960s, the Situationists believed that artists were in the best position to lead the way toward change, converting art from a precious consumable object to a principle permeating daily life'.
32. Op designs were taken up in Britain by fabric manufacturers such as Heals and wallpaper manufacturers such as Sanderson (the Palladio 6 and 7 ranges) from 1963. See Lesley Jackson, *The Sixties: Decade of Design Revolution*, London 1998, pp. 89–90.
33. Plant, 1992, op. cit., p.5.
34. See the comments of Canaday, Picard, Lanes cited earlier in this chapter.
35. John Fraser, *Violence in the Arts*, Cambridge 1974, p.42. Here we see commercialization of art related to notions of technology (in an apparently negative sense) and professionalism.
36. Katherine Whitehorn, 'Instant Pictures', *The Observer*, 3 March 1963.
37. According to film critic John Brosnan, these became rare in the 1960s (John Brosnan, *The Primal Screen: A History of Science Fiction Film*, London 1991, p.131)
38. David A. Kyle, *A Pictorial History of Science Fiction*, London 1976, p.151.
39. John Brosnan, 1991, op. cit., p.126.
40. My account here draws mainly on the work of religious historian Colin Campbell, *The Romantic Ethic and the Spirit of Modern Consumerism*, Oxford 1987.
41. T.J. Clark, *Farewell to an Idea: Episodes from a History of Modernism*, New Haven & London 1999, p.7.
42. Campbell, 1987, op. cit. See also Christopher Breward, *The Culture of Fashion*, Manchester and New York 1995. Breward argues that the first signs of the emergence of a 'fashion system' occurred in the mid-fourteenth century but this did not extend beyond an urban elite until the eighteenth century, following advances in manufacturing and distribution (see p. 110). François Boucher (1987) agrees with Breward's mid-fourteenth century origins of modern fashion.
43. Campbell, 1987, op. cit., p.89.
44. Walter Benjamin, quoted in Susan Buck-Morss, *The Dialectics of Seeing: Walter Benjamin and the Arcades Project*, Cambridge 1989, Mass. p.101 and p.405, note 130.
45. Buck-Morss, 1989, op. cit., p.103.
46. Ibid., p.114. Benjamin here quotes Jules Michelet.
47. Booker, 1969, op. cit., pp.67–68.
48. Picard, 1965, op. cit., p.8.
49. Walter Benjamin, *Gesammelte Schriften*, quoted in S. Buck-Morss, 1989, op. cit., p.144.
50. D'Otrange Mustai, 1965, op. cit.
51. Breward, 1995, op. cit., p.194.
52. Penny Sparke, *Design in Context*, London 1987, p.220.
53. Ibid., p.220.
54. Anon., 'Fashion. Will the real picture please sit down', *Time*, 5 March 1965, p.55. Designer Raymond Loewy had described Betty Grable's kidneys as 'no doubt adorable' in his 1951 autobiography (quoted in Adrienne Berney, 'Streamlining breasts: The exaltation of form and denial of function in 1930s' ideals', *Journal of Design History*, vol.14, no.4, p.329). Both that and the passage quoted here suggest a reversal of notions of the 'abject' that might be thought to be associated with inner organs.
55. It should be noted that Anuskiewicz may have had no hand in designing Lombard's dress, as the author of this article wrongly attributed another outfit to Riley.
56. A photograph of Myles with fabrics copied from these artists' work appeared in *Art in America*, no.2, April 1965. Alternatively, Anon., 'Kandy Kolored jacket gets an Op Art rocket', *Daily Mail*, 4 March 1966, claimed that a designer named Robert Aldritch (probably a reference to Larry Aldridge) was responsible for the dress mentioned in this incident.

57. Robert Kudielka (ed.), *Dialogues on Art*, London 1995, p.70.
58. Ibid., p.69.
59. 'Cool' was a contemporary 'buzz-word' used by McLuhan and applied by art critics to a variety of post-Abstract Expressionist art as well as more generally to attitudes, ideas and fashions currently in vogue. For example, see I. Sandler, 'The new cool-art', *Art in America*, 1965, no.1, pp.96–101.
60. For example, de Beauvoir's *The Second Sex* was translated into English in 1960; Betty Friedan's *The Feminine Mystique* was published in the USA in 1963; Friedan later founded the National Organization for Women (1966). In 1964, the US government founded the Equal Employment Opportunity Commission to end all employment discrimination, including sex discrimination.
61. Sheila Rowbotham, *A Century of Women*, London 1997, p.297.

Chapter 7
The Hermaphrodite and the Gorilla:
The Gendering of [Riley's] Op Art
pp.195-222

1. John Russell in Bryan Robertson, John Russell and Snowdon, *Private View*, London 1965, p.209.
2. Robert Melville, 'The new generation', *Architectural Review*, June 1964b, p.448.
3. See Anne Wagner, *Three Artists (Three Women): Modernism and the Art of Hesse, Krasner and O'Keeffe*, Berkeley CA 1997.
4. Melville also wrote for the *New Statesman*, Russell for *The Times* and *Sunday Times*.
5. Griselda Pollock, *Differencing the Canon: Feminist Desire and the Writing of Art's Histories*, London and New York 1999, p.25.
6. Bridget Riley 'The hermaphrodite' (1973) in Robert Kudielka (ed.), *The Mind's Eye: Bridget Riley Collected Writings 1965–1999*, London 1999, p.39. This may suggest Marcel Duchamp's sometime adoption of the feminized alter ego persona of Rrose Sélavy.
7. Griselda Pollock, 1999, op.cit. p.25. The notion that only men can 'transcend' their own sexuality to represent an idealized 'Humanity' is not, of course, limited to debates on art: it lies at the heart of the debate in the Anglican and Roman Catholic churches about the suitability of women for the priesthood. It is a myth, in the Barthesian sense of 'depoliticized speech', where what is culturally constructed is made to appear 'natural'.
8. I shall, however, use the term 'man artist' where appropriate here.
9. See Bridget Riley, 'Perception is the medium', *Art News*, October 1965, pp.32, 33, 66.
10. The chess board suggests both the tiled floors of Renaissance paintings, used to create perspective as well as to display the painter's grasp of the relevant mathematics, and the grid so often used as a base in modernist art; it is reminiscent of Cézanne's (male) chess players and successive, male, international champions who fascinate the mass media (which give little attention to the game itself).
11. Paradoxically, the idea of the mad genius is also associated with both art (van Gogh) and science (the fictional Dr Strangelove).
12. Jonathan Miller, 'à la Mod', *New Statesman*, 29 May 1964, p.853.
13. T.J. Clark argues that for critics in the 1860s Manet's *Olympia* did not seem appropriately 'feminine', and quotes a French journalist, in 1865, who described the figure of Olympia as 'a sort of female gorilla'– again as though one would not expect a gorilla to be female. See T.J. Clark, *The Painting of Modern Life*, 1984, p.94.
14. Griselda Pollock, *Vision and Difference: Femininity, Feminism and the Histories of Art*, London 1988, p.24.
15. Jeremy Lewison, *Interpreting Pollock*, London 1999, p.69. Lewison was Director of Collections at London's Tate Gallery at the time of the Pollock retrospective there in 1999.

16. I have covered this in some depth in other chapters. See, e.g. Thomas B. Hess, 'You can hang it in the hall', *Art News*, 1965, Vol. 64 No 2, the title of which alludes to the notion that Op art was too disturbing to hang anywhere where it would be viewed constantly.
17. Andreas Huyssen, 'Mass culture as woman: Modernism's other' in *After the Great Divide – Modernism, Mass Culture and Postmodernism*, London 1986, p.53.
18. Ibid., p.53.
19. Ibid., p.55.
20. Peter Wollen, *Raiding the Icebox: Reflections on Twentieth Century Culture*, London and New York 1993, p.19. I am grateful to Tag Gronberg for drawing my attention to this text.
21. Luce Irigaray, French feminist.
22. Mary Anne Doane, *The Desire to Desire: The Woman's Film of the 1940s*, London 1987, p.23.
23. Ibid. Doane discusses how cinema conveyed images of clothing and household appliances to American women in the 1940s.
24. Colin Campbell, *The Romantic Ethic and the Spirit of Modern Consumerism*, Oxford 1987, p.89.
25. '"Statistics have proved that 85% of the buying is done by women", announced Jack T. Chord in 1931' (Chord was the author of a manual on window display). Cécile Whiting, *A Taste for Pop: Pop Art, Gender and Consumer Culture*, Cambridge and New York 1997, p.13.
26. See Cora Kaplan, *Sea Changes: Culture and Feminism*, London 1986, p.17.
27. Quoted in Sheila Rowbotham, *A Century of Women: The History of Women in Britain and the United States*, London 1997, p.338.
28. Mary Quant quoted in Juliet Gardiner, *From the Bomb to the Beatles*, London 1999, p.133.
29. Anon. Item in a gossip/trivia page, *Daily Mail*, 10 September 1963.
30. See Chapter 5.
31. Quoted in Robert Kudielka (ed.), *Bridget Riley Dialogues on Art*, London 1995, chapter 4, 'A reputation reviewed' (broadcast radio conversation with Andrew Graham Dixon), p.70.
32. Andreas Huyssen, 1986, op.cit., p.55.
33. Robert Kudielka (ed.), 1995, op.cit., p.73.
34. Andreas Huyssen, 1986, op.cit., p.53.
35. Bridget Riley, 1965, op.cit. All quotations from p.32.
36. Andreas Huyssen, 1986, op.cit., p.51.
37. Ibid., p.53.
38. Cora Kaplan, 1986, op.cit., p.121.
39. Anon., 'Kandy Kolored jacket gets an Op art rocket', *Daily Mail*, 4 March 1966. The *Mail* was incorrect in the name of the manufacturer responsible for plagiarising Riley's painting *Hesitate* – he was Larry Aldridge, not Robert Aldritch.
40. Lil Picard, 'Op-report', *Kunstwerk*, July 1965, p.8.
41. Walter Benjamin, 'The work of art in the age of mechanical reproduction' (1955) in Gerald Mast, Marshall Cohen, Leo Braudy, *Film Theory and Criticism*, New York & Oxford 1992, p.673.
42. Cécile Whiting, 1997, op.cit., p.200.
43. Ibid., p.205. At 34 in 1964, Marisol was rather older than most fashion models. She had studied art in Paris and the USA and had been exhibiting in New York since 1958.
44. Ibid., pp.209–210.
45. Ibid., p.211.
46. Director: Carol Reed (1965) for Twentieth Century Fox.
47. Jeremy Lewison, 1999, op.cit., p.70
48. Robert Kudielka (ed.), 1995, op.cit., p.69. Joyce Egginton, writing in *The Observer*, 28 February 1965, ('Fashion follows Op art') noted the prevalence of Op-derived fabrics in New York's fashionable Fifth Avenue stores.
49. In the following year, 1966, Riley took issue with the British chain Richard Shops, which had used window backdrops based on paintings such as *Crest* (1964) – see Robert Kudielka (ed.), 1995, op.cit., p.69 and Anon., 'Kandy Kolored jacket gets an Op art rocket', *Daily Mail*, 4 March 1966.
50. Cécile Whiting, 1997, op.cit., pp.193 and 195.
51. S. Rowbotham, 1997, op.cit., p.348.
52. Ibid., p.367.
53. Quoted in ibid., p.371.
54. Photographer Norman Parkinson was later to say, 'I was one of the first to take the scent-laden atmosphere out of photographs and the first to get girls to run, to jump, to stretch, to let air through their knees' – quoted in David Alan Mellor and Laurent Gervereau, *The Sixties*, London 1997, p.108. The authors note that John Cowan 'photographed model Jill Kennington swinging from a parachute, on horseback, leaping into the sky, running in the Trocadéro (1963–4)' while 'Ronald Traeger illustrated Op ... fashions on girls in full movement, making images that were frozen moments of kinetic fashion ballet' (p.108).
55. Hilary Radner, 'Introduction' in Hilary Radner and Moya Luckett (eds), *Swinging Single: Representing Sexuality in the 1960s*, Minnesota 1999, p.12.
56. Ibid., p.14.
57. For example, sprawled with tense energy in the centre of *Continuum* (1963, Fig. 21) or emerging from it in white jeans and black sweater, looking up at the camera with what appears to be a sceptical expression (cover).
58. *Women's Wear Daily*, vol. 110, no 91, 11 May 1965.
59. *Tatler*, 17 June 1964.
60. Illustrating Hilary Spurling, 'Bridget Riley's colour explosion', *The Times*, 21 July 1971.
61. Illustrating Isabel Carlisle, 'Four decades of a life lived in the abstract', *The Times*, 11 November 1998.

62. Illustrating Richard Cork, 'Her brilliant career', *The Times Magazine*, 12 June 1999, pp.16–24. This article is illustrated with a variety of shots of Riley with her work, in several of which she is shown handling/dragging large canvases.
63. It could be argued that in New York Riley did not have a studio to be photographed in, but this restriction did not apply to British photographers and would not have prevented her dealer circulating such shots to the US press.
64. Sidney Tillim, 'Optical art: pending or ending?', *Art Magazine*, January 1965, pp.16–23.
65. See for example Jeremy Lewison, 1999, op.cit., p.69.
66. Lisa G. Corrin 'Continuum: Bridget Riley's 60s and 70s, a view from the 90s' (1999) in L.G. Corrin, Robert Kudielka and Frances Spalding, *Bridget Riley Paintings from the 1960s and 70s*, 1999, pp.38–39.
67. Ibid., p.39.
68. Cécile Whiting, 1997, op.cit., p.210.
69. See Chapter 4 regarding the comments of Jerrold Lanes (1965). In fact, this was after Riley's face and one of her paintings had appeared on the front cover of *Tatler* magazine. The media coverage of 'The Responsive Eye' nonetheless seems likely, by its sheer profusion, to have had a significant effect on public perceptions of Riley.
70. Barry Curtis has pointed out that references to judo, in relation to Riley, may have been inspired by associations with Emma Peel, a central character in the television series, *The Avengers*, popular in both the US and the UK.
71. Christopher Booker, *The Neophiliacs*, London 1969, p.232.
72. Goldsmiths College London and the Royal College of Art.
73. Robert Melville, 'Pom-pom', *New Statesman*, 6 August 1965, p.196.
74. Ibid.
75. Ibid.
76. Riley expressed her views in 'The hermaphrodite'. Bridget Riley, 1973, op.cit., p.39.
77. The *Mail* was certainly no friend of feminism – earlier in the century, it had coined the uncomplimentary term 'suffragettes'. Sheila Rowbotham, 1997, op.cit., p.11.

Postscript
pp.223-226

1. Michael Archer, *British Art Since 1960*, London 1997, p.164.
2. Norbert Lynton, 'London letter', *Art International*, October 1963, pp.64–85.
3. Jasia Reichardt, 'Op art' (1966) in Nikos Stangos (ed.), *Concepts of Modern Art*, London 1981, pp.239–243, see p.243.
4. John Canaday, 'The Responsive Eye: Three cheers and High Hopes', *The New York Times*, 28 February 1965.
5. Bridget Riley, 'Perception is the medium', *Art News*, October 1965, p.66.
6. Ibid., p.66.
7. 'A reputation reviewed' (conversation between Riley and Andrew Graham Dixon) in Robert Kudielka (ed.), *Bridget Riley Dialogues on Art*, London 1995, p.70.
8. The choice of Riley to represent Britain in the 1968 Venice Biennale, and her winning the International prize for painting, are early strong indications of the lack of negative impact of earlier commercialization on her career.
9. Ron Hunt, 'Andreas Gursky' in *Modern Painters*, 1999, vol.12, no.1, p.120.
10. As T.J. Clark (*The Painting of Modern Life: Paris in the Art of Manet and his Followers*, London 1984) has shown in the case of Manet.

Bibliography

Articles and Reviews in Periodicals

Amaya, Mario. 'When Op becomes Pop', *Financial Times*, 26 May 1965.
'The Stuyvesant contribution', *Financial Times*, 21 November 1967.

Anon. 'Gallery Guide', *The Observer*, 27 May 1962.

Anon. 'Painters who explore the mechanics of vision', *The Times*, 1 October 1963.

Anon. Untitled item in a gossip/trivia page, *Daily Mail*, 10 September 1963.

Anon. 'Is amateurism a management illness?', *The Times*, 1 April 1964.

Anon. 'Op art: pictures that attack the eye', *Time*, 23 October 1964, pp. 42–44.

Anon. 'Painters of the urban world', *The Times*, 2 April 1964.

Anon. 'Something to blink at', *Time*, 1 May 1964, p.45.

Anon. 'The gestures British artists make', *The Times*, 29 July 1964.

Anon. 'Two French painters : Mr Victor Vasarely', *The Times*, 17 April 1964.

Anon. 'Art in New York', *Time*, 26 March 1965.

Anon. 'Decorative arts: Op fabrics', *Art in America*, no.2, April 1965.

Anon. 'Fashion. Will the real picture please sit down', *Time*, 5 March 1965, p.55.

Anon. 'Miss Bridget Riley and Optical art', *The Times*, 19 April 1965.

Anon., 'Uptown', *Time*, 5 March 1965, p.6.

Anon. 'Kandy Kolored jacket gets an Op Art rocket', *Daily Mail*, 4 March 1966.

Atkinson, Liz. 'Enter the fashion that dances before your eyes', *Daily Mail*, 9 June 1965.

Banham, Reyner. 'Ad or art?', *New Society*, 7 April 1966, p.4.

Baro, Gene. 'British painting: the post-war generation', *Studio International*, 1967, pp.133–141.

Berney, Adrienne. 'Streamlining breasts: The exaltation of form and denial of function in 1930s' ideals', *Journal of Design History*, vol. 14, no 4, 2001.

Bracewell, Michael. 'A plea for painting', *The Guardian Weekend* supplement, 15 March 1997, p.14.

Brett, Guy. 'Personal image', *The Guardian*, 31 October 1963.
'Optical energy subtly used', *The Times*, 26 July 1969.

Burn, Guy. 'The New Generation', *The Arts Review*, 4–18 April 1964, p.10.

Canaday, John. 'The Responsive Eye: Three cheers and High Hopes', *The New York Times*, 28 February 1965a.
'That's right. It's wrong,' *The New York Times*, 14 March 1965b.

Carlisle, Isabel. 'Four decades of a life lived in the abstract', *The Times*, 11 November 1998.

Collings, Matthew. 'Waiting for Robo', *Modern Painters*, Spring 1999, pp.78–82.

Cork, Richard. 'Dazzled by the life of Riley', *The Times*, 23 June 1999.
'Her brilliant career', *The Times Magazine*, 12 June 1999, pp.16–24.

Coutts-Smith, Kenneth. 'London: The New Scene', *Arts Review*, 17 April–1 May 1965.

Cumming, Laura. 'Riley, ace of stripes', *The Observer Review*, 15 November 1998.

D'Otrange Mustai, M. L. 'The foundations of "Op" art', *Connoisseur*, July 1965, p.215.

Denny, Robyn. 'London Letter', *Art International*, May 1964, p.53.

Egginton, Joyce. 'Fashion follows Op art', *The Observer*, 28 February 1965.

Ehrenzweig, Anton. 'The pictorial space of Bridget Riley', *Art International*, February 1965, pp.20–24.

Faulkner, Simon. 'Art, cigarettes and visual culture in the sixties: the Peter Stuyvesant Foundation and the "New Generation" exhibitions, 1964–66', *Visual Culture in Britain*, vol.1, no.1, 2000.

Forge, Andrew. 'Presentation', *New Statesman*, 24 April 1964, p.655.

Forge, Andrew and Sylvester, David. 'A kind of anarchy', *Encounter*, vol. Xxiii, 1964, pp.44–48.

Fried, Michael. 'Art and Objecthood', *Artforum*, Summer 1967, vol.5, no.10, pp.12–23.

Gardner, Martin. 'Mathematical games: On the relation between mathematics and the ordered patterns of Op art', *Scientific American*, July pp.100–103.

Golding, Martin. 'An echo in the body: Painting, experience and still life', *Modern Painters*, vol.11, no.1, Spring 1998, pp.110–113.

Gosling, Nigel. 'The shapes of the Sixties', *The Observer*, 10 February 1963, p.21.
'Seduced by Riley', *The Observer*, 27 July 1969.

Greenberg, Clement. 'The decline of Cubism', *Partisan Review*, vol.XV, no.3, 1948, pp.366–369.
'The plight of our culture: industrialism and class mobility', *Commentary*, 15 June 1953.

Hess, Thomas B. 'You can hang it in the hall', *Art News*, vol.64, no.2, 1965, pp.41–43, 49–50.

Hickling, Alfred. 'The life of Riley', *The Guardian*, 17 November 1998.

Kozloff, Max. 'British painting today', *Encounter*, vol.xxii, no.1, January 1964.

Krauss, Rosalind. 'Bridget Riley, Richard Feigen Gallery', *Artforum*, June 1966.

Lanes, Jerrold. 'Current and forthcoming exhibitions: New York', *Burlington Magazine*, April 1965, vol.92, no.745, pp.219–220.

Lucie-Smith, Edward. 'Introduction' in the catalogue for 'One Year of British Art', Arthur Tooth & Son, London, 21 January–9 February 1963.

'Bridget Riley's Venice success', *The Times*, 29 October 1968.
Lynton, Norbert. 'Bridget Riley', *Art International*, September 1962, p.47.
'London letter', *Art International*, October 1963, pp.64–85.
'London letter', *Art International*, Summer 1964a, p.73.
'London letter', *Art International*, October 1964b, p.60.
'Optical art', *New Statesman*, 29 May 1964c, p.853.
Maharaj, Sarat. 'Pop art's pharmacies: kitsch, consumerist objects and signs, the unmentionable', *Art History*, vol.15, no.3, 1992, pp.334–350.
Marmer, Nancy. 'Los Angeles: New British painters', *Art Forum*, December 1964, pp.11–12.
'Bridget Riley, Feigen Palmer Gallery', *Art Forum*, December 1965.
McCormick, Carlo. 'pOPTOMETRY', *Artforum*, November 1985, pp.87–91.
Melville, Robert. 'Miscellany', *Architectural Review*, August 1962, pp.132–4.
'Surrealists and others', *The Architectural Review*, February 1964a, vol.135, no.804.
'The new generation', *Architectural Review*, June 1964b, pp.447–449.
'Summer pickings', *New Statesman*, 7 August 1964c.
'Abstract Illusionism', *New Statesman*, 16 October 1964d, p.588.
'Pom-pom', *New Statesman*, 6 August 1965, p.196.
'Paraphrases', *New Statesman*, 5 August 1966, p.208.
'An art without accidents', *New Statesman*, 23 July 1971, p.121.
Miller, Jonathan. 'à la Mod', *New Statesman*, 29 May 1964, p.853.
Mullins, E. 'London in September: modern exhibitions', *Apollo*, September 1963, vol.78, no.19, pp.232–233.
Oster, Gerald and Nishijima, Y. 'Moiré patterns', *Scientific American*, May 1963, pp.54–63.
Picard, Lil. 'Op-Report', *Kunstwerk*, July 1965, p.8.
Pick, Hella. 'New York's Responsive Eye', *The Guardian*, 13 March 1965.
Prendeville, Brendan. 'Merleau-Ponty, realism and painting: psychological space and the space of exchange', *Art History*, vol.22, no.3, 1999, pp.364–388.
Jasia Reichardt. 'London: Bridget Riley', *Architectural Design*, August 1963.
Riley, Bridget. 'Perception is the medium', *Art News*, October 1965, pp.32, 33, 66.
Rose, Barbara. 'Beyond vertigo: Optical art at the Modern', *Artforum*, April 1965, pp.30–32.
Rosenthal, Nan. 'New York: Gallery notes', *Art in America*, no.1, 1965, pp.114–116.
Russell, John. 'Towards grown-up greatness', *The Times*, 3 February 1963a.
'Hazard is everywhere', *The Sunday Times*, 15 September 1963b.
'Downright professional', *The Sunday Times*, 19 July 1964.
'The newest thing in London', *Art in America*, no.1, 1965, pp.139–142.
Sainsbury, John. 'Introduction', *British Painting in the Sixties*, Tate and Whitechapel Galleries, June 1963.
Sandler, Irving. 'The new cool art', *Art in America*, no.1, 1965, pp.96–101.
Seldis, H.J. 'With Op art the eyes have it', *Los Angeles Times*, 3 October 1965.
Shaw-Miller, Simon. '"Concerts of everyday living": Cage, Fluxus and Barthes, interdisciplinearity and inter-media events', *Art History*, vol.19, no.1, 1996, pp.1–25.
Simon, Sidney. 'From England's green and pleasant bowers', *Art News*, vol.64, no.2, April 1965, pp.28–31.
Spencer, Charles. 'What is the quality of a woman's vision?', *The Times*, 5 June 1968.
Spurling, Hilary. 'Bridget Riley's colour explosion', *The Times*, 21 July 1971.
Stevens, Elizabeth. 'Bridget Riley', *Art News*, vol.64, no.2, April 1965, p.14.
Sylvester, David. 'Fences', *New Statesman*, 25 May 1962.
Thompson, David. 'London Commentary: Concentric circles', *Studio International*, June 1966a, p.268.
'From Caliban to Ariel', *Observer*, 3 July 1966b.
'International recognition for British painting', *The Times*, 31 December 1963.
'Introduction' catalogue to *Peter Stuyvesant Foundation: The New Generation 1964*, Whitechapel Gallery, London March–May 1964.
Tillim, Sidney. 'Optical art: pending or ending?', *Art Magazine*, January 1965, pp.16–23.
Tucker, A. 'Prize show', *The Guardian*, 23 November 1963.
Whitehorn, Katherine. 'Instant pictures', *Observer*, 3 March 1963.
Whitford, Frank. 'London Galleries: British painters', *Arts Review*, 23 January – 6 February 1965, p.8.
Whittet, G.S. 'G.S. Whittet says ... ', *The Studio*, no.847, November 1963. *Womens' Wear Daily*, vol.110, no.91, 11 May 1965.

Books and Catalogues

Aldred, Nanette. 'A Canterbury tale' in David Mellor (ed.), *A Paradise Lost: The Neo-Romantic Imagination in Britain 1935–1955*, Lund Humphries/Barbican Art Gallery, London 1987.

Anderson, Benedict. *Imagined Communities – Reflections on the Origin and Spread of Nationalism*, Verso, London 1983/1991.

Archer, Michael. *British Art Since 1960*, Thames & Hudson, London 1997.

Argüelles, Jose A. *Charles Henry and the Formation of a Psychophysical Aesthetic*, University of Chicago Press , Chicago and London 1972.

Arnheim, Rudolf. *Art and Visual Perception*, Faber and Faber, London 1954.

Bakhtin M. 'Rabelais and his world' (extract) in Pam Morris (ed.), *The Bakhtin Reader: Selected Writings of Bakhtin, Medvedev and Voloshinov*, Edward Arnold, London 1994.

Banham, Reyner. *Los Angeles: The Architecture of Four Ecologies*, Pelican, London 1973.

Barnard, Malcolm. *Fashion as Communication*, Routledge, London 1996.

Barrell, John. *The Dark Side of the Landscape: The Rural Poor in English Painting 1730–1840*, Cambridge, New York & Melbourne: Press Syndicate of the University of Cambridge, 1980.

Barrett, Cyril. *An Introduction to Optical Art*, Studio Vista, London 1971.

Bataille, Georges. 'The notion of expenditure' in Georges Bataille, *Visions of Excess: Selected Writings 1927–1939*, Manchester University Press, Manchester 1985, orig. pub. 1933, pp.116–129.

Bell, Clive. 'The aesthetic hypothesis', first published 1914, reprinted in *Art in Theory 1900–2000*, in Charles Harrison and Paul Wood (eds), Blackwell, Oxford 2003 pp.107–109.

Benezra, Neal. 'To speak another language: The critique of painting and the beginnings of Minimal and Conceptual art' in Christos M. Joachimides and Norman Rosenthal (eds), *American Art in the Twentieth Century*, Royal Academy of Arts/Prestel, London 1993, pp.117–124.

Benjamin, Walter. 'The work of art in the age of mechanical reproduction', first pub. 1955, reprinted in Gerald Mast, Marshall Cohen, Leo Braudy, *Film Theory and Criticism*, Fourth edn, Oxford University Press, New York/Oxford 1992.

Berger, John. *Ways of Seeing*, BBC/Penguin, London 1972.

Berghaus, Günter. 'Happenings in Europe: Trends, events and leading figures' in M.R. Sandford, *Happenings and Other Acts*, Routledge, London 1995.

Bernasconi, Robert. 'Maurice Merleau-Ponty' in Ted Honderich (ed.), *Oxford Companion to Philosophy*, Oxford University Press, Oxford 1995, p.554.

Bogart, Michelle H. *Artists, Advertising and the Borders of Art*, University of Chicago Press, Chicago 1995.

Bogdanor, Vernon. 'The Labour Party in opposition 1951–1964', *The Age of Affluence 1951 to 1964*, Bogdanor, Vernon and Skidelsky, Robert (eds). Macmillan & Co., Basingstoke 1970.

Bois, Yve-Alain and E. Krauss, Rosalind. *Formless: A User's Guide*, Zone Books, New York 1997.

Booker, Christopher. *The Neophiliacs: A Study of the Revolution in English Life in the Fifties and Sixties*, Collins, London 1969.

Bowness, Alan. *Recent British Painting The Peter Stuyvesant Collection*, Lund Humphries, London 1967.

Breward, Christopher. *The Culture of Fashion*, Manchester University Press, Manchester and New York 1995.

Briganti, Giuliano. 'Cultural provocation: Italian art of the early sixties' in Emily Braun (ed.), *Italian Art in the Twentieth Century*, Prestel-Verlag and Royal Academy of Arts, Munich and London 1989.

Brosnan, John. *The Primal Screen: A History of Science Fiction Film*, Orbit Books, London 1991.

Buck-Morss, Susan. *The Dialectics of Seeing: Walter Benjamin and the Arcades Project*, Mass: MIT Press, Cambridge 1989.

Campbell, Colin. *The Romantic Ethic and the Spirit of Modern Consumerism*, Blackwell, Oxford 1987.

Cawthorne, Nigel. *Sixties Source Book: A Visual Guide to the Style of a Decade*, Quantum Books, London 1998.

Clark, T.J. *Image of the People: Gustave Courbet and the 1848 Revolution*, Thames & Hudson, London 1973, 1982.

'Arguments about Modernism: a reply to Michael Fried', orig. pub. 1983, reprinted in Francis Frascina (ed.), *Pollock and After: The Critical Debate*, Harper & Row, London 1985.

The Painting of Modern Life: Paris in the Art of Manet and his Followers, Thames and Hudson, London 1984.

Farewell to an Idea: Episodes from a History of Modernism, Yale University Press, New Haven & London 1999.

Cockcroft, Eva. 'Abstract Expressionism, weapon of the cold war', orig. pub 1974, reprinted in F. Frascina and J. Harris (eds), *Art in Modern Culture*, Open University/ Phaidon, London 1992.

Compton, Michael. *Optical and Kinetic Art* (catalogue), Tate Gallery, London 1967.

Compton, Susan. 'Anthony Caro and sixties abstraction' in Susan Compton (ed.), *British Art in the Twentieth Century*, Royal Academy of Arts/Prestel, London 1987.

Connor, Steven. 'Bataille, Georges' in Michael Payne (ed.), *A Dictionary of Cultural and Critical Theory*, Blackwell, Oxford 1997, pp.48–50.
Corrin, Lisa G. 'Continuum: Bridget Riley's 60s and 70s a view from the 90s' in Lisa G. Corrin, Robert Kudielka and Frances Spalding, *Bridget Riley Paintings from the 1960s and 70s*, Serpentine Gallery, London 1999.
Crow, Thomas. *The Rise of the Sixties*, Weidenfeld & Nicolson Ltd, Everyman Art Library, London 1996.
Davie, Grace. *Religion in Britain since 1945*, Blackwell, Oxford 1994.
Debord, Guy. *The Society of the Spectacle*, orig pub 1967, trans by Donald Nicholson-Smith, Zone Books, New York 1995.
Doane, MaryAnne. *The Desire to Desire: The Woman's Film of the 1940s*, Macmillan, London 1987.
Donaldson, Frances. *The British Council: The First Fifty Years*, Jonathan Cape, London 1984.
Ehrenzweig, Anton. 'Introduction', Catalogue to Bridget Riley's one person show at Gallery One, May 1963.
The Hidden Order of Art: A Study in the Psychology of Artistic Imagination, Weidenfeld & Nicolson, London 1967.
Feaver, William in Mary Banham and Bevis Hillier (eds), *A Tonic to the Nation: The Festival of Britain 1951*, Thames & Hudson, London 1976.
Fer, Briony. 'Poussiere/peinture: Bataille on painting' in Carolyn Bailey Gill, *Bataille: Writing the Sacred*, Routledge, London and New York 1995.
On Abstract Art, Yale University Press, New Haven and London 1997.
Briony Fer, David Batchelor, Paul Wood, *Realism, Rationalism, Surrealism: Art Between the Wars*, Yale University Press in association with the Open University, New Haven and London 1993.
Fraser, John. *Violence in the Arts*, Cambridge University Press, Cambridge 1974. Michael Fried, *Art and Objecthood*, University of Chicago Press, Chicago and London 1998.
Fry, Roger. 'An essay in aesthetics', orig. pub. 1909, reprinted in Charles Harrison and Paul Wood (eds), *Art in Theory 1900–2000*, Blackwell, Oxford 2003, pp.75–81.
Gardiner, Juliet. *From the Bomb to the Beatles*, Collins & Brown, London 1999.
Garlake, Margaret. *New Art New World*, Yale University Press, London and New Haven 1998.
Goldberg, RoseLee. *Performance Art: From Futurism to the Present*, Thames and Hudson, London 1979.
Gombrich, E.H. *Art and Illusion*, Phaidon, London 1960.
The Image and the Eye, Phaidon, London 1982.
Green, Jonathon. *Days in the Life: Voices from the English Underground 1961–1971*, Pimlico, London 1988/1998.
All Dressed Up: The Sixties and the Counterculture, Pimlico, London 1999.
Greenberg, Clement. 'Abstract, representational and so forth', *Art and Culture Critical Essays*, orig. pub. 1961, Beacon Press, Boston 1992.
'Avant garde and kitsch', orig. pub. 1961, edited reprint in *Art and Culture Critical Essays*, Beacon Press, Boston 1992.
'Modernist painting' (Radio broadcast, 1961), reproduced in Francis Frascina and Charles Harrison (eds), *Modern Art and Modernism, A Critical Anthology*, London 1982, pp.5–10.
Avant-garde Attitudes: The John Power Lecture in Contemporary Art, University of Sidney, 1969.
Gregory, R.L. *Visual Perception*, Oxford University Press, London 1973.
Guilbaut, Serge. *How New York Stole the Idea of Modern Art: Abstract Expressionism, Freedom and the Cold War*, University of Chicago Press, Chicago 1983.
Harper, J.G. 'Product and Response: The Painting of Bridget Riley', Unpublished MPhil dissertation, Birkbeck College, London University, 1982.
Harrison, Charles. 'Modernism and the transatlantic dialogue' in Francis Frascina (ed.), *Pollock and After: The Critical Debate*, Harper & Row, London 1985.
English Art and Modernism 1900–1939, Yale University Press, New Haven & London 1994.
Harrison, Charles and Wood, Paul. 'Modernity and Modernism reconsidered' in Paul Wood, Francis Frascina, Jonathan Harris, Charles Harrison, *Modernism in Dispute: Art Since the Forties*, Yale University Press and the Open University, New Haven and London 1993.
Hewison, Robert. *Culture and Consensus: England, Art and Politics Since 1940*, Methuen, London 1995.
Huxley, Aldous. *Brave New World*, orig. pub. 1932, reprinted Flamingo Modern Classic, London 1994.
The Doors of Perception, orig. pub. 1954, reprinted Flamingo Modern Classic, London 1994.
Huyssen, Andreas. 'Mass culture as woman: Modernism's other' in *After the Great Divide: Modernism, Mass Culture and Postmodernism*, Macmillan, London 1986.
Innes, Christopher. 'Modernism in drama' in M. Levenson, *Cambridge Companion to Modernism*, Cambridge University Press, Cambridge 1999.
Ittelson, W.H. *The Ames Demonstrations in Perception*, Hafner, New York 1968.
Jackson, Lesley. *The Sixties: Decade of Design Revolution*, Phaidon, London 1998.
Kaplan, Cora. *Sea Changes: Culture and Feminism*, Verso, London 1986.

Krauss, Rosalind E. *The Optical Unconscious*, Cambridge, Mass. and London, England: MIT Press, 1993.

Kudielka, Robert (ed.). *BridgetRiley: Dialogues on Art*, Zwemmer, London 1995.

The Mind's Eye: Bridget Riley Collected Writings 1965–1999, Thames & Hudson/Serpentine Gallery/De Montfort University, London 1999.

Kyle, David A. *A Pictorial History of Science Fiction*, Hamlyn, London 1976.

Lechte, John. *Fifty Key Contemporary Thinkers*, Routledge, London and New York 1994.

Levin, Bernard. *The Pendulum Years: Britain and the Sixties*, Pan Books, London 1970.

Lewison, Jeremy. *Interpreting Pollock*, Tate Gallery Publishing, London 1999.

Lippard, Lucy R. (ed.). *Pop Art*, Thames and Hudson, London 1970.

Livingstone, Marco. 'Pluralism since 1960' in David Britt, *Modern Art, Impressionism to Post-Modernism*, London 1989, pp.359–405.

Pop Art: A Continuing History, Harry N. Abrams, New York 1990.

Lucie-Smith, Edward. *Art Today*, Phaidon, Oxford 1989.

Lynton, Norbert. *The Story of Modern Art*, Phaidon, London 1989.

Maitland, Sara (ed.). *Very Heaven: Looking Back at the 1960s*, Virago Press, London 1988.

Malbert, Roger. 'Exaggeration and degradation: Grotesque humour in contemporary art' in Timothy Hyman and Roger Malbert, *Carnivalesque*, Hayward Gallery Publishing, London 2000.

Marwick, Arthur. *British Society Since 1945*, Penguin, London 1996.

The Sixties: Cultural Revolution in Britain, France, Italy and the United States c.1958–c.1974, Oxford University Press, Oxford 1998.

Massey, Anne. *The Independent Group: Modernism and Mass Culture in Britain 1945–59*, Manchester University Press, Manchester 1995.

McLuhan, Marshall. *Understanding Media*, Routledge Classics 2001 edition, London 1964.

Melechi, Antonio (ed.). *Psychedelia Britannica: Hallucinogenic drugs in Britain*, Turnaround, London.

Mellor, David. *The Sixties Art Scene in London*, Phaidon/The Barbican, London 1993.

Merleau-Ponty, Maurice. *Phenomenology of Perception*, orig. pub. 1945, trans. Colin Smith, English edition, Routledge and Kegan Paul, London 1962.

'Eye and Mind', orig. pub. 1960, reprinted in G.A. Johnson and M. Smith (eds), *The Merleau-Ponty Aesthetics Reader*, Northwestern University Press, Illinois 1993.

Moore, Barbara. 'New York intermedia: Happenings and Fluxus in the 1960s' in Christos M. Joachimedes and Nigel Rosenthal (eds.), *American Art in the Twentieth Century*, Royal Academy of Arts and Prestel, London.

Moorhouse, Paul (ed.). *Bridget Riley*, Tate Publishing, London 2003.

Morson, Gary Saul, and Emerson, Caryl. *Mikhail Bakhtin: Creation of a Prosaics*, Stanford University Press, Stanford California 1990.

Naifeh, Steven and White Smith, Gregory. *Jackson Pollock: An American Saga*, Barrie & Jenkins, London 1989.

Nochlin, Linda. 'Lost and found: once more the fallen woman' in *Women Art and Power and Other Essays*, Thames & Hudson, London 1989.

Nuttall, John. *Bomb Culture*, MacGibbon & Kee, London 1968.

Harold, Osborne. *Abstraction and Artifice in Twentieth Century Art*, Clarendon Press, Oxford 1979.

Pevsner, Nikolaus. *The Englishness of English, Art*, Architectural Press, London 1956.

Plant, Sadie. *The Most Radical Gesture: The Situationist International in a Postmodern Age*, Routledge, London 1992.

Pollock, Griselda. *Vision and Difference: Femininity, Feminism and the Histories of Art*, Routledge, London 1988.

Differencing the Canon: Feminist Desire and the Writing of Art's Histories, Routledge, London & New York 1999.

Priestman, Martin. 'A critical stage: drama in the 1960s' in B. Moore Gilbert and John Seed (eds), *Cultural Revolution? The Challenge of the Arts in the 1960s*, Routledge, London 1992.

Radner, Hilary and Luckett, Moya (eds). *Swinging Single: Representing Sexuality in the 1960s*, University of Minnesota Press, 1999.

Read, Herbert. *To Hell with Culture And Other Essays on Art and Society*, orig. pub. 1963, Routledge, reprinted, London 2002.

Reise, Barbara M. 'Greenberg and the Group: A retrospective view' in Francis Frascina and Jonathan Harris, *Art in Modern Culture: An Anthology of Critical Texts*, Open University/Phaidon, London 1992.

Robbins, David. Jacquelynn Baas (eds), *The Independent Group: Postwar Britain and the Aesthetics of Plenty*, MIT Press, Cambridge Mass. and London 1990.

Robertson, Bryan, John Russell and Snowdon, *Private View*, Thomas Nelson & Sons, London 1965.

Rosenberg, Harold. *The Anxious Object*, orig. pub. 1964/1966, University of Chicago Press, Phoenix edition, 1982.

Rosenblum, Robert. 'British twentieth-century art: A transatlantic view' in Simon Compton (ed.), *British Art in the Twentieth Century*, Royal Academy of Arts/Prestel, London 1987, pp.89–98.

Rosenthal, Norman. 'American art: a view from Europe' in Christos M. Joachimedes and Norman Rosenthal (eds), *American Art in the Twentieth Century*, Royal Academy of Arts/Prestel, London 1993.

Roszak, Theodore. *The Making of a Counter Culture: Reflections on the Technocratic Society and its Youthful Opposition*, Faber & Faber, London 1970.

Rowbotham, Sheila. *A Century of Women: The History of Women in Britain and the United States*, Viking, London 1997.

Sandford, Mariellen R. *Happenings and Other Acts*, Routledge, London 1995.

Sausmarez, Maurice de. *Bridget Riley*, Studio Vista, London 1970.

Seitz, William. Catalogue to 'The Responsive Eye', Museum of Modern Art, New York 1965.

Shone, Richard. *The Century of Change: British Art since 1900*, Phaidon, Oxford 1977.

Sillars, Stuart. 'Caro verbum factus est: British art in the 1960s' in B. Moore Gilbert and John Seed (eds), *Cultural Revolution? The Challenge of the Arts in the 1960s*, Routledge, London 1992.

Sked, Alan and Cook, Chris. *Post- war Britain: A Political History*, Third edn, Penguin, London 1990.

Sontag, Susan. 'Film and theatre', orig. pub. 1966, reprinted in Gerald Mast, Marshall Cohen, Leo Braudy, *Film Theory and Criticism*, Oxford University Press Inc. New York 1992, pp.362–74.

Sparke, Penny. *Design in Context*, Quarto.

Stangos, Nikos, (ed.), *Concepts of Modern Art*, Thames and Hudson, London 1981.

Stich, Sidra. *Yves Klein*, Hayward Gallery, London 1995.

Sussman, Elizabeth (ed.). *On the Passage of a Few People Through a Rather Brief Moment in Time: The Situationist International 1957–1972*, MIT Press, Boston, Mass. 1989.

Sylvester, David. *About Modern Art: Critical Essays 1948–97*, Pimlico Editions, London 1997.

Thompson, David. 'Bridget Riley' (introduction to Riley's catalogue for her work shown at the XXXIV Venice Biennale, 1968).

Thomson, David and Warner, Geoffrey. *England in the Twentieth Century (1914–1979)*, orig. pub 1965, rev. edn, Penguin, Harmondsworth 1981.

Tisdall, Caroline. 'Materia: the context of Arte Povera' in Emily Braun (ed.), *Italian Art in the Twentieth Century*, Prestel-Verlag and Royal Academy of Arts, Munich and London 1989.

Wagner, Anne. *Three Artists (Three Women): Modernism and the Art of Hesse, Krasner and O'Keeffe*, University of California Press, Berkeley, CA 1997.

Walker, Alexander. *Sex in the Movies*, Penguin, Harmondsworth 1968 (originally published as *The Celluloid Sacrifice* 1966).

Wallach, Alan. 'The museum of modern art: the past's future' in Francis Frascina and Jonathan Harris, *Art in Modern Culture*, Phaidon Press, London 1992, pp.282–291.

Wheale, Nigel (ed.). *The Postmodern Arts*, Routledge, London 1995.

Whiting, Cécile. *A Taste for Pop: Pop Art, Gender and Consumer Culture*, Cambridge University Press, Cambridge and New York 1997.

Wiener, Martin J. *English Culture and the Decline of the Industrial Spirit 1850–1980*, orig. pub. 1981, reprinted, Penguin Group, London 1992.

Wilkie, Tom. *British Science and Politics Since 1945*, Blackwell and Institute of Contemporary British History, Oxford UK and Cambridge, Mass. 1991.

Wilson, Andrew. 'Moving times – new words – dead clocks: Sigma, London counter-culture' in David Alan Mellor and Laurent Gervereau (eds), *The Sixties*, Philip Wilson, London 1997.

Wollen, Peter. *Raiding the Icebox: Reflections on Twentieth Century Culture*, Verso, London & New York 1993.

Wright, Elizabeth (ed.). *Feminism and Psychoanalysis, A Critical Dictionary*, Blackwell, Oxford 1992.

Websites

http://bcfservices.org.uk (British Chess Federation)

www.chesscenter.com/british2000.html

www.fi.muni.cz/~toms/PopArt/Biographies/marisol.html

www.lunarsociety.org.uk www.scholarly-societies.org/history/1775Rsb.html

www.thewho.net/pete/www.uiowa.edu/~ournews/2000/january/0110picard.html

www.warholstars.org/chron/andydies68n33.html

Bridget Riley Paintings illustrated

Fig. 1
Movement in Squares 1961
48 × 48 inches | 122 × 122 cm
Tempera on hardboard
Arts Council of Great Britain

Fig. 2
Horizontal Vibration 1961
17½ × 55½ inches | 44.5 × 141 cm
Tempera on hardboard
Collection Manfred Wandel, Reutlingen

Fig. 4
Black to White Discs 1962
70 × 70 inches | 178 × 178 cm
Emulsion on canvas
Stolen in 1965 and destroyed

Fig. 5
Tremor 1962
48 × 48 inches | 122 × 122 cm
Emulsion on board
Private collection

Fig. 6
Burn 1964
22 × 22 inches | 56 × 56 cm
Emulsion on board
Collection of the artist

Fig. 8
Climax 1963
36 × 39½ inches | 91.5 × 100.5 cm
Emulsion on wood
Collection of artist

Fig. 9
Shuttle 1 1964
44 × 44 inches | 112 × 112 cm
Emulsion on board
British Council
(for Gulbenkian Foundation)

Fig. 10
Straight Curve 1963
28 × 24½ inches | 71.2 × 62.2 cm
Emulsion on board
Private collection

Fig. 11
Shift 1963
30 × 30 inches | 76.2 × 76.2 cm
Emulsion on hardboard
Helga and Edzard Reuter

Fig. 12
Blaze 1 1962
43 × 43 inches | 109.4 × 109.4 cm
Emulsion on board
Private collection

Fig. 13
Fall 1963
55½ × 55¼ inches | 141 × 140.5 cm
Emulsion on board
Tate Gallery

Fig. 14
Current 1964
58⅜ × 58⅞ inches | 148.5 × 149.5 cm
Emulsion on board
Museum of Modern Art, New York
(Philip C. Johnson Fund)

Fig. 15
White Discs 1 1964
52 × 52 inches | 132 × 132 cm
Emulsion on board
Private collection

Fig. 16
Shiver 1964
27⅛ × 27⅛ inches | 69 × 69 cm
Emulsion on board
Private collection

Fig. 17
Loss 1964
46 × 46 inches | 117 × 117 cm
Emulsion on board
Private collection

Fig. 18
Ascending and Descending Hero 1963
72 × 108 inches | 182.9 × 274.3 cm
Emulsion on canvas
The Art Institute of Chicago;
Michigan Ave at Adams St; Chicago,
Ill. 60603

Fig. 19
Pause 1964
44 × 42 inches | 112.2 × 106.6 cm
Emulsion on board
Collection of artist

Fig. 20
Crest 1964
65⅜ × 65⅜ inches | 166 × 166 cm
Emulsion on hardboard
The British Council

Fig. 23
Fission 1963
34¼ × 35 inches | 88.8 × 86.2 cm
Tempera on board
Donated to MOMA, New York
by Philip Johnson, 1969

Fig. 24
Disturbance 1964
68 × 68 inches | 173 × 173 cm
Emulsion on linen
Private collection

Fig. 28
Where 1964
42 × 44½ inches | 107 × 113 cm
Emulsion on board
Private collection

Fig. 29
Uneasy Centre 1963
15⅜ inches | 39 cm
Emulsion on wood
Private collection, London

Fig. 52
Arrest 1 1965
70 × 68¾ inches | 178 × 174.5 cm
Emulsion on canvas
Hokkaido Museum of Modern Art,
Sapporo, Japan

Fig. 53
Arrest 3 1965
69 × 75½ inches | 175 × 192 cm
Emulsion on canvas
Art Gallery & Museum, Kelvingrove,
Glasgow

Acknowledgements

A number of people have given me advice, encouragement and support in the writing of this book.

I am indebted to Bridget Riley for her interest and encouragement, for copies of catalogues for her recent shows and invitations to her private views, and in particular for access to her personal archive and for granting permission for the reproduction of paintings in the text. I am also grateful to Karsten Schubert for his faith in my approach to the project and his constant encouragement and help.

My editor Eileen Cadman gave much invaluable advice and guidance in the development of the text for publication, and it has been significantly improved thereby. I am also grateful to Caroline Thompson for her expert work in finding the illustrations, to Adam Gahlin and Douglas McFarlane for their work in tracking down some of these, and to Adam Gahlin for his help in checking the proofs. Richard Hollis designed the book and its cover and his work speaks for itself.

Dr Tag Gronberg of Birkbeck College, London University, provided sensitive but persistent guidance while I was researching the thesis on which this book is based. Her unfailing support and encouragement, as well as practical suggestions and criticisms, were invaluable. I would also like to thank Emeritus Professor William Vaughan for his perceptive, useful comments as the thesis progressed, and Professor Barry Curtis of Middlesex University and Dr Brendan Prendeville of Goldsmiths College, who examined the thesis and both of whom made most detailed and useful criticisms of it, some of which I have tried to address.

The staff at Birkbeck College Library, University of London Library at Senate House, Tate Library and the British Museum periodicals collection at Colindale have all, at various times, given much needed help with tracing necessary references.

In producing this book I have endeavoured to correct some of the shortcomings of the original thesis; in a subject which turned out to be of much greater complexity than I had ever anticipated, many must remain and are, of course, entirely my own responsibility.

Only those who have embarked on a project such as this can appreciate the amount of patience, forbearance and support which one's partner is called upon to provide, and my enduring admiration for and gratitude to Alan Butler, for so unstintingly providing all three, must be noted – but cannot be satisfactorily expressed – here.

Picture credits

Figs. 1–20, 23, 24, 28, 29, 52, 53
Works by Bridget Riley
by kind permission of Bridget Riley ©Bridget Riley 2004

Photographs of paintings
Fig.**14** Brompton Studios
Figs.**4,5,8,11,15,16,19,28,29,52,53** Prudence Cuming
Figs.**9,17,18, 24** Robert Horner
Figs.**1, 2, 6, 12, 13, 23** John Webb

Other Illustrations
Figs.**25, 49** Photography courtesy of *Vogue Australia*
Figs.**26, 35** Getty Images
Fig.**27** Taken from an article that first appeared in *New Society*, 7 April 1966
Fig.**30** 'The Time Tunnel' © 1966 Twentieth Century Fox Television and Irwin Allen Properties, LLC. Used with permission. All rights reserved
Figs.**31,32** © The Woolmark Company /images supplied by London College of Fashion
Fig.**33** Getty Images /Hulton Archive
Fig.**34** © 1965 S. Hatami, Courtesy of Westwood Gallery, New York City / © The *Observer*,
Fig.**36** V&A Images / V&A Museum, Photograph John French
Fig.**37** Courtesy of Bath and North East Somerset Council – The Museum of Costume, Bath,
Fig.**39** Cecil Beaton Studio Archive, Sotheby's
Fig.**40** © Courtesy Duane Michals / PaceMcGill Gallery, New York
Figs.**41,42** Gordon Parks / Time Life Photos / Getty Images
Fig.**43** © Corbis Sygma / Rudolph Burckhardt
Fig.**44** (centre) Horst/*Vogue* © Conde Nast Publications Inc.
Fig.**44** (left and right) © Corbis / Conde Nast Archive
Fig.**45** Feigen Gallery, New York
Fig.**46** © The Lewinski Archive at Chatsworth
Figs.**47,48, 51** Images courtesy of the Illustrated London News Picture Library. All effort has been made to trace the copyright holder of these works, and the reproduction has been made in good faith. If you are the copyright holder, or the estate of the copyright holder of this work, please contact the Illustrated London News Picture Library, 20 Upper Ground, London SE1 9PF
Fig.**50** *Women's Wear Daily*, New York

Every effort has been made to contact the holders of copyright material, but if any have been inadvertently overlooked the publishers will be pleased to make the necessary arrangements at the first opportunity.

Index